399

LIBRARY
SAMPSON COMMUNITY C
P. O. DRAWER 318
CLINTON, N.C. 28328

P9-DDO-405

The Rattigan Version

Books by B.A. Young
The Rattigan Version
Cabinet Pudding

The Rattigan Version

Sir Terence Rattigan and the theatre of character

B. A. Young

Atheneum

New York   1988

For Pegs French

Originally published in Great Britain by Hamish
Hamilton Ltd.

Copyright © 1986 by B.A. Young

All rights reserved. No part of this book may be
reproduced or transmitted in any form or by any means,
electronic or mechanical, including photocopying,
recording or by any information storage and retrieval
system, without permission in writing from the Publisher.

Atheneum
Macmillan Publishing Company
866 Third Avenue, New York, N.Y. 10022

Young, B. A. (Bertram A.)
  The Rattigan version.
  Includes index.
  1. Rattigan, Terence—Biography.   2. Dramatists,
English—20th century—Biography.   I. Title.
PR6035.A75Z98   1988   822'.912   [B] 87-37372
ISBN 0-689-11952-6

Macmillan books are available at special discounts for
bulk purchases for sales promotions, premiums, fund-
raising, or educational use. For details, contact:

Special Sales Director
Macmillan Publishing Company
866 Third Avenue
New York, N.Y. 10022

First American Edition

10 9 8 7 6 5 4 3 2 1

Printed in the United States of America

Contents

List of illustrations

With hey! with hey! the thrush and the jay
Are summer songs for me and my aunts.
The Winter's Tale

Acknowledgements

All quotations from the plays come from *The Collected Plays of Terence Rattigan*, published by Hamish Hamilton.

Among the many people who have helped me, I am indebted to Sir John Gielgud, CH, Mr Anthony Powell, CBE, Mr Harold French and Mrs 'Pegs' French, Mr Peter Carter-Ruck, Mr Stewart Trotter, Mr James Morwood, Librarian of Harrow School, and Mr M. G. Tyrrell, its Head of Drama. I am obliged to Mr Richard Price and to the Proprietors of *Punch* for permission to use the extract from 'The Problem of Crocker-Harris', and I am especially grateful to Miss Holly Hill for the manifold assistance I have had from her dissertation.

My thanks are due for permission to use quotations from the following books: *Chips: the Diaries of Sir Henry Channon*, ed. R. Rhodes James; Weidenfeld and Nicolson, 1967. *Clinging to the Wreckage*, John Mortimer; Weidenfeld and Nicolson, 1982. *Confessions of an Actor*, Laurence Olivier; Weidenfeld and Nicolson, 1982. *Diversions of a Diplomat*, Frank Rattigan; Chapman and Hall, 1924. *Faces in my Time*, Anthony Powell; Heinemann, 1980. *I Thought I Never Could*, Harold French; Secker and Warburg, 1973. *Letters to Graham Robertson*, ed. Kerrison Preston; Hamish Hamilton, 1953. *Stagestruck*, Alfred Lunt and Lynn Fontanne; Heinemann, 1965. *Mind, Sex and War*, K. O. Newman; Pelago, 1941. And *The Theatres of George Devine*, Irving Wardle; Cape, 1973.

And my fraternal gratitude goes to my brother Hugh, who has read the proofs and compiled the index.

B. A. Y.

Induction

Terence Rattigan was the boy who never grew up.

He became successful, he became famous; he was on intimate terms with Laurence Olivier and Marilyn Monroe, he lunched with the Queen at Buckingham Palace; he ran a Rolls Royce with a vanity numberplate. He was, for a time, the most celebrated playwright in the English theatre. But these were things he had decided to do as a child. It would be hard to find anyone who drove more directly to his chosen target.

When he was still of prep. school age, he announced to his parents that when he was big he was going to write plays. His father, who was in the Diplomatic, reckoned that he should follow him into that corps, and advanced a usual father's argument that writing plays would never bring him enough money to live on. This must have been hard for the young Rattigan to believe, for he was a constant theatregoer even before he reached his teens. People must have written the plays that he and so many others so much enjoyed watching, and it was hardly likely they would have done it for nothing.

Later in his life, when he was able to analyse his obsession, he explained it simply. 'I began to write plays,' he wrote in the Preface to the first volume of his collected works, 'because I felt I had the gift for writing plays.' He added, 'I also believed myself to have the gift for writing novels and short stories, for I find that the works of this period and earlier were nearly all described as being by "the famous playwrite

1

[sic] and author, T. M. Rattigan".' By 'this period' he meant 'early prep-school vintage' – say nine or ten.

His addiction to the theatre meant watching plays and writing plays. Just as a less exceptional boy would have imagined himself on the footplate of the Flying Scotsman rather than sitting in a corner of a first-class compartment, Terry wanted to be in the driving seat. He took part enthusiastically in school plays, less enthusiastically in Oxford plays. Acting in other people's plays was not the same as creating plays of one's own, and he had been doing this almost since he learnt to write, for his own satisfaction. He was only twenty-two when he saw the first professional production of one of his own works, though this was a work of collaboration with another writer of his own age. He wrote *First Episode*, with a fellow undergraduate, while he was reading history at Oxford. This was indeed an early success by the standards of the time, and rather suggests the fortunes of the leisured young men of the Restoration days (with whom, artistically, Rattigan may in some ways be compared). Congreve and Otway both saw their first plays acted when they were twenty-three; Farquhar saw his at twenty. It is true that *First Episode* confirmed the judgment that playwrights didn't make enough money to live on, for its authors made no money from it at all.

But they had a good time, and, more important, they got good notices. The modest run of about eighty performances was more than enough to confirm Rattigan's belief that writing plays was the destiny fate had marked him down for. He came down from Oxford without a degree, and his father made the sporting offer that he would support him for the next two years while he worked on his plays, on the understanding that he would take some more responsible job if at the end of that time he had not made a success of it. Within two years, he had a second play running in the West End that released him from dependence on his father, and from then on he earned his living as a playwright for the rest of his days.

This sounds like a happy ending, but it has to be qualified. His easy success in the theatre was all that he won. He was indeed a successful playwright, but no more than that. (Where were those novels and short stories?) From his mid-twenties onwards, he could have attained virtually any experience or possession he wanted. He never chose, like Somerset Maugham, to explore the world and examine the way in which people other than the English middle class passed their lives. It never occurred to him to explore the Amazon or Tibet, like Peter Fleming. He served during the war as an air gunner in the RAF, but his only war-based dramas were a romance and a farce. He never married. He never involved himself more than superficially in any current movement. The nearest he ever came to public controversy was in a lively correspondence in the *New Statesman* that he had set off with an article discounting the idea that plays should concern themselves with current concerns. All his life, his relationships with his fellow human beings were fundamentally the relationships of a schoolboy.

This innocence was undoubtedly a disadvantage to him, though with schoolboy assurance he presented it as an advantage. Plays, he maintained, should be about people, not about things. He proved himself to have a great talent for writing plays about people, even though they were generally the kind of people among whom he lived his own life. There is all too little in his work that is not a reflection of his own existence. When he strays from his own world to depict great heroes of history, they assume an unexpected look of well-bred Englishmen. It's true that there was nothing in Rattigan's life like the case of the Archer-Shee cadet, or the campaigns of Alexander the Great or T. E. Lawrence, or the trial for murder of Mrs Rattenbury, which he chose as subjects for plays. But, as he interpreted them, these events emerge as stories he had read, news items in the day's *Times*. Ably as he manipulated the people in his scripts, they were the people he knew from Harrow and Oxford and Hertford Street and Sunningdale and Albany.

By beginning a survey of Rattigan's life in this way, I am breaking a Rattigan rule. 'When you're writing about something you like,' he once said to me, 'but about which you have important reservations, it seems to me that the proper thing is to put your approval at the top of your notice and then bring out the reservations afterwards. People make up their minds from the first thing they read.' He would not, I suspect, have considered the reservation I have put at the front of my book antipathetic. He filled his plays with characters who would be immediately recognizable to his audiences, and gave them language to speak that was the language of those audiences. His special genius was to manipulate these familiar figures in such a manner as to provide the dramatic impact he was after.

His own life was pretty well free from excitement, or pathos, or tragedy, on a scale greater than touches the life of the average successful man. No doubt his father would have been better pleased to see him involved in activities as adventurous as some of his own, but was reconciled to see that he had been mistaken in his estimate of a playwright's earning capacity. His mother was a wisely critical admirer all her life. But the relation on whose opinions he relied more than on any other was an aunt that he invented for himself – his Aunt Edna.

Aunt Edna was not only Terence Rattigan's aunt; she was the aunt in every middle-class family, who kept them in touch with what was going on and what they ought to think. He invented her as a prop in the Preface he wrote to the second volume of his collected plays. Sitting in the stalls at a West End theatre or concert hall, or pacing the floors of the art galleries, she pronounced her judgments on what was new, and it was to extract a favourable judgment from her that Terence Rattigan shaped his work. We shall see her more clearly later on. Meanwhile, one must envisage her looking over the author's shoulder, from his very earliest writing days. No doubt he did not notice her at first, but once she had been spotted, it was her opinions, favourable or not, that he courted. Whether such devotion was good for him is a question that has been long, even acrimoniously, discussed. But there she sat, and even when he wrote something intended to displease her, it was by her standards that he worked.

Terence Mervyn Rattigan was born on 10 June 1911. His father, Frank Rattigan, was in the Diplomatic Service, at that time *en poste* at Tangier, but currently on leave in London. His leave was arranged not only on account of the birth of his son (which seems to have made little impression on him at the time), but also to enable him to attend the coronation of King George V. He had secured himself an appointment as Gold Staff Officer at this ceremony, his duty being to escort the former Grand Vizier of Morocco at the celebrations. Terence was his second son. In a light-hearted autobiographical book, *Diversions of a Diplomat*, that Frank Rattigan wrote after his retirement, he records the birth of neither of them, nor indeed their existence. Nor does he reveal much about his marriage.

Frank Rattigan's father was a distinguished lawyer who practised in India, became Chief Justice of the Punjab, then came home and continued his public life as MP for Lanarkshire, North-East, with a knighthood – Sir William Rattigan. Sir William's father was also a distinguished Indian lawyer, Bartholomew Rattigan, but according to one account he originally went to India from his home in County Kildare as a private soldier.

It would be easy to portray Frank Rattigan disparagingly as a frivolous man whose chief concerns were shooting and other outdoor sports, and who had a weakness for equally frivolous women. But it seems that, as diplomats go, he was not a bad one. He records in his book how, on the day after his arrival in Cairo, he was sent for by Lord Kitchener, who calmly informed him that he was to write the annual report on the Sudan. This was a vast document dealing in detail with every branch of the administration.

'I was absolutely dumbfounded, and merely stared at him without uttering a word. Giving me a sharp but quizzical glance of his keen blue eyes, he said, "Have you any comment to make?" I replied, "No, sir, except that for the moment I know nothing about the Sudan." "Then you are in luck," he retorted, "for when you have finished the report you should know everything that can be known about it. I can give you exactly a fortnight to finish the draft report!"' [And in ten days the draft was done.]

When he applied to Kitchener for a job at the beginning of the 1914-1918 war, his current posting in Berlin having been taken from him by *force majeure*, Kitchener was good enough to write a recommendation that included the factor, 'Your intelligence is about up to the average', no mean compliment from such a difficult man. Certainly Frank Rattigan seems to have displayed initiative and even courage in Berlin at the outbreak of war, in France on the vague military mission that Kitchener had found for him, more especially in Bucharest, which he and his wife had to leave in 1917 by way of Petrograd at the height of the revolution.

Even his early retirement from the Diplomatic Service seems to have shown some determination. He was assistant High Commissioner in Constantinople in 1922. This was the time of a now-forgotten little crisis, the Chanak incident. The question was whether Britain should offer armed assistance to the Greeks against the Turks or remain neutral. Frank Rattigan was strongly in favour of giving armed help to the Greeks. Lord Curzon, the Foreign Secretary, found it embarrassing that our second man in Constantinople should be urging action against the Turks, and Frank Rattigan left the service.

He married Vera Houston in 1905, when she was only seventeen, a strikingly beautiful girl. Her family, like the Rattigans, came of Irish legal stock, though none of the Houstons achieved quite the eminence of Frank's father Sir William. In the present context, perhaps the most interesting of the Houstons was Professor Arthur Houston, a political economy don at Trinity College, Dublin, and an amateur of English drama. (He was not optimistic about its future; writers who had the needful ability to create character, he thought, would prefer the novel to the play – and if you look at the plays and the novels current in 1863, when that judgment was passed, you can understand his belief.)

Terence was devoted to his mother all his life. His elder brother, Brian, was born three years after her marriage; he had a club foot, and died comparatively young, of lung cancer, in the 1950s. The relationship between the brothers must have been close in their early days, for they had to spend a lot of time together without their parents. Vera Rattigan was a model diplomat's wife, sociable and popular, able to restrain in her husband the frivolity that existed in him. She followed him loyally and efficiently from one post to another, all too often separated from her children. Frank and Vera were in Germany for the first half of 1914; in the spring of 1915 they went to Romania, where Frank had been appointed Second Secretary at the Legation. During the war Terence and Brian were left with their grandmother, Lady Rattigan. She seems to have been a favoured refuge for Rattigan children; also on hand were the three children of Frank's brother, who had been killed on the Somme. But, in retrospect, Terence thought of his grandmother without much affection.

In 1916 Romania entered the war on the Allies' side, and before the end of the year the Germans entered Bucharest. The Diplomatic staff found their way to Petrograd, after an appalling journey through starving Romania and revolutionary Russia. Vera Rattigan is mentioned occasionally in Frank's account of their adventures; after four pages about shooting duck, six lines tell us that she 'bore these hardships wonderfully,' and worked for ten months in a French Military Hospital. In Russia, where Frank was laid low with water on the knee, Vera seems almost to have been in charge of the party. 'With roars of good-humoured laughter,' Frank reports, 'the Russians patted my wife on the shoulder, telling her apparently that she ought to be a soldier.' By the time they got back to England, little Terry, now seven years old, might have expected some normal family life, but in 1918 Frank returned to Bucharest as Chargé d'Affaires, and the boys went back to Lady Rattigan.

In 1920 he went to his private school, Sandroyd, to prepare for Harrow. Here at last he could begin to live what passes as a normal life among the young of the well-off. When he had been here two years, his father resigned from the Diplomatic, and it was made clear that Harrow would be out of the question unless he could win a scholarship, and this in due course he did.

At what stage he reckoned on becoming a playwright when he grew up is hard to say, for the decision is wreathed in romance, partly Terry's own. From his earliest years he had been a compulsive theatregoer. His parents took him; an 'indulgent aunt' took him; and when he had enough pocket money and no invitation, he took himself.

What were his immature reactions, sitting by himself in the gallery (or, if he had a little extra spending money, in the pit)? He has explained them in the Preface he wrote for his first volume of *Collected Plays*:

> 'If my neighbours gasped with fear for the heroine when she was confronted with a fate worse than death, I gasped with them, although I suppose I could have had but the haziest idea of the

exact nature of the lady's peril; when my neighbours laughed at the witty and immoral paradoxes of the hero's bachelor friend, I laughed at them too, although I could have appreciated neither their wit nor their immorality; and when my neighbours cheered the return of some favourite actor I cheered with them, even though at the time of their last appearance in London I had, quite possibly, not been born.'

One summer, during the holidays from Sandroyd, the family leased a cottage belonging to Hubert Griffiths, the critic. The only books in the cottage were plays, and Terry, aged about ten, read them greedily. He achieved the admirable ability of turning the words on the page into a theatrical performance in his head. The next thing was to think up words that would turn into a performance of his own invention. The first recorded example was a ten-minute melodrama called *The Parchment*, which he recalls in the Preface to his second volume of *Collected Plays*. 'Turgid and ill-written,' he calls it, 'turgid' being a favourite adjective of his when dealing with his early pieces.

The Parchment is set in an English sitting room and has a cast of seven, so we may see that the young Rattigan had an instinctive understanding of managements. However, he then drifts off into a flashback to the Palace of the Borgias in the 16th century; and his belief in managers, if it really existed, didn't extend to the length of casting, for on the cover of his play he wrote that 'The author wishes it to be known that the following cast might be suitable for a presentation of this work – Godfrey Tearle, Gladys Cooper, Marie Tempest, Matheson Lang, Isobel Elsom, Henry Ainley, Noël Coward.'

As Rattigan explains in his Preface, this star-studded cast was not seriously expected to take part in the performance, nor was any performance seriously expected to happen. But, as he wrote the lines, the author had to visualize the characters, and a suitable way of visualizing them was to imagine a familiar actor in the part.

The Parchment was written in Rattigan's first year at Harrow, where he had gone in 1925, having successfully won his scholarship. Here he encountered his first experience of dramatic criticism. A French master required his class to write a short play in French. Rattigan naturally seized the opportunity to compose a scene from a romantic melodrama. He has left us his own account of it in the Preface to Volume Two of his plays:

'I had seized the theatrical opportunity with both hands . . . and had plunged straight into the climactic scene of some plainly very turgid tragedy. The Comte de Boulogne, driven mad by his wife's passion for a handsome young *gendarme*, rushes in to the Comtesse's boudoir where she sits at her dressing-table having her hair done by three maids . . . and announces, incorrectly, I think, that the *gendarme* of her choice is none other than her long-lost brother, Armand. I do not intend to shame myself by quoting any of the truly hideous dialogue in which the Comte and Comtesse de Boulogne (the *gendarme*, being hidden in the cupboard at the time, happily took no active part in the scene) except the final line, which surely even my unsympathetic master had to admit was syntactically faultless:

> COMTESSE: (*souffrant terriblement*): Non! non! non! Ah non! Mon Dieu, non!'

The French master gave the exercise two marks out of ten, and added, 'French execrable: theatre sense first class.' Rattigan was so concerned with the plot of his little story that he overlooked the need to reduce it to correct language.

This is a quality that remained with him throughout his life. He admits in his first Preface to his servitude to 'the thraldom of middle-class vernacular', and excuses it – no, merely explains it – with the argument that 'if I denied myself my gift for telling a story and delineating character in the terms of everyday speech', the gift would suffer. Sir Harold Hobson once observed that if Rattigan had had better criticism, he would have become a better writer.

The next item of juvenilia that we have dates from a year later; it has the words 'age 15' pencilled on one of the two surviving copies. The item is a play that was originally called *Integer Vitae* (a quotation from Horace's *Odes*) but was later changed to *The Pure in Heart*. One copy, written in ink in a school exercise book, is credited to 'T. M. Rattigan, author of *The Consul's Wife, King's Evidence*', suggesting the existence of previous completed works. The other copy has been typed, and it is on this one that the Latin name has been crossed out in ink and the new title written in. For a fifteen-year-old, it is by no means a bad play.

The ambience, typical of later Rattigan, is the home of a middle-class family. A man who does some vague work in an office (not, one would have thought, the kind of man familiar to the Rattigans) has been threatened with the sack, but reprieved on the ground that he is known for his 'blameless integrity'.

That day, his son comes home to tell his father and mother that he has killed a man who had insulted his girl. If he were to be arrested, of course, this would smirch the integrity on which his father depends for his living, so his father advises him to go abroad. The son agrees to do so, but the evening paper reports that someone else has been arrested for the murder, and (having apparently more integrity than his father) he resolves to give himself up. His father is having none of that, and disapproves of the young man's half-way-house decision to wait for the trial and see if the other man is convicted.

When the trial comes, the son indicates to his father that the verdict has been 'guilty'. The two of them go upstairs to discuss the situation, and the son falls from an unsound balcony and is killed. This is by no means the end of the predicament, however, for once the immediate problems have been cleared up, the boy's mother accuses his father of having killed his son, as he knew that the balcony was unsafe. The verdict at the murder trial, she says, was in fact 'not guilty', and there was no longer any fear of their son giving himself up. She decides that she can no longer live with such a man; but he, after a moment's consideration of suicide, thinks that the best thing he can do is to go back to the office as if nothing had happened, with his reputation for 'blameless integrity' intact.

The author's own blameless integrity is clear in his careless use of murder and suicide to make his dramatic points, but you could say that the play is 'well made' in the way that Rattigan insisted upon in his own, and other writers', work later on, and such theatrical points as he makes are good ones, even if he makes them in a rather naive way.

There are no other survivors from his schoolday compositions, but we learn a little about his critical faculties. He was reputed to have read every play in the school library – including, no doubt, the *Agamemnon* of Aeschylus that later played its part in *The Browning Version*. An essay in the *Harrovian* charts the direction in which his future dramatic ventures were to go. Comparing what later came to be known to him as 'plays about people' and 'plays about ideas', he wrote, 'The Pinero –Jones school – ably being upheld by such excellent craftsmen as Somerset Maugham, Noel Coward, Ben (sic) Levy, Ashley Dukes – hold as their acknowledged criterion the box-office . . . the Shaw school have gone on developing side by side and show no sign of converging.' He was on the side of the Pinero–Jones (Henry Arthur) school, and he remained on their side all his professional life.

An earlier piece of criticism turned up lately. A contemporary of Rattigan's, who shared a room with him in The Park (their house), used to do Rattigan's maths for him, while Rattigan did his English. He was asked one day if he would provide an essay on Edgar Wallace's *The Terror*, and he wrote some of it on two empty pages at the end of the School List for January 1928. The list was subsequently included in a bound volume, and although the binder tried to erase it, some of it survives. It goes like this:

Mr Edgar Wallace tells us that he wrote *The Terror* in three days. I can well believe it. If it is true, he is certainly to be congratulated. But it is emphatically a bad play. But what else can you expect. Could Galsworthy or G.B.S. write a good play in three days? No. Nor can Mr Edgar Wallace. But quite possibly the latter could not write a good play in three years. And so as I say he is to be congratulated upon having written a play, which if it is not good, is at least remarkably effective.

In a prologue reminiscent of the Lyceum in its palmier and more melodramatic days, Soapy S. – cast in durance vile at Dartmoor, vows vengeance. . . .

The binder has deprived us of the rest.

The style is almost recognizable, the opinions too. All that is uncharacteristic is the fact that the young Rattigan didn't know that Noël Coward, one of the excellent craftsmen of the Pinero–Jones school, had written *Hay Fever* in three days, or so he said.

A younger contemporary, two years his junior, remembers Rattigan as 'a very clever boy who quickly went up to the top of the school. He was, of course, most successful not only at work but also at cricket, being in the First XI. Boys of my generation admired and respected him.' He played in the first eleven for three seasons. In 1929 he opened the batting for Harrow in the Eton and Harrow match (29 in the first innings, 1 in the second). The following season his form declined and he was not included in the side, to his (and his father's) great distress. He also played squash and racquets for the school.

He found work easy, and there was room in his mind for other interests besides cricket, the drama and working for a scholarship to Oxford. His politics were fashionable, liberal and inclined towards pacifism. He much resented having to spend his time on OTC parades, and went one better than his contemporaries, who wrote letters to *The Harrovian*, by writing a letter to *The Times*, who printed it. Stanley Baldwin, the prime minister, was himself a Harrovian. No change was made in the twice-weekly schedule of parades.

Rattigan left Harrow at the end of the Summer Term of 1930, with a scholarship to Trinity College, Oxford. He was to read history. His main concern, however, was still the drama.

At Harrow, the school drama society is now called the Rattigan Society – an ample tribute to the respect with which he is held.

One
Oxford and Apprenticeship

Rattigan went up to Trinity in October 1930. Oxford was thick with theatrical talent. George Devine spent all his time at the club rooms of OUDS, and became President in the 1931–32 season. Other members were Giles Playfair, Christopher Hassall, Hugh Hunt, Peter Glenville, Paul Dehn, Frith Banbury, William Devlin, Raymond Raikes. Rattigan joined the society as soon as he was able (it required no more than the ability to pay the subscription), and many of the members became his friends for life. Others of his contemporaries were Angus Wilson, Tony Goldschmidt (with whom he later collaborated), Philip Heimann (with whom he also collaborated) and John Bayliss, a fellow-Harrovian who fed him with enough reliable racing tips to nourish the weakness for betting that had been with him since school.

In his first year, he lived in college. He was not an assiduous worker, but his devotion to the theatre continued unchanged, both as a writer and as a performer. He also wrote criticism of plays and films for *Cherwell*, thus ensuring a foot in both camps.

His indifference to work, as unlikely to be of much value to a playwright, was hardly gratifying to his father. Frank Rattigan, living on his pension and what he could make from dealing in antiques, still saw his boy as an embryo member of the Diplomatic, and on Terence's first long vacation he was dispatched to France to improve his French. The crammer's he went to was in Wimereux, near Boulogne, and was run by a Monsieur Martin, who taught French on the 'direct method'. There

11

were half a dozen other young people there, and the weeks he spent there were profitably employed in putting away as many mental notes as possible in case they might be of dramatic value later on.

Two summers later, he went to a crammer's in the Black Forest to improve his German, but by that time other matters had established their priority and he spent most of his time there working with Philip Heimann on a play.

Rattigan's dramatic activities at Oxford began to mature in his second year. He was a favourite performer in the smokers at OUDS, presenting bitchy little sketches under the name of Lady Diana Coutigan. (The chosen surname shows that he was in no way reluctant to display a tendency to 'camp'. 'Queer as a coot' was a current phrase for homosexuals.) He also wrote an uncharacteristically experimental piece which he submitted to George Devine for OUDS. Devine rejected it, but kindly. 'I'm sure he was right,' Rattigan said later. 'It was a highly experimental piece rather in the vein of Constantine's effort in *The Seagull*. He was very kind. He said, "Some of it is absolutely smashing, but it goes too far." It did.'

His best known undergraduate performance was in the OUDS production of *Romeo and Juliet* in February 1932. This historic production was directed by John Gielgud; Peggy Ashcroft played Juliet, and Edith Evans the Nurse. (Women undergraduates were not allowed to join, and professional actresses were invited to play, though without payment. They were 'put up and loved', in George Devine's phrase. Professional directors were often invited also, but these were generally paid a fee.)

Rattigan was one of the maskers, and was entrusted with the single line, 'Faith, we may put up our pipes and be gone.' Why, neither he nor his director has ever been able to say, but the way he spoke the line made the audience laugh. The legend is that he spoke it differently each subsequent night, but it always got the laugh. It proved to be the last line that he ever spoke on the stage; from that time on, he was interested only in writing plays – though he acted them to himself, as he wrote.

From his second year on, he moved out of college and into digs at Canterbury House in King Edward Street. Peter Glenville moved in at the same time, and so did Philip Heimann, a young South African who was reading law. Heimann was having an affair with a woman undergraduate, Irina ('Va-va') Basilewich who, at twenty-six, and already once married and divorced, must have seemed immensely sophisticated. (Heimann was twenty-one.)

To Rattigan the situation was irresistably theatrical, particularly as his friendship with Heimann had reached a stage of intimacy that could justify a kind of eternal-triangle plot. (Heimann, years later, used the plot in a novel.) The two of them discussed it endlessly but not unduly seriously. The play that the two of them wrote together is more concerned with undergraduate jokes than with three-sided romance, and this proved to be a handicap. But the ambience in which it was written made a light-hearted treatment inevitable – first, their daily life at Oxford, then the flippant routine at Karlsruhe on the edge of the Black Forest, where Rattigan had gone to study German but where Heimann had followed him to go on with the play.

The play, initially called *Embryo* but subsequently rechristened *First Episode*, takes place in a university lodging where four students live, though only two of them really matter, Tony and David. Tony has begun a liaison with Margot, a successful London actress of about thirty. (There are various ages in different sources.) David believes that Tony's affair will not only keep him from passing the exams on which his later career may depend, but – and this is more serious – fracture the deep friendship between them. Tony is persuaded that he must break off his friendship with Margot, especially as she is becoming more and more dominating. When he does so, she blames the break on David, and tips off the proctors that David may be found in bed with his girl Joan at a forbidden hour. David is sent down, Tony is deprived of Margot and Margot of Tony, and Joan is compelled to find solace in a brainless young cricketer called Albert. Such an unfulfilled conclusion became typical of Rattigan later on.

The writers filled the play with student larks, including a drunk scene for David and a great party to celebrate a win on the Derby. (Rattigan, under John Bayliss's tutelage, had twice picked Derby winners, April the Fifth and Windsor Lad.) The result was that, when the play was produced, it was for laughs, and not for the deeper content, the strain on the young men's friendship.

The fact that it was produced at all was unexpected. The authors did not see it as possible material for OUDS, and when they had finished it, they sent it off to a London management. Heimann then returned to South Africa, and was at once replaced in Karlsruhe by John Perry, a friend Rattigan had made during the production of *Romeo and Juliet*. In an unusually short time, by today's standards, the management replied suggesting that the play should be put on at once, and Rattigan flew home.

The play was produced at the Q Theatre, a 'fringe' house in, appropriately, Kew, under the direction of Muriel Pratt. It is likely that the emphasis on the friendship of the two young men may have led to a fear that the Lord Chamberlain would believe that there was a suggestion in the play of homosexuality, a subject that was absolutely taboo on the stage (unless it were contained in plays like Marlowe's

Edward II, written before the Lord Chamberlain was granted his censorship powers). How much homosexuality there is in this kind of attachment is hard to say. Americans take this kind of buddy-buddy friendship for granted, as you see in plays like *Who'll Save the Plowboy* and *That Championship Season*. At any rate, the direction emphasized the almost farcical comedy, and this pleased the critics, none of whom thought that the break-up of David's friendship with Tony was as vital as one of the authors at least must have believed.

The fun pleased *The Times* critic enough for him to forgive 'its rather more than occasional failure to make its development plausible'. There is in fact no reason why any kind of development should have been plausible at that level, for the characters of Tony and David are pretty short of qualities strong enough to prompt them to do anything valid. The comedy, said *The Times*, was as uproarious as *Charley's Aunt*; as Brandon-Thomas's comedy had run almost non-stop for the best part of a century, perhaps the London critics had some justification for their predictions that *First Episode* would have a long run. Even James Agate, who was later so scathing about *French without Tears*, thought it should run. The *Evening News* reckoned it would run for a year. In fact, it transferred from the Q to the Comedy and ran for eighty performances.

Unhappily, Rattigan and Heimann had neglected to read their contract carefully enough, and the only money they got from the play was an advance of £100 (between them) on the transfer to the West End. Rattigan had invested £200 of his own money in the production, but it was never returned. But to a young playwright, money counts less than success, and to have a play running in the West End was enough to confirm Rattigan in his ambition. The University authorities were disturbed by the suggestions, put about by the papers, that this riot of drink, sex and gambling was a picture of contemporary Oxford. *Cherwell* was forbidden to carry any review of the play.

There was only one thing to do. Rattigan wrote to his father to tell him that there was now no longer any question of his working for entrance to the Diplomatic. He would leave Oxford at once and settle down to follow his new calling in London, at an address that he would not divulge. Then he went to the Proctors and announced that he was leaving. The secret address was the flat in Half Moon Street that Heimann had taken when he returned from his home in South Africa for the opening at the Comedy. They had an enjoyable existence *à deux* for a while, but in time life caught up with fiction and Heimann married his Irina Basilewich and returned to South Africa, where he went into the family business he had so disparaged at Oxford. Frank Rattigan had no difficulty in finding out where his son was living. With admirable generosity, he suggested that, if Terence was determined to become a writer, he would do better to become one in his father's home, where he wouldn't have to pay the rent.

Frank Rattigan behaved with notable benevolence, considering what he had invested in his son's education. He moved a writing desk into a room in his flat in Stanhope Gardens and told his son that he would make him an allowance of £200 a year for two years, on condition that if, at the end of those two years, he had not made enough progress in the theatre to ensure that he would be able to keep himself, he would accept anything that his father would find for him. Terence moved into his new work room and began to write plays.

He simply wrote plays as fast as he could go, sending them off to one agent after another. There was a New York production of *First Episode*, but he was unable to go to that. It ran for forty performances at the Ritz Theatre and netted nothing for its authors. An apparently better prospect came when Hector Bolitho invited him to collaborate on a play he was writing.

Hector Bolitho was a writer of travel books and royal biographies. He had also written two novels, and was engaged on the adaptation of a third, *Grey Farm*. This was about a man who is driven mad at the prospect of his nineteen-year-old son marrying a girl student. At its climax, the unhappy man, who has spent most of the evening brooding over his hands, strangles his maid and shoots himself. What else happens in the three acts I can't say, for the play was never done in England, and when it was played in New York in 1940, with Oscar Homolka as the mad farmer, it ran only from 3 May to 1 June and collected terrible notices. 'Hopeless script,' said *Variety*, and, adding a touch of detail to the bare tale of the crazy parent, 'It seems the old man just can't control his thumbs, which, ever since his wife died in childbirth nineteen years before, have been itching to squeeze somebody's neck.'

Bolitho regarded the play as a 'solemn, quiet little piece', and was disturbed by the accounts he had of Homolka's playing. He had turned it, he thought (though he never saw it), 'into a mid-European rodeo'.

This collaboration gave Rattigan no pleasure. He liked neither the story nor its writer; but only a few miles from Bolitho's house at Hempstead was the house at Finchingfield shared by John Perry and John Gielgud. John Perry, an actor and writer who later became a director of H. M. Tennent, had met Rattigan when Gielgud was directing *Romeo and Juliet*, and the two became close friends. Whenever he could, Rattigan would take time off and visit Perry and Gielgud, and this unexpectedly led to a new and much more amenable work of collaboration.

Gielgud had just finished a tour of *Hamlet*, and was working on a production of André Obey's *Noah*, in which he was to play the lead. At the same time, he was planning to make a stage adaptation of Dickens's *A Tale of Two Cities*, in which he was to double the parts of Sydney Carton and the Marquis de St Evrémonde. He had devised a scenario, but he needed someone to add the dialogue, and – probably at John Perry's suggestion – he invited Terence Rattigan to do this.

This was by no means a routine task. One of the characteristics of *A Tale of Two Cities* that distinguishes it from most of Dickens's other novels is that it depends less on dialogue to establish the pattern of the characters. As Dickens explained, his object was 'to provide characters the story shall express, rather than that they should express themselves by dialogue' – much, in fact, as if he were writing for a silent film. In the event, a good deal of dialogue found its way in, though all too much of it is couched in an artificial vein intended to suggest French. 'Where do you go, my wife?' 'I go with you at present. You shall see me at the head of women, by and by.' But there are many passages, notably Charles Darnay's trial at the Old Bailey, where cold narrative sentences present scenes that in the theatre need telling exchanges of speech.

Gielgud's scenario told the essentials of the story, leaving out much of the ornamental documentary decorations that Dickens put in to heighten the sinister colours of revolutionary Paris. Thus there is no storming of the Bastille or assassination of Foulon, the action being confined more closely to the principal actors. Terence Rattigan would have no trouble in providing them with words by which they might 'express themselves'; he had, after all, written at least six plays of his own besides *First Episode*. But in these, the dialogue was to be spoken by characters he had invented himself. To write words for other people's characters, especially characters familiar to English readers, was another matter.

What he wrote was decent straightforward English, with some decent straightforward characterizations for people like Jerry Cruncher ('Recalled to life? Now ain't that a blasted queer answer!') and Miss Pross ('Look at her, I ask you! Would you like to run into that on a dark night if you had half-a-crown in your purse?') Here and there a good English joke appears. 'You don't seem quite to realise what the Bastille is,' Jarvis Lorry accuses Miss Pross. 'It's a prison, isn't it,' she says, 'only French.' Dickens's pseudo-French ('What the devil do *you* do in that galley there?') is rightly exiled.

The script reads well enough. It is Gielgud's scenario that supports the Rattigan dialogue rather than the other way round (though the script is generously headed '*A Tale of Two Cities*, by Terence Rattigan and John Gielgud.') When the first two acts were done, Gielgud sent them to Bronson Albery, and Albery told him that, if the third act were as good, he would certainly produce the play. The third act was completed in a little over a week, and preparations for production began at once. The play would be put on at the New Theatre (now the Albery), and an excellent company was lined up. Fay Compton was to play Lucie Manette, Martita Hunt Miss Pross, Mary Clare Madame Defarge, Leon Quartermaine Dr Manette and George Howe Jarvis Lorry. The Motleys designed an ingenious set for the New stage, which couldn't cope with too many elaborate changes. There was to be a central upper stage with acting areas on each side below. The action was to move alternately between these two, with occasional scenes on the upper stage. A set of this kind was regarded as something of a novelty for a romantic melodrama in those days.

Everything was going forward well when Gielgud got an angry letter from Sir John Martin-Harvey. Sir John had been playing his own adaptation of the same book, *The Only Way*, for many years – in fact, since 16 February 1889 – and he intended to go on playing it in a series of farewell performances. Gielgud took the problem to Albery. Various people were asked for their views, and in the end Albery reluctantly agreed to put the play aside. Martin-Harvey was 72, and it would hardly have been fair to deprive him of his most famous part.

This was not quite the end of the production. At the meeting where it was decided to abandon the project, Gielgud spontaneously proposed an alternative. Peggy Ashcroft and Edith Evans, the Juliet and Nurse in the OUDS production where Rattigan had had such trouble with his line, were now both free. Why not a new *Romeo and Juliet*? Once more there was conflict with other players. Robert Donat was about to play Romeo in a production of his own. So was Laurence Olivier. But this time, matters worked out better. Olivier joined Gielgud's production, and they alternated the parts of Romeo and Mercutio.

The set on which they played was the set that the Motleys had designed for *A Tale of Two Cities*, adapted from eighteenth-century Paris to medieval Verona. There was no way of involving Terence Rattigan, but Albery sent him a cheque for fifty guineas.

A few years later, Rattigan and Gielgud lunched with the directors of H. M. Tennent. 'Terry and I toyed with the idea of a really grand production,' Gielgud recalls, 'for the Coliseum or Drury Lane, coach and horses, big crowd set.' The meeting took the idea even further. 'A lot of incidental music composed in the manner of the Fred Terry melodramas, to emphasize mood and excitement in different scenes, and Louis Dreyfus said "Why don't I take the idea to one of the big American composers and turn the whole thing into a musical?"

'I was quite horrified. Years later, when I saw *Oliver*, I realized what a fool I had been not to do as he had suggested. Well, perhaps it will end up one day as a Rock Opera.'

Terry, as Rattigan was known to his friends, did not come out of the project empty handed, however. When Bronson Albery sent him his cheque, he invited him to let him see any other play he might have written. Albery had already seen a fair number, but there were a couple that had not been read and returned. Rattigan sent him *Gone Away*.

Albery took out a nine-month option for a small fee. Nine months went by, and the play was not produced. This was a disastrous situation, for by now the two years' licence his father had given him were up, and Terry had to find a job. On the strength of *First Episode*, he was employed as a scriptwriter in Warner Brothers' studio in Teddington. In true Hollywood fashion, this involved clocking in at the studio at precise hours, to take on such work as was given rather than to use one's facility for invention. It was not the occupation Terry was looking for, but he had a seven-year contract, at a starting salary of £15 a week – nearly four times what his father was allowing him.

It was fifteen years before anything more was heard of *A Tale of Two Cities*. In 1950 it was broadcast on BBC radio, with Eric Portman in the part of Sydney Carton; and in the same year it was played by the students of St Brendan's College, Clifton. And lately Terry's agent approached John Gielgud, having chanced on a copy of the play, to ask if he would like him to try and place it. Naturally Gielgud said yes. Nothing has happened up to the time of writing.

One of Terry's colleagues at the Warner Brothers studio was the novelist Anthony Powell. 'Rattigan was outwardly very much like the popular notion (as opposed to the usual reality) of a young diplomat,' he has written in his memoirs *Faces in My Time* (Heinemann 1980); 'tall, good-looking, elegant in turnout, somewhat chilly in manner.' For three weeks they worked together to try and produce a story; they never produced one, but they laughed a good deal over their work. Powell has left a perceptive sketch of Rattigan at that period.

> One was always aware in Rattigan of a deep inner bitterness, no doubt accentuated by the irksome position in which he found himself at that moment. In the theatre good publicity such as he was enjoying is something to be taken advantage of without delay. He had a touch of cruelty, I think, and liked to torment one of the male executives of the studio, who showed signs of falling victim to Rattigan's attractions.

When I asked Rattigan if the French crammer's in his play bore any resemblance to that he had himself attended at Wimereux (one specializing in Foreign Office candidates), he replied: 'Not in the least.' This did not bother him at all. He was a thrusting young man whose primary concern was to make himself financially independent, not interested in 'art' so much as immediate effect.

Rattigan would talk entertainingly about the mechanics of how plays are written, always consciously from a 'non-artist' angle, though in a manner never to bring in doubt his own grasp and intelligence. One of his favourite formulas was: 'Take a hackneyed situation and reverse it.' His own natural abilities always seemed to me to conflict with this disregard for more than popular success, even if a popular success designed to be a cut above run-of-the-mill banalities.

It is interesting to see how much of that character sketch of Terence Rattigan in his early twenties remained valid through the rest of his life.

Two
French without Tears

Terry was never quite positive about the number of plays he wrote in the Stanhope Gardens period. When Albery had asked him for a play, his final choice was between the light comedy, *Gone Away*, and a romantic piece called *Black Forest*, which he has described in the light of later judgment as 'a turgid drama about tangled emotions'.

As an insatiable theatregoer he would have known the plays that had found most public favour at the time. Merton Hodge's *The Wind and the Rain* had played 1001 performances at the St Martin's. Anthony Armstrong's *Ten Minute Alibi*, Anthony Kimmins' *While Parents Sleep*, Rudolf Besier's *The Barretts of Wimpole Street*, St John Ervine's *The First Mrs Fraser*, had clocked up runs of more than a year. The emphasis seemed to be on popular entertainment rather than tangled emotions. Encouraged by his mother, Rattigan sent off *Gone Away*.

Black Forest was well described by the mature Rattigan. It is set in a hotel in the Black Forest, but contains no hint of reference to Rattigan's own days there. In the Hotel Schönblick, an ageing schoolmaster, William Bryant, is on holiday with his family. He has chosen the Black Forest for its splendid air, and for the chance it will give him and his two sons John (at Cambridge) and Peter (at the school where he is himself a housemaster) to brush up their German. Besides his wife, of whom we see very little, and his sons, his party also includes his daughter Mary, twenty-six and unmarried, and her would-be fiancé David Pleydell, who hopes to succeed to Bryant's house in due time.

Also at the hotel, to Bryant's dismay, is Edward Watherstone, whom he had to sack from school when he was discovered making love to a kitchen maid in a churchyard ('a most unsavoury case'). As if this were not enough, Watherstone has written a school story full of libels, and is now wandering around Germany (perhaps to escape the writs) with a German girl, Toni, also of 'the servant class'. You can hardly be surprised that Pleydell finds him 'a thundering cad'. (Pleydell is obviously a name borrowed from Dornford Yates.) Bryant orders that his party may have no contact with Edward or Toni but, in the course of a busy three days, John has become friendly enough with Toni to propose marriage, and Mary has rediscovered a youthful passion for Edward so powerfully that they agree to elope together. Both these projects are scotched when Toni, her earlier loyalties not so easily discarded as she supposed, goes missing. Of course Mary and Edward believe that she must have killed herself, but she turns up in the morning, having slept in the woods. Alarmed by such contacts with brutal reality, Edward, Toni, Mary and John abandon their hastily contrived romances, and the former unhappy contacts are resumed, for better, for worse, in what was to become a characteristic Rattigan open ending.

These affairs are very superficially drawn. All the characters are stereotypes, even fourteen year-old Peter, whose function is to demonstrate how to the innocent eye impropriety may seem harmless.

The pros and cons of *Black Forest* need concern us no longer, however, for once *Gone Away* had been launched on its career, it was not heard of again.

Gone Away had begun life as *Joie de Vivre* (a title that it briefly assumed years later when it was ill-advisedly turned into a musical). Then it was retitled *French Chalk*. It had already been sent to a number of managements, possibly including Albery's. This time, Bronson Albery read it himself, and it made him laugh.

While Albery failed to exercise his option, Terry worked his 10-till-6 routines at the studio. Film scripts were not at the time among his abilities. One script that he took to Irving Asher, in charge of the studio, expecting a word or two of praise, was torn in half before his eyes, and a more experienced writer was deputed to take him away and show him how scripts ought to be written. That event was subsequently elaborated into a legend that the script in question was *Gone Away*. It was in fact an adaptation of Lady Eleanor Smith's novel *Tzigane*, a romance of gipsy life. But *Gone Away* was indeed offered to the studio later on. Terry did not find it easy to live on £15 a week, and he offered all rights in his play for £200. Warner Brothers were not interested.

21

Albery and Wyndham had not forgotten the play, however. At the Criterion, one-of their three London theatres, a play called *The Lady of La Paz* was foundering before they had anything to put on in its place. *Gone Away*, with a cast of ten (small by the standards of the time) and one set, would keep the house open until something more important was ready. The option was renewed.

If its author thought that this spelt immediate freedom from his work in the studio, he was mistaken; he was under contract to Warner Brothers and they had no intention of releasing him. Harold French was appointed to direct the play, and casting began, but without any consultation with Rattigan, who continued his routine activities. Indeed, it was not impossible that these activities might be made all the more onerous as the result of his play's forthcoming production. As Anthony Powell recalls, 'One of the most oppressive of Hollywood's methods imported into the UK (like working on a Saturday afternoon) was that an actor or writer, under contract to one studio, might be hired out to another ... Rattigan's present good fortune made a repetition of such borrowing probable.'[1] He was not ultimately released from his contract until some weeks after the play had opened at the Criterion.

Actually, when Harold French was asked to direct the play, most of the casting had already been done by Bronson Albery, as the production was wanted in a hurry. Kay Hammond, Jessica Tandy, Percy Walsh and Robert Flemyng were engaged, and they were followed (after a momentary protest from Kay Hammond) by Rex Harrison. Next came Trevor Howard, twenty years old, a French actress named Yvonne André and Guy Middleton. Two parts remained to be filled, one of them only a walk on, the other allotted to Roland Culver. The first read-through was held in Albery's office on 15 October 1936. Terry was there, the meeting having been arranged late enough for him to attend without depriving Warner Brothers of his services for too long; but for a time nobody noticed him. He sat quietly in a corner, beyond the semicircle of actors facing Harold French and Bronson Albery. Harold French reckoned that he was probably an assistant stage manager making a note of the props that would have to be found. Only when there was a coffee-break at the end of the second act did anyone think to introduce him to his director.

Harold French has given a good account of the play's opening in his autobiographical book, *I Thought I Never Could* (Secker and Warburg 1973). When the reading was over, he took Rattigan to the Green Room Club. In spite of the experience he had had with *First Episode* and his acquaintance with the lower levels of the film world, Terry was still

[1] *Faces in My Time*

fan-struck. 'As members – most of them household names – strolled from group to group, he would ask, "Isn't that so-and-so?" When I assured him that his guess was correct, he would mutter an awed "Good Lord!" as though he believed dreams could come true.' None of the cast of *Gone Away* was exactly a household name. Their top salary was £25 a week (Rex Harrison asked for, and was refused, £30 – more than Rattigan's pay at the studio, but not in the category of the eminent players surrounding him in the club.).

After a drink or two, Harold French brought up a point that had been worrying him. Why was the play called *Gone Away*? This was a hunting phrase, and there was nothing in the play, or in any of its characters, to suggest a hunting connection. Rattigan, French reports, was silent for quite a while, and then asked for time to think about it. As it was the play's third title, there was no doubt something to think about.

At 1.30 the following morning, he telephoned French at home. 'This is Terry Rattigan here. I'm terribly sorry to disturb you, but I've been thinking, and you're quite right. This is only an idea, kick it out if you don't like it, but would *French without Tears* be any good?' The new title was agreed at once.

On the day before the dress rehearsal, when Terry was dining with his director, he asked him if it were possible to make an alteration at the end of the last act. As the director still had some notes to give to the company, he was prepared to listen. The way the play stood, Diana, a girl who is always on the look-out for a fresh conquest, is preparing to chuck her last venture in favour of another who sounds more exciting. A new student is about to arrive at the crammer's – a lord, no less. Diana takes up her position near the door, where she cannot fail to be seen, a siren in a bathing-suit. With all the appropriate amount of offstage brouhaha, Lord Heybrook is heard arriving. He enters – in Rattigan's phrase, a 'blond, swishy queer' – leading a Dalmatian on to the stage with the unlikely line 'Come along, Alcibiades'.

The point is made, the man-eating Diana is baulked of her prey. But as Terry could see, this moment of vulgarity was alien to the rest of the play. Homosexuals, when they were allowed on the stage at all at that period, were for low comedy.

'What alternative have you?' French asked.

Terry had one. You can inherit a peerage at any age, he pointed out. When Lord Heybrook comes on, why shouldn't he be just a young boy? The same point is made, with equal validity, but without the music-hall vulgarity of the blond, swishy queer and his dog.

Changing the script is one thing, changing the production is another. French, delighted by the alteration, agreed to put it up to Albery. There was only a day before the dress rehearsal. George Astley, the actor who had had his hair specially dyed for the part, had to be laid off. A boy had to be found, auditioned and rehearsed. However, on the credit side – apart from the improvement to the play – a boy actor would be paid less than a man, and the Dalmatian wouldn't have to be hired. Bronson Albery consented to the changes. A teenage actor called William Dear was engaged (everyone knew him as Billy Dear, which sounded so much like a nursery appellation that when he became an adult he had the sense to change the whole name), and stayed with the play throughout its run.

He was lucky. The dress rehearsal was a disaster. It was seriously suggested by one of the players that they shouldn't open. Here is Harold French's account in *I Thought I Never Could* (Secker & Warburg, 1973).

> Trevor Howard dried on his second line, Rex Harrison played as though he were constipated and didn't care who knew it, Roland Culver put in more 'ers' than he had done at the reading, Jessica Tandy was so slow she might have been on a modern strike, Percy Walsh forgot he was playing a Frenchman and every now and then lapsed into an Oxford accent; only Guy Middleton and Kay Hammond played as though they knew what it was all about.

In the stalls were Albery and the people who had put up the £1 500 it cost to put the play on. Albery went back to his office when the curtain fell and arranged for another play to come into the Criterion as soon as possible. He reckoned *French without Tears* couldn't run more than a week. The other punters were busy trying to sell off their investments. Rattigan had brought his mother, who was partly responsible for his having chosen the play to submit to Albery. There had not been so much as a titter the whole evening.

Harold French is not a good loser. Anger overcame his misery in a few moments, and he stormed on to the stage, where the cast were standing about, consoling one another. In a quarter of an hour, he said, there will be another complete dress rehearsal.

He was by no means sure that the company would do what he asked. They might simply have gone off home and cursed their luck. But by the time French had collected Rattigan, whom he found loitering mournfully in the foyer, and returned to the stalls, there were encouraging sounds coming from behind the curtain. The second dress rehearsal was played exactly as he wanted it. 'Thank you,' he said when it was done. 'Sorry to have kept you so late.' There didn't seem to be anything else to say.

The first night was a total success. The laughs began almost at once, at Guy Middleton's appalling French accent as he ordered his breakfast, at his classic translation:

KENNETH: If you're so hot, you'd better tell me how to say she has ideas above her station.

BRIAN: Oh, yes, I forgot. It's fairly easy, old boy. Elle a des idées au-dessus de sa gare.

After that, the mood was set, the laughter was continuous throughout the evening. When the final curtain came down, there were cries of 'Author! Author!' But where was the author? He had brought his mother and father, but did not sit with them. Now he was nowhere to be seen. Harold French went through the Pass Door to congratulate the cast, and found Rattigan leaning against the back wall of the theatre and showing signs of emotional exhaustion. 'Get on the stage!' he told him. 'They're calling for you.'

Rattigan went on, prepared, as he said afterwards, to make the extempore speech that he'd been working on for at least five hours. The stage hands, not warned of his appearance, were taken by surprise. The curtains closed across the stage, impaling him from either side.

The company gathered at Kay Hammond's flat and sent out for the morning papers. They were not disappointed. With one exception, the critics were uniformly approving. 'A brilliant little comedy,' said the ultra-conservative *Morning Post*, 'gay, witty, thoroughly contemporary without being unpleasantly "modern".' (How lucky that that blond, swishy queer had been sacrificed.) 'The gift of real lightness is a rare one in the theatre,' the *Daily Telegraph* said, 'and Terence Rattigan is a lucky young man to have it.' 'Sly, cool and delightfully opportune dialogue,' said *The Times*. Of the morning papers, only the *Daily Herald* came down against it. 'It has no conceivable relation to British Drama,' its critic thought.

The weeklies followed suit, though there were some powerful exceptions. In the *Observer*, Ivor Brown complained of 'little construction and no freshness or fun', though he conceded that the play was 'never flagging in jovial absurdity'. The main antagonist was James Agate of the *Sunday Times*. He could not understand this kind of play and acting, he complained, and confessed that he had left the theatre before the end. (It was said, but not by him, that he arrived after the beginning, and only stayed for about half an hour.) Perhaps to persuade his readers that being in a minority was not necessarily a sign of being wrong, he continued to salt his columns week after week with occasional jibes at the play until, after they had been going on for eighteen months during which time it was virtually impossible to buy a stall at the Criterion, John Gielgud wrote a letter of protest.

'It seems a pity,' he wrote, 'that your critic, not content with having dismissed this play contemptuously on its first production, should lose no opportunity since to belittle or sneer at its success.' Agate wrote a pompous reply, shifting his responsibility to George Jean Nathan, from whose *The Morning After the First Night* he quoted 'This finer theatre that so many of us bores have our hearts set on will never emerge from the critical encouragement of things like *French without Tears*.' His argument was that to praise the lightweight would result in the theatre's being swamped with more lightweight work, leaving no room for the serious work he visualized.

His assault on *French without Tears* did more harm to himself than to Terry, however, for he was attacked from all sides for his unfair treatment of the play. Finally he shut up, and the play ran for its final year without another barb from his pen.

How does the play seem from today's standpoint, when its success in the West End has been followed by success in dozens of other productions all over the country, and indeed in other countries?

The plot is certainly unimportant. It doesn't generate real tension; no one has seriously tangled emotions. Diana, who, at the age of twenty-two or so, confesses frankly that 'having men in love with me is my whole life', tries to induce Kit, Lieutenant-Commander Rogers and Alan to fall in love with her, and is only discouraged from adding Lord Heybrook to their number by his lack of years. As plots go, this is no more than a rack to hang the characters on.

But sub-plots abound. There is Alan, an ambassador's son bound for a career in the Diplomatic, who would rather give it all up and write novels (of which he has one already going the rounds of the publishers). There is the education of Lieutenant-Commander Rogers, who is as shy of his younger fellow students as they expect to be bored by him, until both sides discover that it is possible for youth and maturity to get on well together. There is the exceptional case of Brian, who believes that the way to win a woman's love is to purchase it at 50 francs a throw. Most complex is the conversion of Kit; Kit believes himself in love with Diana, but is beloved by Jacqueline, Maingot's daughter. Kit is not at all in love with Jacqueline – 'I'm frightfully fond of her, but somehow – I don't know – I mean you couldn't kiss her or make love to her.' However, as the result of Alan's machinations, they talk about the possibility of their loving one another, even rehearse the dialogue they would exchange if such an unlikely situation should arise. And at once it does arise, though they compromise by calling themselves sentimental friends.

Whether we believe that they intend to marry and settle down together is up to us. 'Summertime sweethearts, where do they go in the fall?' ran an American song of the time. The happy endings of comedies would look very different if we could see beyond the final curtain. But what is fascinating about the final curtain of *French without Tears* is that, as far as Alan and Diana go, there is no happy ending. Diana, when she was called on to resolve the question whether she was in love with Kit or the Commander, resolved it by telling them she was in love with Alan, thus adding an extra charge to Alan's existing half decision to chuck his exams and go home to be a novelist. He is packed and ready to leave when Lord Heybrook arrives and deprives Diana of her alternative prey. Then this happens:

DIANA: Come and help me pack, someone. I'm going to catch that London train or die. (*She disappears through door at back.*)

ALAN (*pursuing her despairingly*):   No, no, oh, God, no! (*Turning at door.*) Stop laughing, you idiots. It isn't funny. It's a bloody tragedy.

So the chase may still be on, on another ground. If we could peep into a hypothetical Act Four, though, I suspect she would still be among the boys at Maingot's establishment, perhaps lowering her age limit in favour of Kenneth, who, after all, has little function in the play except to provoke others to utter good lines. One wouldn't even have been surprised if Kenneth had followed Alan back to England as well, so notable is his devotion to the intellectual leader of the pack. The truth is that the emotion so generously described as 'love' by all concerned is no deeper than a schoolboy, or schoolgirl, crush such as the author may well have experienced at Harrow and at Oxford.

This does nothing to devalue the story, which is about young people of undergraduate age (apart from Commander Rogers, who was evidently suffering from too little time ashore). Schoolboy and schoolgirl crushes, impinging on virgin territory, can seem the most piercing affections of a lifetime. But their functions in the play are almost solely to effect dramatic coups, not to ask us to weep over unresolved longings, any more than over unwritten essays. Every little peak in the course of events is shaped and timed with a certainty remarkable in so comparatively inexperienced a playwright.

In Anthony Powell's recollections that I quoted earlier, he said that Rattigan spoke always of the mechanics of playwriting, not of the art. The early drafts of Terry's plays in those days concentrated on the mechanics, while the art remained in his head. 'Three-minute dialogue between A and B. C enters unexpectedly with news. Fifteen-second silence. Four-minute angry discussion. C leaves. B changes mind in long one-minute speech' – that sort of thing, into which the words were duly dropped. Each important moment was carefully led up to; it arrived, not necessarily where the dialogue logically took it, but a little before or a little after to give it an extra effect. Diana's confession of love for Alan in the middle of a quarrel between Kit and Rogers over which of them she loves best is a good example.

ALAN: Diana, these two gentlemen have good reason to believe that you have been trifling with their affections. You have told Kit that you are in love with him and are bored by Bill, and you have told Bill that you are in love with him and are bored by Kit. So now they naturally want to know who exactly you are bored by. Are you going to answer their question?

DIANA: Certainly not. Whom I love and whom I don't love is entirely my own affair. I've never heard such insolence.

ALAN (*turning to ROGERS and KIT*):   Insolence! She's good, this girl, she's very good.

DIANA: May I please be allowed to go to my room?

ALAN: Not until you've answered our question.

DIANA: I think you'd better let me go.

ALAN: Just as soon as you've given a straight answer to a straight question.

Pause. DIANA at length takes a step back.

DIANA: All right. You want to know who I'm in love with. Well, I'll tell you. (*To ALAN*) I'm in love with you.

There is a dead silence.

We have exactly the right amount of delay before Diana makes her unexpected declaration. And here, too, is an illustration of the much-quoted maxim about taking a well-known romantic situation and turning it on its head. This is a principle that Terry constantly uses, not only in situations, but in dialogue.

ROGERS: We must scupper her with a plunging salvo.

ALAN: Oh, no, don't let's do that.

And at the end of Act 1, when the loving, unlovable Jacqueline has arranged her hair in glamorous imitation of Diana's:

JACQUELINE: You think I ought to keep it like this?

KIT: Keep what?

JACQUELINE: My hair.

KIT: Oh, don't be such a bore about your hair, Jack. Yes, keep it like that. It'll get a laugh anyway.

In less than a year after the London opening, *French without Tears* opened on Broadway at the Henry Miller Theatre. After the show, the company converged on Terry's suite at the Waldorf. There would be a review on the radio. The company clustered round the set.

'A little English comedy called *French without Tears* opened at the Henry Miller Theatre this evening,' said the critic. 'The English actor Frank Lawton had the last line, "It's not funny! It's a tragedy!" And how right he was.'

The New York critics were not all as savage as that, but they were not really encouraging. In the *New York Times*, Brooks Atkinson conceded that 'the style was an attractive one', but only after he had written that the situations were commonplace and the characters unprepossessing. Richard Watts condemned the play in the *Herald-Tribune* as 'escapist', but allowed that it had 'charm, vivacity and engaging amiability'. As these qualities were all it was meant to have, a review like this would not have discouraged London audiences, but New Yorkers like an element of seriousness even in their comedies. English comedies that have packed London theatres often flop in New York (and it's only fair to point out that American comedies, even by writers as eminent as Neil Simon, achieve only moderate success in London). In New York, *French without Tears* ran for 111 performances.

Terry, with one success under his belt, decided to put the New York critics right, and contributed to the *New York Times* a piece called 'Drama without Tears' in which he defended escapist drama. He went so far as to suggest that plays designed to put over a message succeeded only on their dramatic, not their political or sociological, merits. 'English audiences listened to Shaw because he made them laugh. They went to Galsworthy's plays because he was a superb technician and gave them characters that were real and situations which they found exciting. I can't honestly believe that they cared much for the messages which either of these dramatists contributed.'

These are a young man's opinions, easily countered. The long, silent scene of Falder in his cell in Galsworthy's *Justice* ultimately resulted in changes in the use of solitary confinement in English prisons, for instance. But they remained his opinions for the rest of his life, even

29

after the great theatrical renaissance of the mid-1950s commonly associated with John Osborne. 'I believe that the best plays are about people and not about things,' he wrote in the *New Statesman and Nation*, when some years later, after a good deal more experience, he again took up the problem of meaningful theatre. Even questions that he himself felt strongly about were not ventilated in his plays; or if they were, only under a veil of disguise.

Yet in *French without Tears*, the only play by which he was known to the public, there is an instance of overt propaganda unparalleled in the whole corpus of his work. It comes in Act Two, where Alan tells the plot of his much-rejected novel. This is what he says:

ALAN: It's about two young men who take a vow to desert their country instantly in the case of war and to go and live on a farm in Central Africa. War breaks out and they go. One of them takes his wife. They go, not because they are any more afraid to fight than the next man, but because they believe violence in any circumstances to be a crime and that, if the world goes mad, it's their duty to remain sane.

COMMANDER: I see. Conchies.

ALAN: Yes. Conchies. When they get to their farm one of them makes love to the other's wife and they fight over her. . . . But in fighting for her they are perfectly aware that the motive that made them do it is as vile as the impulse they feel to go back and fight for their country. . . . The characters in my book have the honesty not to rationalize the animal instinct to fight, into something noble like patriotism or manliness.

Alan, the spoiled diplomat with literary aspirations, is, as it were, the first person in the story of the play. When Terry was at Oxford, he was one of the 275 members of the Union who voted for the notorious motion proposed by C. E. M. Joad, 'That this House will in no circumstances fight for King and Country.' Drawing on himself for his character, it is reasonable that the character should voice the creator's opinions.

But there is no further pursuit of the pacifist argument, nor is it taken up in subsequent work as if it lay near the author's heart. Indeed, in a year or two, when Terry had himself joined the armed forces, he wrote two pieces dealing sympathetically with men (and women) who were fighting for their King/President and country, both plays free from perceptible pacifist leaning. No 'ideas' even as strong as Alan's outburst appear in any of the subsequent plays, unless you count the mockery of Hitler in *Follow My Leader*. There isn't even the kind of social criticism that the Restoration writers put into such plays as *The Country Wife* and *The Recruiting Officer*. If Terry had any idea of writing plays of ideas, he certainly laid it aside in his next play, *After the Dance*, which he began to write in New York during the run of *French without Tears*.

Three

After the Dance and Flare Path

During the whole run of *French without Tears*, Terry was still under contract to Warner Brothers – more correctly, Warner Brothers British, a separate company – who continued to pay him at his agreed rate, £15 a week. His initial lack of promise forgotten, they now found him a great bargain, for without raising his pay they were able to sublet him to other studios for much higher rates.

Besides that meagre figure, however, Terry was now making more than £100 a week from the Criterion production, and in due course this was augmented by productions in Paris and New York. Paramount (not Warner Brothers) ultimately bought the film rights at a five-figure sum.

So Terry was no longer the younger son, working for his living. He moved out of his workroom in Stanhope Gardens, and took a flat in Hertford Street, a quiet Mayfair thoroughfare near Shepherd Market. He became the man he had always seen himself, spending money lavishly on clothes, parties and gambling. It was said that he made over £20,000 out of that one play, and spent it all.

Warner Brothers had no intention of relinquishing their hold on this unexpected goldmine. However, they gave him leave to visit New York in September 1937 to see the New York production of his play, and Terry, being Terry, took a suite at the Waldorf Astoria. Life in New York suited him very well, and when his specified leave came to an end he was in no mood to go back to London.

As it happened, however, that risk was not imminent. A worse fate threatened him. Irving Asher, his employer at the studios, followed him to New York and announced that he had sub-contracted him to Hollywood, and what was more, a sleeper had been booked for them both on that evening's train. In consideration of the higher cost of living, his salary would be increased by fifteen per cent, bringing it up to the dollar equivalent of £17 5s. a week, hardly an income in the Hollywood class.

Terry flatly refused. There was a heated interview in Irving Asher's hotel. Asher insisted that he was legally bound to go with him; the contract was perfectly clear. Terry said that he had no intention of going anywhere, and as for the contract, Warner Brothers were perfectly entitled to sue him if they wanted to. So Asher went on to Hollywood on his own, to apologize for failing to bring his paragon with him and no doubt to consult his lawyers over the question of the broken agreement. In the end, no case was ever brought. Terry went back to the London studios when he was ready; and later the firm went out of business and all the contracts were scrapped.

There was a particular reason why Terry had not wanted to leave New York. Hubert Gregg, who was playing Kit Neilan in the New York production, was invited to go and see Rattigan in his suite at the Waldorf Astoria. 'I was very good-looking in those days,' Hubert Gregg remembers, 'and I wasn't sure what was on.'

What Terry wanted was to show him a draft of a new play that became *After the Dance*. It was an interesting draft to look at, almost diagrammatic, such as I have described. There would be a brief stage direction, something like 'They sit together on the sofa laughing'; under that a vertical line down the page marked a space labelled 'three minutes dialogue'; then there would be another direction, followed by another space for dialogue, all carefully timed. Terry talked his ideas over with Hubert Gregg, and he was duly given a part in the production the following summer.

Curiously enough, *After the Dance* proved to be a play of ideas, of social criticism, though Terry didn't seem to have been very sure what the ideas were that he proposed to illustrate. He was determined not to be 'escapist', the word the American critics had applied to *French without Tears*; but to say that he was making a firm statement that another war was coming was neither anti-escapist, nor particularly perspicacious, in the winter of 1937.

The people to be blamed for the next war were the people who had just missed the last one, the Bright Young People of the 1920s, 'would-be bohemians who blame the war for their failings, though it didn't concern them much', as Terry told *The Times*. The people to whom we were to turn for salvation were 'the serious-minded and well-mannered young of today'. 'When I was at Oxford,' he told the *Evening Standard*, 'youth had done with the frivolity of the previous generation and was exceedingly serious.' So in his new play, he would be backing his own generation (he was twenty-six) against the next generation above it.

Let's see how he goes about it (and let me say at once that there is nothing about the next war):

The spokesman for the former Bright Young Things is a thirty-eight-year-old writer, David Scott-Fowler (a name possibly meant to suggest Scott Fitzgerald, who was drinking his way through literature at the time). David is married to Joan, of the same class and the same age; and living permanently with them is John Reid of their generation, whose function in the play is to act as Charles-his-friend whenever required.

David takes on as his secretary a young cousin, Peter (this was Hubert Gregg). Peter is engaged to a girl called Helen. These are the representatives of the serious-minded and well-mannered younger generation, but they do not go about their tasks either seriously or politely. Helen decides that it is her duty to reform David, who is more concerned with giving parties than he is with writing his life of King Bomba of Naples (in the style of Hector Bolitho, Rattigan says bitchily). Her scheme for doing this is to separate him from his wife Joan and to marry him herself. She calmly tells the unhappy Joan about this proposal. 'Let's have a quiet little divorce,' Joan suggests, 'with only the family as guests.'

Joan is a well-disposed woman at heart. John tells her (and it is an interesting early example of the need for love that Rattigan illustrated later in *Variation on a Theme*), 'All he wants is someone in love with him.' 'But not me,' Joan says. She has been concealing the serious side of her nature through the twelve years of her marriage because she feels that David would be bored by a serious wife. When she tells David this, he confesses that he has been hiding the serious side of his life because he thought it would bore her. The ultimate consequence is that, at the climax of a gay party, she walks out on to the balcony and throws herself to the pavement.

And the younger generation? Helen suffers the same social fate as her predecessor. David, reluctant to disappoint her by failing to reorient his ways, decides to destroy himself by continuing on his rackety life, having taken a look at the fatal balcony and concluded that it's not for him. Moreover, as John points out to him, Helen is already beginning to bore him; far better to show her the bad side she knows about than let her believe he is still in love with her. As for Peter, he has by now discovered that the carefree life around him is just what he was after, and resolves to take part in it himself. Of them all, John, of the Bright Young Thing generation, is the only one that ends up with a decision to settle down and work.

Terry's fate was already looming over him. When he tried to write about the real world, he revealed that he didn't know enough about it. David and Joan, and Peter and Helen, were such people as had surrounded him since his new affluence engulfed him. No one in the play is engaged in any serious pursuit, any more than people in Noël Coward's plays are, or Frederick Lonsdale's. There is no reason why Rattigan should not have written a piece about the wasters and parasites who had flocked about him in his bounteously-spending days; but it is too much to claim that it has any great relevance to the state of society.

After the Dance opened at the St James's Theatre on 21 June 1939. *French without Tears* had ended its record run only a few weeks earlier, and Terry was ready for a fresh supply of income. (Some years later he told Kenneth Tynan that he took all he had saved of his sudden wealth and lost it on the tables in France.) The critics received the new play well. Plays about the marital fluctuations of the wealthy had been standard fare in the West End for decades, and Rattigan could hardly be blamed if he followed the example of his elders. These frivolous people were on the whole accepted as valid symbols of the society of the time. Only in *The Era* was there any disparagement of the character drawing; George Bullock wrote, 'The chief weakness of this very thoughtful piece is in the character-drawing of David and Joan . . . these two people are not representative of the worthless crowd Mr Rattigan is seeking to portray. They are too fundamentally decent and sincere.'

Others were generous. *The Times* approved the 'thoughtful' studies of the principals. 'His selection of incident,' their critic wrote, 'is never so adroit nor so fresh as his portraiture.' W. A. Darlington in the *Daily Telegraph* wrote of the 'extraordinary fidelity' of the characters. Ivor Brown in the *Observer* praised the drawing of Joan. The *New Statesman*'s critic thought Helen a 'brilliantly caught character'. Even James Agate in the *Sunday Times* was moved to approval. 'I see nothing here that is not praiseworthy,' he reported. 'Worthy of respect.'

The conflict between the generations was commented on by G. B. Stern in a *Daily Telegraph* article. She saw clearly what Rattigan was getting at, but seems to have been misled by the quality of the conversations. 'This superannuated-at-forty brigade, still potential for mischief if for nothing else, overlapping a present younger generation who might be children of another planet, with their serious good sense, their powers of self-discipline, their clear code of moral responsibility, their slightly priggish scorn of the generation before them,' she wrote. But was it Helen's 'clear code of moral responsibility' that led her to interfere with David's marriage, and so ultimately to Joan's suicide? Was it Peter's 'powers of self-discipline' that allowed him, when temptation offered, to join the excesses of his elders? The truth is that Terry was overcome by his own creatures. He began with a theme (the *New Statesman* thought it more suitable for a comedy than a melodrama), and his characters took over. Those talents that G. B. Stern admires are spoken of in the dialogue, but the bearers of them have wills of their own.

Whether or not the play lives up to the arguments that Terry had claimed for it, it is a worthwhile piece by the standards of the day, its dialogue sensitive and witty. But July 1939 was no date to launch a play on a long run. War was just round the corner, and everybody knew it. People weren't going to the theatre. *After the Dance* closed on 12 August after a run of 60 performances. On 3 September war broke out, and all the theatres for a time were closed.

Terry was in poor shape. Despite all that had happened on the Continent, despite the Anschluss and the rape of Czechoslovakia and the Sudetenland, he was still a pacifist, though hardly so pronounced a pacifist as he had been earlier. The prospect of war was abhorrent to him. Moreover, he had more personal problems to cope with. He reckoned he was hard up (and judging from his earnings in the three previous years, indeed he was); he wondered if he would ever be able to write another play. Since coming home from America, he had suffered from a 'writer's block'.

Fortunately, the work that awaited him in the spring of 1940 did not involve a great deal of creativity. He had already drafted a film script for *French without Tears*, and he now set to work on it with Anthony Asquith, who was to direct. Anthony Asquith, commonly known as 'Puffin', was an enthusiast for the play and, with his help, Terry turned out a film script better than any he had done for Warner Brothers. They became close friends, and worked together as often as they could. Asquith directed a dozen films from Rattigan's scripts, and in the theatre he directed *Flare Path* and *While the Sun Shines*.

It was he who coaxed Rattigan through the script of *French without Tears* with his endless bubbling good-humour and, at the end of it, it was he who persuaded Anatole de Grunwald that Terence Rattigan was the man to work with him on the script of Esther McCracken's *Quiet Weekend* (which Asquith directed). But at the end of it all, Terry still had his block.

After finishing *After the Dance*, he'd had what seemed to him a good idea, a farcical burlesque making fun of the European dictators rather as Charlie Chaplin was to do in *The Great Dictator*. But the idea was as far as he could go. As he said afterwards, 'I brooded over the plot for so long that I completely forgot how to hatch. I didn't know what was funny any more.' The solution was to take a collaborator with the same sense of humour. There was someone available who answered all the requirements – Tony Goldschmidt, a fellow-Harrovian who had gone up to Oxford at the same time as he, with whom he had been on close terms ever since. Goldschmidt was delighted at the idea, and they retired together to a cottage that Rattigan had rented in Surrey and began work on *Follow My Leader*.

The feeling of the play suggests derision but surprisingly little hatred. Clearly neither writer knew very much more about Hitler than they would have picked up from the headlines in the newspapers, and what they wrote suggests a revue sketch extended to a couple of hours. The nation where the action takes place is called Moronia. The neighbouring nation is called Neurasthenia. Moronia is governed by sinister politicians called Baratsch, Slivovitz and Quetsch. They need a mouthpiece, and for this purpose they choose a convenient plumber, Hans Zedesi. Zedesi becomes the puppet-president of Moronia; where Germans would greet one another with a raised arm and a greeting of 'Heil Hitler!' the Moronians would greet one another with a cry of 'Up Zedesi!'

Two or three scenes reach a higher level than this schoolboy punning. The best of them is the visit of the British Ambassador, whose Embassy has been blown up by a wild terrorist called Riszki, who thought it was the Neurasthenian Embassy. His formal clothes in tatters, the Ambassador reports, in well observed diplomatic language that Rattigan had no doubt learnt from his father, that Whitehall will take no hasty decision on the matter, 'but it is conceivable that they may instruct me to deliver a formal protest.'

There is a good scene, too, borrowed from Rostand's *Cyrano de Bergerac*, where the illiterate Zedesi makes a great speech from a balcony, his words dictated to him line by line. 'I am not the man who can be dictated to by any one!' Zedesi assures the Moronian plebs.

When the play was done, they sent a copy to the Lord Chamberlain for his approval, Tony Goldschmidt's name being changed to Anthony Maurice for the occasion, in case anyone might think he was a German. The Lord Chamberlain banned the play completely. 'It would give offence to a friendly nation,' he ruled. Terry was disappointed; it was surely the moment for an anti-Hitler play, however frivolous.

He had nothing else in his mind, and *After the Dance*'s short run had left the world cheerless. Terry began to wonder if he had not made a mistake to imagine that his talent would support him all his life. He grew so depressed that he consulted a psychiatrist.

He chose Dr Keith Newman of Oxford City and County Hospital. He was, in fact, an Austrian, originally called Odo Neuman. Newman's patients remember him as having exercised an almost mesmeric influence on them, and there is no doubt that he achieved considerable authority over Terry which persisted for some time. His advice was to join the RAF and give his talents for command and invention some practical use.

Once war was declared the Lord Chamberlain's office relented. *Follow My Leader* was given a week's trial in Cardiff, then brought as quickly as possible to London. It opened at the Apollo on 16 January 1940. This was too late, of course. A year earlier it would have seemed funny; now it just seemed to be repeating a lot of saloon bar jokes. The papers were kind but not enthusiastic, apart from the *Manchester Guardian*, whose critic thought it was three times as funny as *French without Tears*. It ran for ten days. No one wanted to go out in the blackout to hear the kind of jokes they were making themselves.

Little help came from the New York production of *Grey Farm* at the Hudson Theatre on 3 May. It got the most appalling notices. 'It is impossible to imagine trash on a more wholesale and boring scale than *Grey Farm*,' wrote John Mason Brown. 'We lunched, frugally, on the royalties, and learned to forget,' Bolitho said. The play came off on 1 June.

In April of that year, Hitler invaded Denmark and Norway, and in the next month the 'phony war' came to an end as the Germans advanced into Holland and Belgium, and through the gap in the Maginot Line between Sedan and Mézières. No one could sit about in England and watch this happening without showing some reaction. Many of Terry's friends were already fighting. The smart people in the smart places began to turn up dressed as ensigns in the Guards, or as airmen, or as Ordinary Seamen. Terry at last took Newman's advice, and applied to join the RAF.

Why Newman should have chosen the RAF for him is difficult to say. It was not Terry's kind of service. He was not a mechanically-minded man and he was a snob. The RAF had become a very democratic service since the introduction of short-service commissions. 'They're the kind of people who eat curry with a knife and fork,' I was told when I asked one short-service officer what his associates were like. What's more, officers and sergeants were more or less interchangeable members of air crew, both in the air and on the ground. Terry would have been more at home in the Guards or the Rifle Brigade; but it was harder, and took longer, to get a commission in the Army, with all the initial training, and then the OCTU. If he had made up his mind earlier and gone to some such regiment as the Artists

Rifles or the HAC, widely favoured by theatre people, he might have found himself an officer more quickly. But, under Newman's mysterious spell, he chose the RAF, and Newman was proved right. Rattigan was fascinated by the details of all the new techniques he had to absorb. He learnt quickly and performed well. In a letter he wrote to Newman, quoted in Newman's book *Mind, Sex and War – Blackouts, Fear of Air Raids and Propaganda* (Pelago, 1941), he wrote of his training as if it were vitally important to him:

> 'I have passed my tests 100 per cent which is not unprecedented or anything like it. . . . Such exercises aren't at all difficult. What is difficult is to do correctly all the 100 little things connected with the whole business – to forget none of them or, if one does (and one nearly always does) forget one, to be able to find the fault and not to panic. . . . However, I become a bore on the subject and indeed think and talk of nothing else.'

To think and talk of nothing else was a familiar disposition in the Services during the war, and no one thought Pilot Officer Rattigan a bore. He was well liked and did his job well. When his training was done, he was posted to Calshot, near Southampton, as an air gunner wireless operator. He would be flying in the tail end of a Sunderland flying boat in day-long reconnaissances over the Atlantic.

He remained under the spell of Keith Newman, who seems to have been a bizarre, almost sinister, figure. Not only did he have Rattigan and Puffin Asquith entranced by his personality, but later, when his treatment had had its effect, and a new play had been written, the play was dedicated to him and – most curious of all – Rattigan entrusted to the same hands his young leading actor, who became another Newman addict.

The play was written in appropriately warlike circumstances. Terry had been posted to a squadron in Freetown in Sierra Leone, but bad weather delayed the takeoff for a couple of weeks. In the comparatively unsympathetic surroundings of RAF Calshot, he began to fill an exercise book with his draft. He had done the first act when it became possible to fly, so he tucked his exercise book in his kitbag. Over the Bay of Biscay, a German fighter appeared out of the sky and scored one or two hits with cannon shell. The damage was not serious, but it meant waiting at Gibraltar for a time. Terry unpacked his exercise book and set to work on Act Two.

In the end that flight never reached Freetown, for over the Atlantic one of the engines packed up. One engine out of four did not mean immediate disaster, and the captain decided that if all excessive weight were lost, he could reach Bathurst in the Gambia. 'Excessive weight' meant not only sundry disposable parts of the aircraft, but the personal effects of the crew. Terry was put in charge of the unhappy task of collecting everything not vital to survival and dropping it all into the Atlantic Ocean. There were books and framed photographs and souvenirs, and, at the last moment, he remembered the exercise book in his kitbag. Apologizing to the rest of the crew, who had seen their most precious belongings consigned to the deep, he pulled it out, ripped the pages away from their hard cover, and stuffed them into his jacket. The rest went overboard. The Sunderland limped on towards Africa, and is said to have arrived at Bathurst with no more than two minutes' fuel in the tanks.

There was leisure to spare at Bathurst and, in circumstances more suggestive of Graham Greene than of a boulevard playwright, Terry wrote his third act. When the aircraft was fit to fly again, it moved on to Freetown, and there he made a fair copy of his interrupted opus in another exercise book. The new play, entitled *Flare Path*, was dispatched to London to A. D. Peters, his agent. Peters had great faith in his young client (he had invested both in *French without Tears* and in *After the Dance*), and he believed that in *Flare Path* he had another potential winner. The first two managements he approached turned the play down. The third was H. M. Tennent. They accepted the play, and its production marked the start of a long and profitable association.

Terry had managed to get enough leave to take part in the preliminary stages of the production, and he persuaded Tennent's to appoint Puffin Asquith to direct, something he had not done in the theatre before. When they auditioned their leading man, which they did at the Savoy, Newman was there.

The leading man was Jack Watling, who had been on the stage since he was twelve (as an Italia Conti Frog in *Where the Rainbow Ends*). Why he should have been treated as he was by Asquith, and why Tennent's should have allowed it, is hard to understand. Once it was decided that he would fit the part of Flight-Lieutenant Graham, Terry said to him, 'Now, Puffin Asquith will be directing the play, but Keith Newman will direct you.'

And so it was. Jack Watling remembers it with dislike. 'Newman was an extraordinary chap. He seemed to have control of everyone. Later on, when I was an ordinary AC plonk, he took me to a symphony concert. I was in my uniform, he was wearing an old sweater, and there were all these people in dinner jackets. Newman went up to Adrian Boult, who was conducting, and he said "Boult, we need tickets for tonight", and Boult gave them to him at once.'

Newman not only directed Jack Watling in his part, he went to see the play every day for several months. He published his conclusions in a book called *250 Times I Saw a Play, or Authors, Actors and Audiences.* Ultimately he went mad.

Flare Path was an immediate success. There was a four-week tour, and then it opened at the Apollo on 13 August 1942. Ever since the Battle of Britain, the RAF had been great public favourites, and a play about their lives had never been done before. Romances about the army were an established thing, and *Journey's End* clinched the ideal. The navy, less easy to display on the stage, had established naval officers as the *beaux idéals* of fighting men, almost as romantic as legionnaires of the French Foreign Legion. But the RAF was the fashionable and popular novelty. Terry not only introduced the world to a new class of people they had not encountered before, he reproduced their lives from first hand experience. And by way of an extra bonus, his story was unashamedly romantic, indeed unashamedly sentimental to a degree that he never quite reached anywhere else. The backbone of the story is a very simple triangular affair. Peter Kyle, a successful film actor, has flown over from Hollywood to tell his mistress, a not very successful actress, Patricia Warren, that his wife has at last divorced him and they can now get married. In the year that they have been apart, however, the war has broken out, old loyalties have been tucked aside, new loyalties formed overnight, and Patricia has married a young bomber pilot, Teddy Graham.

In the scales of her choice, Patricia finds that the greater weight is on the side of chucking Teddy and going back to the old happiness she knew with Peter. But when Teddy comes back from the raid his flight have been making over Germany, and confesses to her the terrible feelings of funk that may make it impossible for him to go on flying any more operational missions, the scales are suddenly weighted the other way. She will stay with him. Peter walks out like a gentleman.

There are two parallel sub-plots. Count Skriczevinsky has gone on the raid with an aircraft of the Polish squadron. Sergeant 'Dusty' Miller has gone on it as Teddy's tail gunner. Each of them has left a wife waiting for his return. The Count's wife is a nice plump girl who was a barmaid until she married him, and has honest doubts about her future after the war, when the Count has ceased to be a Flying Officer attached to the RAF and has returned to Poland to be a rich landowner. Dusty's wife is a gloomy woman doing war work in a laundry, who has taken much trouble to be with her husband for this one night, only to find it snatched from her by the RAF's decision to mount an unscheduled operation. Dusty comes back from the raid, the Count does not – well, not when he is expected.

41

There are also a property landlady, a property handyman (aged fifteen) and a property middle-aged non-flying Adjutant. All the action takes place in the lounge of a country pub with a view over a bomber station. Everyone talks RAF slang whenever the opportunity occurs.

The slenderness of the plot does not mean that the play is at all short of action. At its lowest level, we have a forced landing by a Stirling (a type of bomber that seems to have dropped out of legend altogether); there is a distant German air raid; we hear the take-off of four Wellington bombers (nothing romantic about those nowadays, either), one of which is attacked by a German night-fighter and crashes on the runway. We don't see these things unless the electrician cares to devise some necessary fireworks with his lights. But we hear the sounds, still a little daunting to the oldsters who can remember them in earnest, and the detail is filled in, by RAF experts or their equally expert wives or by civilian would-be experts like the boy Percy.

The play is symmetrically balanced around the operation in which Teddy, Dusty and the Count take part. The aircraft take off – or don't take off – in Act 2, Scene 1; they return – or they don't return – in Act 2, Scene 2. Act 1, apart from the little *coup de théâtre*, no more really than a *frappe de théâtre*, when the Adjutant arrives to break up the party with news of the unexpected order from Group Headquarters, is devoted to introducing the characters.

They are not convincingly introduced. They fulfil their several functions, but you wonder what they are like when they are anywhere else. Peter Kyle is given no personal idiosyncrasies of his own; he is an ordinary middle-class Englishman, slightly too well dressed for the country, aged 'about thirty-five' according to the stage direction, 'forty-one' and too old for stardom according to himself. Could it be that his age was not the real reason why the studio had decided to dispense with him? What I have said about Peter Kyle applies, *mutatis mutandis*, to Patricia. Both of them are given interesting things to do, but neither of them is an interesting individual. As for Teddy, who at twenty-four is a flight-lieutenant with a DFC, as far as personality goes he is a *tabula rasa*, with nothing in his mind beyond his crush on Patricia and his attention to his duty. As it happens, he is given one of the two most interesting speeches in the play, but it comes spurting out like champagne from a water tap. Count Skriczevinsky is just a stage foreigner, capable of nothing much beyond comic broken English until the end of Act Three, when he is promoted to the dual role of hero and comic. His plane has not returned to the station, and it is believed that it has crashed. There is some rather elementary fun going on about Dusty Miller's wife feeling it her duty to report that she has seen her husband's Wellington and it has 'a great big hole' in the tail, when the

Count appears quietly at the door, still in flying-kit, but dirty and wet.
'Is – please – my wife – in home?' he enquires.

To universal acclaim he is made to tell of his experience, and he does
so in a brand of broken English designed to split the ears of the
groundlings. 'Please – we fall in se drink,' he begins, but while Patricia
goes to fetch his wife, he continues less convincingly. Truncated a
little, the conversation runs like this:

TEDDY: You fall in the drink. What happened then?

COUNT: We – land – pumkek.

TEDDY: Pancake. Yes ——

COUNT: We – not hurt – not much. We go pouf ——

SWANSON: You go pouf?

COUNT: (*helplessly*) We go pouf.

TEDDY: I've got it. They inflate their rubber dinghy.

In their dinghy, they row for three hours, see a plane but are not seen
themselves. After another two hours:

COUNT: We walk in se ruddy water.

DUSTY: They wade ashore, sir.

COUNT: We see – a pheasant.

SWANSON: What's a pheasant got to do with it? You saw a
pheasant on the beach?

COUNT: Not – on – beach. By – gottage.

SWANSON: I still don't see ——

TEDDY: He means peasant.

Such easy misunderstandings are really not valid in what was meant as
a serious moment in a serious play. Apart from anything else, they are a
grievous indictment of the intelligence of the RAF personnel in the
scene, who have to simulate incomprehension simply to allow the
Count to move on to his next gag. You would have thought one of them
might at least have offered him a glass of whisky.

The Count's safe return was vital in a play about the Royal Air Force
at that time, but dramatically it is rather cheap. A shade of tragedy
might have added depth to what is a simple boys' paper tale; but a war

play that involved a hero going to his death would not have done at all. On the other hand, the belief that the Polish crew had crashed opens the way to the best scene in the play.

When the Count left on his mission, he left a farewell letter with his wife, to be opened in the event of his not coming back. The Countess cannot read it, for it is not written in English. It is not written in Polish either, but in French, a language more likely to be accessible to someone in the hotel. The Countess asks Peter Kyle to read it to her, and it proves to be an avowal of eternal devotion that would have persisted after the war as it flourished during the war. This is a specially significant sentiment to her, for earlier in the day she has overheard Peter suggesting that the Count's loyalty to her will only last as long as the war keeps him in Britain.

The letter also has a personal significance for Peter. He realizes that Patricia's marriage to Teddy has something in common with the Countess's to her Pole, but in reverse. How will she feel about him when he ceases to be a heroic young bomber pilot? If he had been present at the scene where Teddy confessed how scared he was, how unsure he was of his ability to go on, and seen the loyalty she displayed then, he might have known; but the case of the Skriczevinskys persuades him that fidelity is not a passion to be lightly impaired, and he leaves to fly back to the States and resume his film career.

The critics received the play with general enthusiasm, mixed with fairly common doubts about the truth of the characters. Patricia, said Ivor Brown in the *Observer*, 'seems to be quite unbelievably unimaginative'. 'The characters of hypersensitive hero and erring wife have never been roundly drawn by the dramatist,' James Redfern complained in the *Spectator*. But audiences in London in the autumn of 1942 were not concerned with dramatic subtleties. They wanted to see our boys (and their allies) winning the war and relaxing with satisfactory romances. *Flare Path* gave them that in spades, and Tennent's were rewarded with a run of 679 performances. The two managements who had refused the play on the ground that people didn't want war plays must have felt pretty silly.

The first night was decorated with hosts of senior RAF officers anxious to tell Flying Officer Rattigan how well he had done. The Chief of the Air Staff, Air Chief Marshal Sir Charles Portal, summoned him to his box to offer his congratulations. Such high level approval of Terry's artistic talent did not prevent his being sent to New York with his squadron, however. When he came back in the New Year, he went, unheralded, to the theatre to see how the production was faring. It was the night that Winston Churchill was in the audience; but no one knew Rattigan was in the house, so they were not brought together. Churchill went backstage afterwards to meet the company. His comment, as reported in the *Daily Sketch*, was: 'I was very much moved by this play. It is a masterpiece of understatement. But we are rather good at that, aren't we?'

Terry's visit to New York was partly due to Eleanor Roosevelt's recommendation of the play in her column, 'My Day'. 'I am glad it is to go to the United States,' Mrs Roosevelt wrote, 'because it is a true and moving picture of the RAF.' It opened at the Henry Miller on 23 December; but the Americans thought nothing of it. 'It seems to be another case of an English hit destined to become an English miss,' Robert Coleman said in the *Daily Mirror*. In the *New York Times*, Lewis Nichols thought 'the drama seems sentimental, slow and confused'. Not for the last time, George Jean Nathan, in the *Theatre Book of the Year, 1942–43*, launched into a scathing onslaught on the English theatre:

> They come pretty bad at times, these English imports that have achieved big success in London, but they do not often come quite so entirely bad as this. If the play has so much as even one half of one redeeming feature, it has eluded this critical cunning. The author's purpose and intention is to pay tribute to the valor of the Royal Air Force; what he achieves, so trivial being his equipment, is something that rather puts that admirable body into a ridiculous light.

The New York run lasted fourteen days, and no one discerned any special quality in the young actor Alec Guinness, who played Teddy. *First Episode*, even *Grey Farm*, had run longer than that. Apart from the blow to his pride, Terry had no need to worry. He was making a great deal of money, not only from the West End production but from touring and foreign productions. The RAF was only too pleased to give him leave, or to arrange a secondment, that allowed him to work on film scripts. And he was already working on his next play.

Four
While the Sun Shines

Flare Path virtually put an end to Terry's days as a practising airman. The official treatment of artists in the Services was a great deal more civilized in the Second World War than in the first. The musicians, poets and artists who had died in the trenches were not followed by an equal oblation of talent in the second war, if it could be helped. During 1942, Terry had been seconded to an organization, the RAF Film Unit, that would have given Haig a heart attack. For it he wrote the script of a picture about the resistance in Norway, *The Day Will Dawn*, which was directed by Harold French; and he was also given time to work, in collaboration with Rodney Ackland, on *Uncensored*, a film about the triumph of love over loyalty, directed by Puffin Asquith. In the following spring, he was teamed up with the American Richard Sherman to work on a film about the transfiguration of an airfield that is handed over by the Royal Air Force to the US Air Force.

Work on this film (which after some years' work ended as *The Way to the Stars*) enabled him to live much more in the style to which he was accustomed: he had the use of chambers in Albany belonging to Roger Machell; he sported a long cigarette holder and a gold cigarette-case by Fabergé. 'The style to which he was accustomed' needed a good deal of adjustment to current London conditions. But London was full of interesting new people, Americans and other birds of passage, and the general feeling was that unless you were actually hit by a bomb, this was the time to enjoy yourself if you could.

Terry's former neuroses were cleared away by a way of life more active than he had ever known before, and no doubt by his continued association with Keith Newman, who maintained his authority over him. There was time to spare when he was working on his films. He was fascinated by the animated life going on around him, and as soon as an opportunity arose, he sat down and wrote a play about it.

Naturally his hero was a young man living in Albany. He was an earl with a fortune of two million pounds, serving as an Ordinary Seaman because he could not reach the Navy's officer standards. Terry said frankly that the play was 'a desperate attempt to copy *French without Tears*', an admission that needs qualifying only over the word 'desperate'. (He told Kitty Black in Tennent's office that he tore up his first draft and threw it away and began all over again.) In fact it's a better play than *French without Tears*.

Like its model, *While the Sun Shines* deals with three young men in pursuit of the same girl, while another, more accessible, girl, stands by. A senior figure completes the pattern, though the Duke of Ayr and Stirling has little in common with Monsieur Maingot. Ordinary Seaman the Earl of Harpenden is on leave in his rooms, awaiting his interview at the Admiralty and his marriage to Lady Elisabeth Randall, a clerk in the WAAF and daughter to the Duke. Both the interview and the marriage are imminent; they are planned to take place on consecutive days, the day depicted in Act 1 and Act 2, and the day that has just begun in Act 3. But Bobby Harpenden, as we soon learn to call him, is in no way alarmed by this dual prospect. He has spent the previous night at the Jubilee Club, and when the play opens his bed is occupied (offstage, the Censor being no less adamant in wartime) by a young American officer, Joe Mulvaney, who, to make matters more complex, is mistaken by Harpenden's manservant Horton for Mabel Crum, a frequent inhabitant of that resort.

The first act is put together with the competent precision of an army movement order. Harpenden, in generous vein, offers Mulvaney the services of Mabel Crum while he himself is away on his honeymoon, and invites her on the telephone to come and meet him. She has a day off, and agrees to come at once. Mulvaney is then kept offstage while Lady Elisabeth Randall pays an unexpected call, and in a very short time begins to badger her fiancé about Mabel Crum, of whose activities she claims to know. She does not know that Mabel Crum is just about to show up; and she does not know that Mulvaney is staying in the chambers, for she has undertaken to ask Bobby if a young French officer she has met overnight may stay there. As if this were not tricky enough, she is followed by her father, the Duke, who has come to complain of a lack of generosity in the marriage settlement. So there, either present or invited, are all the characters in the play.

It need hardly be said that Mulvaney and Colbert, the Free French officer, both fall in love with Lady Elisabeth, and Harpenden, believing that he has lost his fiancée to the American, proposes to Mabel Crum, who accepts him; nor that all misunderstandings are cleared up by the end of Act 3, which shows Mulvaney and Colbert competing for the privilege of being Harpenden's best man at his wedding (to Lady Elisabeth). The simplicities of the plot are decorated with a number of vagaries that stem from the characteristics of the assorted participants, for the characters are more interestingly drawn than their earlier versions in *French without Tears*. There are also many references to the way life went on in London at the time that must have pleased audiences anxious to be shown how to laugh at what were inconveniences or worse.

We meet the first of them at once:

HARPENDEN: Oh, Horton, bring another breakfast, will you? . . . What have you got?

HORTON: Well, there's some spam.

HARPENDEN: No, don't waste the spam; it's too useful for sandwiches, late at night. What about sausages?

HORTON: I can manage one, my Lord.

That was Mulvaney's breakfast. Harpenden's own should have had an egg with it – 'my grandmother's other egg'. He was as much pained to hear that Horton had accidentally broken the one egg he had thought remained from the presents from his grandmother, outside the ration, as he was subsequently disconcerted when he realized that he must shave before going to his interview at the Admiralty, and had 'only one saw-toothed old razor-blade'. That was 1943, even among the rich.

On the other hand, there was the question of lunch with Lady Elisabeth: 'One o'clock at Prunier's.' And Mabel Crum's evening with Mulvaney: 'We went to the Hippodrome and had dinner at the Savoy.' And at Albany, whisky and gin seem endless. The wartime life of the wealthy was well observed – and many people, suddenly changed from office-workers or lawyers into captains and majors, felt themselves wealthier than they had ever been.

Of the characters, Terry has had more fun with the less important than with the principals. There is nothing in Harpenden's behaviour, apart from his having chambers in Albany and a manservant, that distinguishes him from an average young rating hoping for a commission. Mulvaney is a stock American with a normal obsession for women and Scotch. Colbert has a little more individuality; he is a socialist and his attitude to Elisabeth and Harpenden, whom he regards as inadequately in love and so headed for a disastrous marriage, is eccentric, yet on the whole he is characteristic of the Frenchman in an English fiction. As for the girls, Elisabeth, though described as 'very young, and seemingly unconscious of the fact that she is very beautiful', is also very ordinary by the standards of decent young women in the theatre.

Mabel Crum, an amateur tart, is amusing, and has the gift of instant friendship with anyone she fancies. As played by Brenda Bruce, she made instant friends of audiences for two years. When the 7th Armoured Division, Churchill's 'dear Desert Rats', went to France in 1944, the caravan in which the Operations staff worked was labelled on the front bumper, 'Mabel Crum'.

Terry was not as a rule very good with domestic servants, but Horton has been given some unusual qualities. Though impeccably proper in his modes of address, he is inclined to lapse into speech more apt to a batman than a manservant who has been with his master all his life, and before that with his father. He defends the wealthy aristocracy when Mulvancy says that it doesn't seem right 'that a guy should be worth all that money and not to have had to work for it.' 'It happens in your country too, sir,' he says respectfully. He adds that he is himself an American, born in America of an American father. His mother was a housemaid with the Morgans and married an American opera singer. 'I fancy I inherited my mother's talents rather than my father's,' he explains. Terry makes no further use of this detail.

The most amusing of the supporting characters is the Duke of Ayr and Stirling. He is dressed as a Colonel and has an appointment as Liaison Officer with the Poles. He reveals an interest in racing, a pursuit which seems hardly to pay its way. He is, in fact, a committed gambler. When, at the end of Act 2, he comes upon Harpenden, Mulvaney and Colbert playing craps to decide which of them is to have the privilege of proposing to Lady Elisabeth, he joins in the game; and at the beginning of Act 3, four hours later, he and Harpenden are still playing and he is five hundred and ninety pounds, ten shillings to the good.

The dialogue is all couched in Terry's middle-class vernacular, with the necessary concessions to France and the United States. It is not salted with jokes like *French without Tears*'s '. . . des idées au-dessus de sa gare', and there are no witty phrases à la Wilde. The manner was compared in the *Manchester Guardian* with 'P. G. Wodehouse at his best', and this is a very just comparison, for Wodehouse's jokes do not usually fall in his dialogue but in his narrative, and in his situations. You would have to look hard in *Where the Sun Shines* to find a line that you could extract and use to raise a laugh in bar, club or drawing room.

On the other hand, the play raises endless laughs in the theatre with simple play on ordinary things; Harpenden observes sympathetically to Lady Elisabeth, who has just come down from Sergeant to Corporal, 'Funny, we're neither of us awfully good at our jobs, are we?'

> ELISABETH: Oh, I'm quite good at mine. I just have bad luck. That's all.
>
> HARPENDEN: What did you do this time?
>
> ELISABETH: I lost the plans of the Station Defence.
>
> HARPENDEN: Good Lord!
>
> ELISABETH: Well, we found them again all right. I'd only left them in the Ladies.

In Act 2, Colbert comes in when Harpenden, Mulvaney and the Duke are having a confidential dispute. Never a man to forget his manners, Harpenden greets him, 'How are you? I'm so glad you came. Nice to see you. I wonder if you'd mind awfully going up to the kitchen for a moment?'

In Act 3, when Harpenden has airily proposed to Mabel Crum ('Because if I don't marry somebody this leave I'm going to get into trouble with my Captain'), she does her best to make him see sense:

> MABEL: Still, before I definitely commit you, hadn't you better think hard and see if there really isn't someone you'd rather marry than me?
>
> HARPENDEN: All right. (*He shuts his eyes and ponders for a second.*) No. There's only Lucy Scott, and she's taller than I am.

Out of context, there is nothing in those extracts to double anyone up with laughter. They are the everyday exchanges of society, and the secret is the context, and the timing.

H. M. Tennent, at any rate, found the play funny enough. They had *Flare Path* running at the Apollo, and they began casting for the new piece as soon as they could. Anthony Asquith was to direct, Harpenden was Michael Wilding, Mulvaney was Hugh MacDermott, Lady Elisabeth was Jane Baxter, the Duke was Ronald Squire, Mabel Crum was Brenda Bruce. During the month's preliminary tour, there were doubts in the director's mind as to whether Brenda Bruce was quite right. She had come to the company from the Birmingham Rep., where she had been playing more serious roles, and she seemed to be having trouble making herself sufficiently vivacious. It was not helpful when Noël Coward, who had money in the production, came to see it at Oxford and told her in front of the company that he thought her a 'dim little actress'. Brenda Bruce, not unnaturally, broke down and asked if she could be allowed to go back to Birmingham. She stayed with the company, however, and was given helpful coaching by Ronald Squire (who was playing the Duke) and by Terry himself, who went through her lines with her, and changed them when she found them difficult. He gave her a lot of personal attention in off-duty times as well, to make sure that she was happy with the company. Terry must have looked romantic in his RAF uniform, which he always wore.

The play opened on Christmas Eve of 1943, at the Globe, next door to the Apollo, where *Flare Path* had already run for sixteen months. The date was cunningly chosen by Tennent's to ensure a first-night audience in high spirits. The reviews were solidly enthusiastic, give or take occasional sniping at detail. The *New Statesman*, for example, thought that the French officer Colbert was painted with 'a queer vindictiveness' – though the egalitarian socialism that Terry gave him was something that he himself might have thought sympathetic ten years earlier. Most curious of the notices was James Agate's in the *Sunday Times*.

He began by quoting Shaw on Wilde: '"In a sense, Mr Wilde is our only playwright. He plays with everything, with wit, with philosophy, with drama, with actors and audience, with the whole theatre." The same might be said today of Mr Rattigan,' Agate went on, 'a playwright with the brains not to take himself seriously.' To have reacted so favourably towards *While the Sun Shines* after his unrepentent coldness to *French without Tears* suggests a lack of seriousness towards either play. 'One cannot grow from nothing into Oscar Wilde between one light comedy and the next,' Rattigan remarked, 'especially if the second has been modelled on the first.'

At least Agate allowed himself to say that the play was 'a little masterpiece', and other critics used phrases like 'the wittiest play in town', 'this gay farce', 'a dramatist of genius' and so on. Ivor Brown in the *Observer* and Beverley Baxter in the *Express* both complained that the author was retracing old steps. In *Time and Tide*, Philip Hope-Wallace lamented that Rattigan had made an unacceptable mixture of comedy and farce: 'You cannot start your audience looking for human relationships, and at the same time claim the indulgence due to farce.

51

You have to choose between human relationships and naughtiness, at any rate in the theatre.' This intellectual criticism was evidently unobserved by the mass of theatregoers who flocked to the Globe in their thousands. The run of 1154 performances, which beat the run of *French without Tears* by 115, actually outlasted the war. It put Terry into the so-far unchallenged position of having written two plays that had run for over a thousand performances.

There was less admiration for *While the Sun Shines* when in September 1944 it opened at the Lyceum in New York. Rattigan's old enemy, 'sea change', was enormously magnified by the fact that London was a city at war swarming with strangers, from America, Canada, Australia, France, Belgium, that it was beset with wartime restrictions and exposed to enemy bombing, whereas New York, though to some extent also on a war footing, was essentially the familiar New York. Films of American servicemen on leave in the wartime Big Apple allow them a fairly unhindered good time.

Moreover, the characters would have been more or less unfamiliar to American audiences. Bobby Harpenden himself must have seemed something of a freak, with his wealth and his inability to find promotion; the wandering Frenchman would have been a figure virtually unknown; and the Duke must have seemed a figure of pure farce, whereas in English comedy (and indeed in English life, if you look in the right places) he would have been recognizable enough.

Consequently the American critics cared more about the mechanics of the plot and less about the reflections of current life than the British did. '*While the Sun Shines* is not a good play basically,' wrote Lewis Nichols in the *New York Times*, 'for it is contrived as though by a ruler, pencil and a pair of shears' – a judgement that recalls Hubert Gregg's account of the early stages of *After the Dance*. George Jean Nathan decided that 'Mr Rattigan, whose play amounts to little more than a machine-made-box-office tool, rusted, has gone deep into the old wastebasket for his observations and his characters', which to some extent Terry would not have denied.

But Nathan made a curious concession in his notice (which appeared in *The Theatre Book of the Year, 1944–45*). 'Unlike so many other young English playwrights,' he wrote, 'he deals with the emotions of normal people, which comes as a relief. For some years now we have been treated in English imports to so much degeneracy, perversion and psychopathic aberration that the mere sight of a character putting his arms around a woman and kissing her is in the nature of a sensational dramatic event.'

Now it is true that Rattigan made nothing of it, but in *While the Sun Shines* we are given scenes in which (albeit out of sight) young men sleep together. Such casual conjunctions were undoubtedly common in blacked-out London, and no doubt were perfectly innocent as often as not. But to have hit on normality as the chief merit of a play in which a girl is lightheartedly passed from bed to bed and in which two, or even three, young men speak of sleeping together, is bizarre.

Innocent or not, the play pleased not the multitude, and closed after thirty-nine performances. By that time, Terry had a third play heading towards the West End.

Five
Love in Idleness

In the spring of 1943, Rattigan was working on the film he had been asked to do by the RAF Film Unit about the handover of an RAF airfield to the Americans. It was going through fundamental changes. To begin with, William Wyler was no longer to be the producer. The script as it stood, however, seemed promising enough, and a new producer was found, Filippo del Giudice, the producer of the film version of *French without Tears*.

The film was now to be called *Rendezvous*, and Rattigan worked with Asquith and with Anatole de Grunwald adapting the script to the new story. It was ready for shooting in September 1944, which, as del Giudice could see, meant that it was lagging fatally behind the schedule of the war in Europe. By the time shooting was done and the film was edited, the war might very well be over.

The solution was to show the hand-over in flashback. The film began with an abandoned airfield, overgrown and neglected, which came to life to reveal the events that had taken place during the previous five years, the British aircrews settling in as the crews had settled in at *Flare Path*, and then their American successors. Such flying as there is in the film is cosmetic; it was not a war film but a celebration of the alliance between Britain and the United States. It was ultimately released under the title *The Way to the Stars*, a reference to the RAF motto, *Per Ardua ad Astra*. The Americans, who had not the same loyalty to the Royal Air Force, called it *Johnny in the Clouds*. It was an immense success on both sides of the Atlantic.

In the autumn of 1944, Terry was posted to another RAF film, *Journey Together*, which was to be directed at Pinewood by John Boulting, with Richard Attenborough and Jack Watling (both of them currently serving airmen) in the leading parts. But in spite of working on the two films, Terry still found time for work of his own.

Private hospitality, too, flourished among those that could afford it, in spite of the V1 and V2 rockets that had replaced bombing raids. There was already a feeling that the war was coming to an end, at any rate in Europe. Children who had been sent abroad by their parents to keep them away from the fighting were starting to come home again with the idea that they should join in before the show was over. Their families, the worst of the danger being over, were generally agreeable to their return.

Among such families was that of Henry ('Chips') Channon, the Member of Parliament for Southend, who had evacuated his son in 1940 and was now anxious to have him home. Channon, born an American, was a man of tireless hospitality, with an eye for new names to launch in society. On 30 September dining with Juliet Duff (he was indiscreet enough to keep a diary, which in due time was indiscreetly published) he met 'Master Terence Rattigan', and fell for him at once.

Soon they were spending much time together, and Terry must have known how much Channon wanted to be reunited with his boy, whom he reckoned already ripe for coaching in his father's vocation so that he might one day follow him into Parliament.

As Master Paul Channon had been five years old when he sailed for America and nine when he returned, he did not offer promising material as a character in the next Terence Rattigan comedy; but his situation was a fertile one. Suppose he had been, say, thirteen when he left, he would now be old enough to join the forces. What's more, he would have been observant enough both before and after his absence to notice the changes that had taken place while he was away. For example, Chips Channon and his wife were no longer together. How would this impress the newly-sophisticated creature in this hypothetical scenario?

The play as Rattigan wrote it concerned a boy who had left for Canada at twelve and returned at seventeen. There were changes on the young man's side; he had turned from an unpolitical schoolboy into a left-wing opponent of the capitalist society. But the more important changes were in the home. His father had died, and his mother was living with a married man. Terry mentioned the plot to Gertrude Lawrence at a casual meeting, and she encouraged him to write it so that the part of the mother would suit her.

So, at any rate, Terry always maintained. But in the event, when the play was done and handed to Binkie Beaumont, things went wrong. Gertrude Lawrence was bewildered to be shown a new comedy and told, 'Here's the play Terry Rattigan has written for you.' She had no recollection of ever having encouraged him to do so, and in any case she had to go back to America. The whole affair passed from her mind in a moment. In her biography by Sheridan Morley, the matter isn't mentioned.

To Terry, this rejection was disastrous. Everything in that play had been written specifically to suit that special actress. Since *Private Lives* in 1930 had put the peak on her reputation, anything she did, in London or New York, was a predestined success. She was an actress of great talent, with an individuality that wrapped itself around any part she took, to make the character as much herself as the part the author had devised; and every quality Terry had put into his heroine was made to measure for her. To him, *Love in Idleness* without Gertrude Lawrence would have been like the Sistine Chapel without Michelangelo.

Help fell unexpectedly from the heavens, in the shape of a V1 that landed on the Aldwych Theatre. The current production at the Aldwych was a play by Robert Sherwood, *There Shall Be No Night*, in which the leads were played by Alfred Lunt and Lynn Fontanne. The theatre was empty when the V1 fell, and the damage was not disastrous; but there was no hope of the production going on. On the other hand, the Lunts had no intention of quitting their English season for the loss of a theatre. They planned to revive their production of Molnar's *The Guardsman*; but what they really wanted was an English play. Ivor Novello told them that Terry Rattigan had a play looking for a home, and they gave him enough encouragement for him to arrange a meeting.

The subsequent collaboration has been described in detail by Maurice Zolotow in his dual biography, *Stage Struck: The Romance of Alfred Lunt and Lynn Fontanne* (Heinemann, 1965). The play that Rattigan brought to the Lunts was a showpiece for the leading lady, Olivia, a doctor's widow in her thirties. (The manuscript is alas lost.) The only part available for Alfred Lunt was that of Olivia's lover, a cabinet minister with a hint of dubious finance in his history. Terry said frankly that this was not meant to be more than a supporting part. The main comedy would be between Olivia and her seventeen-year-old son, who has returned from evacuation full of youthful Marxism. Even if he could have stood his mother's association with a married man, the fact that this man was also a Conservative and a capitalist put him irrevocably beyond the pale.

Alfred Lunt did not find this a serious objection. 'Sometimes Lynn has the play,' he said, 'and sometimes it's my play.' He took the script away with him; and two days later he told Terry that he would like to start rehearsals at once. He would direct, and he would be glad if Terry could be at hand to make 'a few adjustments here and there'.

'A few adjustments' hardly describes the work that had to be put into the play by everyone concerned with it. 'We are working our little heads off over it,' Alfred Lunt wrote to Graham Robertson, the artist, 'and I hope it will turn out well, though I must say that rehearsing a new play on tour is not altogether satisfactory. What with travelling on Sunday and eight performances a week on weekdays, we have so little time or energy to give it what we want. It must be acted with the touch of a feather duster, and I seem to have nothing to bring to the job but an old iron shovel.' That letter came from Glasgow, where they had just arrived from Liverpool. They were playing *There Shall be No Night*, and at the same time they were rehearsing *The Guardsman* and *Love in Idleness*.

For Terry, who was also involved in writing film scripts for the RAF Film Unit, the difficulties were no less. 'He is delighted by Alfred and Lynn's work on the play,' Graham Robertson reported, 'and the progress of rehearsals.' The delight was genuine enough, but it was only achieved by a road that ran uphill all the way. 'I didn't realize,' Terry said later, 'that he was asking me to write a new play. In the end he was right. I wrote a far better play because of his suggestions. But at the time it was rather a trying experience.' It was always Lunt's way to examine every point in terms of whether or not the audience would like it. This is how Terry described the subtleties that he was asked to incorporate in his script:

'Sir John Fletcher, the minister, that was Alfred's part, well, isn't he a little brutal here? And my, but he was a dreadful reactionary, and in this passage here he was such a disagreeable Tory, and "they won't like that, you know". And he'd lose the audience in this scene here.' And so it went on until the play had become a vehicle for the Lunts, the 'supporting part' had turned into a lead, the unattractive lover had been infused with charm, the boy had become a quarrelsome and bitter little monster. Now and then, Lunt would worry that they might be spoiling 'a perfect gem of a play', but whatever his answer to that problem may have been, he went on doing it.

Love in Idleness opened in Liverpool in November 1944, and received poor notices. Three further weeks of touring followed; and the notices remained poor. Noël Coward, who had money in the play, paid it a visit, and was so alarmed by what he saw that he advised Lunt to withdraw it. Tact was never one of Coward's long suits; while

Rattigan sat with Alfred Lunt in his dressing room, the Master, clearly audible through the wall, picked the play to pieces for Lynn Fontanne's benefit in hers. When the post mortem was done, each of the Lunts took Terry aside for a moment's confidence.

'Nothing that Noël has said, or will say,' Lynn Fontanne told him, 'can affect me. This is an enchanting play, and we're going to do it in London.'

'Lynn,' Alfred Lunt said, 'is disheartened by Noël's reactions. She's going to want to close the play. But no matter what Lynn says, we shall do it.'

It opened at the Lyric Theatre on 20 December 1944. On one side of it, *Flare Path* was playing at the Apollo. On the other side, *While the Sun Shines* was playing at the Globe. Only the Queen's, between the Lyric and the Globe, made a gap in the exclusive devotion of the west side of Shaftesbury Avenue to the drama of thirty-one-year-old Terence Rattigan. The Queen's got a bomb through the foyer.

The notices were not enthusiastic. 'Mr Rattigan has on this occasion been insufficiently inventive, and perhaps insufficiently witty, for his theme,' *The Times* said. The feeling was that the Lunts, and not the play, made the evening. In the *Daily Telegraph*, W. A. Darlington wrote, 'Probably this is not Mr Rattigan's best play, but it is difficult to tell. The dramatist who is lucky enough to provide a vehicle for Lynn Fontanne and Alfred Lunt is almost out of the critic's reach.' 'Played by a less brilliant company,' Philip Page wrote in the *Daily Mail*, 'this slender yarn . . . would have been far less entertaining' – though he had committed himself to phrases like 'a hilarious evening' and 'a clever comedy'. In *Time and Tide*, Philip Hope-Wallace conjectured that, 'with other actors, one would feel the piece too superficial and too static'. 'A thin little play,' Desmond MacCarthy called it in the *New Statesman*.

One at least of the more influential critics spoke well of it. '*Love in Idleness* may not prove, when it passes into other hands, to be Mr Rattigan's most successful piece, but to me it certainly seems his best,' Ivor Brown wrote in the *Observer*. In the event, it never did pass into other hands. So let us have a closer look at this thin little play that Mr Brown thought so well of.

In construction, it is a thoroughly conventional three-act light comedy. The first act begins with barefaced plotting. It is not the traditional housemaid giving the family particulars on the telephone, but the mistress herself, Olivia Brown, who is busy organizing a dinner party, her first guest being the Chancellor of the Exchequer. (Her facility in doing this during the last years of the war reminds us of Terry's friendship with Chips Channon, who never wanted for luxury.)

Her seventeen-year-old son wires to announce his imminent return from Canada, where he has been evacuated. How will she cope with the fact that she is living with Sir John Fletcher, a minister in the government, married, and the owner of the house (of 'tasteful opulence') where we now see her? She has no time to think the matter over, for before Sir John Fletcher has had time to pack for a discreet night at his club, the boy Michael arrives. He proves to have pronounced left-wing views and a strong disapproval of the new tank for which Sir John's Ministry is responsible.

This does not strike me as a well-written act. You hear the machinery clanking away under the surface rather too clearly. Moreover the dialogue, intended to represent the talk of the smart set of Park Lane, is not very funny. We are left, all the same, with a very useful situation: a son who resents his mother's second marriage, and who dislikes her new choice not only on personal but on political grounds.

In the next act, where most of the good comedy is concentrated, Terry plays some amusing variations on the theme. Michael is consciously playing Hamlet, and Olivia and John realize it. He has bought a book on poisons, from which he can learn whether John had any hand in his father's death. He wears a black tie every day in belated mourning. He invites Olivia and John to a play, a thriller called *Murder in the Family*. He contrives a 'closet scene' with his mother, inviting her, if not in those actual words, to look on this picture and on this. At the end of it, though, the strain is too much for him. With no Polonius lurking behind the arras, his emotions give way and he bursts into tears. 'Don't go on with it, Mum!' he begs her. 'I can't bear it.'

With a sudden resurgence of maternal feeling, Olivia begins to understand him. As she waits to receive the distinguished guests at her dinner, she breaks it to John that in the conflict between him and Michael, she had decided for Michael. She will go back with him to their little flat in Baron's Court.

The short third act is designed only to work out a happy ending. It is set in Baron's Court, where Olivia, an apron over her skirt, is cooking dried-egg omelettes for her son and teaching herself to type and so prove to him that she is no longer a parasite. (She borrows a line from Sir James Barrie to make her point.) The resolution of the plot could hardly be called subtle. Michael has gone out to dinner with his current girlfriend Sylvia; while Olivia is practising her 'Now is the time for all good men', John creeps silently into the room behind her, Michael having left the door unlocked. It barely needs saying that Michael has been stood up by Sylvia and comes home unexpectedly to the flat. Sylvia has gone to the Savoy with another friend. With a generosity that does him infinite credit, John sets himself to deliver the boy out of his distress. Why do they not, all three of them, go and dine at the Savoy, where he will get the table next to the table where Sylvia and her friend are sitting? With an astonishing *volte face*, Michael agrees to this at once, forgetting his belief that the kind of people who dine at the Savoy are parasites and will be, in Professor Laski's phrase, 'pushed overboard'.

If you can make such a sociological reverse so smartly, there need no longer be any objection to Olivia's association with John, particularly as John has persuaded his wife to give him a divorce, so that what had been a case of living in sin can now become a case of marriage. To ask what would be the likely position of the three of them in five years' time is to break the rules of light comedy. In any case, in 1944 no one had enough confidence to examine life as far ahead as that.

Very well, a thin little play, its plot carried by too many conveniently inconvenient entrances, its emotional peaks dependent on facile changes of mind over fundamental matters – Olivia in Act 2, everyone in Act 3. Compared with *While the Sun Shines* from the previous year, it is indeed short of wit and invention. Yet it holds the attention in a new way for Rattigan. For the first time, he is writing about the interests of adult people.

Adults in his earlier plays have never been taken seriously. They tend to be the kind of parody figures the young imagine the old to be. Monsieur Maingot in *French without Tears* is a joke. Count Skriczev-insky and Squadron-Leader Swanson in *Flare Path* are puppets from stock. The Duke of Ayr and Stirling in *While the Sun Shines* is just a comic peer. What is more, they operate from the sidelines, while events are monopolized by the young. In *Love in Idleness*, the adults are at the centre of things, while the representative of modern youth is the parody figure. For the first time, Terry had to construct an adult character who could be taken seriously.

What is more, in the conflict John wages against the coming generation, he has to appear as the superior character. We only once see him at his work for the Ministry of Tank Production, when he is dictating notes for a speech. To be honest, it sounds like a pretty dire speech, but it was the kind of speech public men were making at the time. More to the point, the new tank for whose production he is responsible is reported to be a success. In his private life, he is instinctively sympathetic to the young; no sooner has he met Michael than he offers him a drink and a cigarette. When Michael shows his real face, his ill-informed leftism, his politically-based discourtesy, John is resolutely patient with him. He behaves with generosity to Olivia when she walks out on him, and with a kind of generosity to his wife when he wants to persuade her to divorce him. He can be amusing in his conversation, he is cultured enough to spot Hamlet in Michael's behaviour, even to quote appropriate lines.

I can't go so far as to hold up Olivia as another well-drawn adult; she belongs among the young in spite of her seventeen-year-old child, and when for a moment, at the beginning of Act 3, she seems to be heading for maturity, she is still pretty silly, and her resolve to join the ranks of the New World, simply to fall in line with her son, reveals her as a woman no less irresponsible than, say, Mabel Crum.

Are we to suppose that there is any connection between Michael's juvenile left-wing thoughts and Terry's own liberal feelings as a young man? Surely not. Michael is as much a figure of fun as Monsieur Maingot, his politics the dramatic equivalent of Maingot's academic rectitude. If John were to be a cabinet minister, it was necessary that he should be conservative, if not actually Conservative. For a viable opponent it was therefore necessary to create a left-wing figure. In fact, Terry has done it neatly, with his references to what Professor Harold Laski wrote in *The Labour Monthly*, with the confidence Michael exhibited in the *obiter dicta* of Canadian contemporaries no better informed than he. It is quite easy to make fun of what one believes in, by directing attention towards the ambient foolishness without mocking the essential creed.

Insofar as he was interested in politics at all in later life, Terry's sympathies were always directed to the left, no matter how much he might complain about such things as income tax. This does not mean that he thought, still less talked, like Michael. Today, if he could be bothered, he would probably have joined the Social Democratic Party. To suggest that Michael's laughable ideas and his instant negation of them when offered a politic dinner at the Savoy represent a movement of Terry's ideas away from the liberal ideas of his younger days won't do. You might as well say that Lieutenant Mulvaney's American ignorance of the British aristocracy in *While the Sun Shines* is a sign of Terry's contempt for the Americans.

Whether or not this was the effect of his work with the Lunts, *Love in Idleness* marks the end of Terry's youth-oriented writing. The exposure to mature, experienced players had shown him how much more dramatic value there was in the lives of adult people than in the emotional affairs of the under-thirties. His next play, eighteen months later, the weight of the war lifted from his shoulders, was *The Winslow Boy*. It might indeed be said that there was a youngster at the heart of it – Ronnie Winslow is described in a stage direction as 'about fourteen' – but the youngster's feelings are given little attention in the play. He is no more than the golfball with which the adults are playing golf. The adults' varying abilities at the game proved far more pliable material for the author than the amatory fortunes of the young. And, as he had found in sculpting Sir John Fletcher from Alfred Lunt, he discovered that characters made from his imagination were far more useful than characters based on the students or the fellow officers of his own intimate circle.

Six
The Winslow Boy

Terry had certainly not been mulling over the idea of making a play about the Archer-Shee case, though he was interested in famous trials and found this case moving. However, he was not short of work. The British film industry was busy at its task of presenting to the world the better features of British life. *Journey Together* and *The Way to the Stars* marked the end of Terry's wartime stint, but his career was enriched by the support of the producer Anatole de Grunwald and the director Anthony Asquith, and he need never have been short of an offer to write a film script if he had wanted one.

The Winslow Boy grew out of what was originally meant to be a film. De Grunwald suggested that Terry and Puffin Asquith might work together on a film about British Justice. Famous trials are not always the same thing as justice; but Terry was interested, and gave de Grunwald a book on the Archer-Shee case.

The case concerned a thirteen-year-old cadet at the Royal Naval College, Osborne. The youngest son of a prosperous family, with a brother in Parliament, the cadet was accused of having stolen a postal order from another boy, and in spite of his denials was expelled from the College. His father believed in his son's protestations of innocence and took the matter up, first with the Commander of the College, then, when he was offered no satisfaction, at increasingly high levels. There was in those days no way of taking action against the Crown, for traditionally the King could do no wrong, and the courts were the

King's own. Osborne, being a part of the Royal Navy, was also a part of the King's domain. What was required was a Petition of Right. This would have to be presented through the Home Office and, if endorsed by the Attorney-General, put before the Crown. The Crown, as an act of grace, might then grant whatever had been requested.

What Archer-Shee wanted was that his son should not be adjudged guilty out-of-hand, but that some show of justice should be made to establish guilt or innocence. His case was handled by Sir Edward Carson, a celebrated and colourful silk. (He had led for the prosecution against Oscar Wilde.) Such an elaborate concern over so trivial a matter was certain to attract a great deal of public attention. Archer-Shee won his case, and the former cadet, now officially innocent, grew up to be killed in the first world war – serving in the Army.

De Grunwald gave Terry his book back with the verdict that the case was too dull. Terry, for whom 'the facts of the Archer-Shee case . . . had so fascinated and moved me that unlike many ideas that will peacefully wait in the store-room of the mind until their time for emergence has come, it demanded instant expression', retorted that if de Grunwald didn't want it as a film, he would write it as a play. Puffin Asquith, though not going so far as to call the matter dull, warned that he thought it would be hard to bring all the legal business to the stage attractively enough. There would, he supposed, be a great trial scene at the climax.

If he had thought more about the dramatic principles that his friend had already demonstrated in the theatre, he would have seen that the play was unlikely to turn out that way. Terry's fundamental doctrine was that plays were about people before plots, that the plot only develops from the characteristics of the people involved in it. In the Archer-Shee case, he was presented with a ready-made plot, indeed – if he had wanted them – with ready-made people. Either the plot or the characters had to go. The respectable, conservative Archer-Shee family might have wandered into a quite different plot. On the other hand, the people who constructed the Archer-Shee plot might have been quite different people. Terry being the kind of writer he was, the historical participants of the case were replaced with a completely new set who were set to work in their own way towards the triumphant success of the Petition of Right.

Of the original case, three factors were retained, two important and one incidental. The long struggle to secure a trial is of course the most important, and the progress of the case as Rattigan presents it corresponds with the actual proceedings. Carson did in fact come and examine the boy at home, and Terry has, not surprisingly, used this encounter, leading with it to one of the best *coups de théâtre* of modern theatre. And it is a fact that on the day the case was won, young Archer-Shee was at the theatre, and so was young Ronnie Winslow, though the theatre has become 'the pictures'.

From here on, invention takes over. Arthur Winslow as the activator of the case, remains a prosperous man of the upper middle class, but his family (apart from the eponymous boy) has suffered a sea change. Archer-Shee's elder son was a major and a Tory MP, and his daughter was as Tory as he. So uniform a family would be slow to suggest incident; so Terry has turned the elder son into Dickie, a frivolous Oxford undergraduate aimed, somewhat dubiously, at the Civil Service, and his sister Catherine into a suffragette of left-wing views. Grace, Arthur Winslow's wife, is a woman of faint convictions, interested only in the trivia of daily life.

To add colour to their existence, he has Catherine engaged to John Watherstone, an army officer whose father dislikes any kind of public display, while at the same time she is loved by Desmond Curry, the not-very-interesting family solicitor, and indeed even arouses a hint of affection in the breast of Sir Robert Morton, KC, briefed for the defence. By way of variety, there is Violet, the comic housemaid, a stock character, I have to admit.

Terry has advanced the date from 1908 to 1912–1914, to increase the suggestion that the case is embarrassing the Admiralty when the Admiralty had quite enough on its plate with the German fleet. The legal process is presented only in as far as it would be seen by an intelligent member of the public. Apart from an explanation of the function of a Petition of Right, technicalities are avoided. What we have is a characteristic English drama of tension among the middle classes such as might have been written by Maugham or Galsworthy. It is superior in craftsmanship to any of Rattigan's other early plays.

The character at the centre of the plot is Ronnie Winslow (originally the name was Hamilton). He plays comparatively little active part in the play, and indeed spends most of one act asleep on the sofa. But it is his play, and so the action properly begins with him, alone in the sitting room, home from Osborne without warning and with a letter in his pocket from his Commander to say that he has been expelled for stealing a five-shilling postal order from another cadet. Afraid to meet his family, he goes into the garden, where it happens to be pouring with rain.

There he remains, seemingly forgotten, while with masterly skill the whole gathering is brought on, including Violet the housemaid, John the fiancé and Desmond the family lawyer. All the family relationships are made clear. Tension reigns, for only Violet has seen Ronnie before he retreated into the garden; and after he has made his timid return, told his sister why he is there and gone upstairs with his mother to get out of his wet uniform, his presence is still unknown to his father until it is accidentally revealed at the moment when everyone is about to toast Catherine and John on their engagement. Ronnie is typically offstage at that moment; it is one of his characteristics to be out of sight when his destinies are being decided by the adults. The most significant thing he says in this act is 'I didn't do it!', which he says often, sometimes in response to inapposite questions.

His family's attitudes vary. Dickie doesn't think that pinching things matters much; at school, everyone did it. Catherine is concerned only at the heartless way in which the case has been dealt with. John explains that this is the way things are done in the service. Grace, Mrs Winslow, cares about his damp clothes. And when Arthur Winslow receives him, rather as if he were a commanding officer interviewing a defaulter, all he wants to know is if the accusation is right. Reassured that it is not, he goes straight to the telephone and asks for the Royal Naval College, Osborne.

The second act of the four is usually played continuously with the first after a short curtain. Nine months have passed, enough time to have harmed both Winslow's health and his prosperity. The case has made some public impact. There are letters in the papers, about 'the scandalously high-handed treatment by the Admiralty' and 'this ridiculous and sordid little storm in a teacup'. Exactly what has taken place we learn when Winslow is interviewed by a woman journalist, more interested in the curtains than the case (another stock figure). What is to take place we learn when Sir Robert Morton, KC, comes to interview the boy and decide whether the case deserves his attention. (It is in this passage that the question of a Petition of Right is first raised, and Morton first speaks the magic phrase in a merely conversational line: 'It is interesting to note that the exact phrase he uses on that occasion is: Let Right be done'.)

We proceed with Morton's examination of the boy, with its magical curtain line. (Terry was never afraid of a curtain line.) The examination has begun with routine questions to hear Ronnie's account of the business. Then this happens:

SIR ROBERT: I suggest, that the time has at last come for you to undo some of the misery you have caused by confessing to us all now that you are a forger, a liar and a thief!

RONNIE: I'm not! I'm not! I didn't do it —

ARTHUR: This is outrageous, sir —

SIR ROBERT (*To DESMOND*):   Can I drop you anywhere? My car is at the door.

DESMOND: Er – no – I thank you —

SIR ROBERT: Well, send all this stuff round to my chambers tomorrow morning, will you?

DESMOND: But – but will you need it now?

SIR ROBERT: Oh yes. The boy is plainly innocent. I accept the brief.

Nine more months have passed when Act 3 opens. Dickie has had to leave Oxford, and it looks as if Violet may have to leave Courtfield Gardens. It is 10.30 at night, and in the House of Commons the Winslow case is being debated. It is not going well, as we learn from the accounts read from the evening papers. Ronnie finds it hard to stay awake as his father reads the speeches to him. Grace Winslow, for the first time, begs her husband to give up the fight, in which she has never shown much interest, and which is ruining their lives. Winslow refuses; but later, when he reads a letter from John Watherstone's father saying in vigorous terms that he will use all his persuasion to stop his son marrying into such a family, he realizes that it is not only his domestic life that is at stake but the future life of his daughter, and reluctantly concedes that in the circumstances he must give up.

But by that time Morton has paid a surprise visit. He intended to ask what further steps Winslow would take if the vote went against him in the House, to which the newly-despondent Winslow replies that he would take none. But a telephone call tells Morton that F. E. Smith has spoken on his side in the debate, the atmosphere has altered, and the First Lord, afraid of a defeat at the division, had undertaken to instruct the Attorney General to endorse the Petition of Right.

In the fourth act, as Puffin Asquith had forecast, the time has come for a great trial scene. But we don't have it on stage. Reports of the hearing are given piece by piece by Grace and Catherine, who take it in turns to go to the court and to attend Mr Winslow, now reduced to a wheel chair. The shouts of a newsboy heard through the window tell of the successful result, and a first-hand description of the scene is given by Violet (who has come remarkably fast from the court to South Kensington).

The winding-up of various side issues follows. Dickie is doing all right in his bank, and has joined the Territorials, to remind us of the impending war. John has visited the trial so that he might meet

Catherine and tell her that he's marrying another girl. Desmond proposes to Catherine, without much hope. He tells her, though he should not have, that Morton was so determined to see the Winslow case through that he had declined the appointment of Lord Chief Justice. Later, when Morton comes for a farewell conversation, Terry handles this sentimental-heroic touch with his usual understatement:

SIR ROBERT: My attitude to this case has been the same as yours – a determination to win at all costs. Only – when you talk of gratitude – you must remember that those costs were not mine, but yours.

CATHERINE: Weren't they also yours, Sir Robert?

SIR ROBERT: I beg your pardon?

CATHERINE: Haven't you too made a certain sacrifice for the case?

SIR ROBERT: The robes of that office would not have suited me. . . . And what is more, I fully intend to have Curry expelled from the Law Society.

The play opened at the Lyric on 23 May 1946, after a successful tour. The part of Sir Robert Morton had been offered to John Gielgud, but he had declined it. It was then offered to Eric Portman, but he declined it too. The part is not a long one, effective though it is at its high points. Morton doesn't appear until two thirds of the way through Act 2, though he certainly has a splendid time when he does. In Act 3 his flamboyance has worn off a little, though he is given the exciting climax. In Act 4 he only has a mopping-up operation to conclude, with some telling exchanges with Catherine. The part was taken by Emlyn Williams. Catherine, a part potentially as striking as Morton, was played by Angela Baddeley, and Frank Cellier played her father. For the record, Michael Newell was Ronnie.

From the beginning, the play established itself as a success – with the public, but less so with the press. There seemed to be some resentment that Terry had not taken the theme of a small man's victory over an oppressive Government department and elevated it into a general plea for civil liberties. In the *Tatler*, Anthony Cookman lamented '. . . it turns what might have been a big play into a highly successful one'. Terry never had any intention of making it a 'big' play, and indeed never wrote such a thing, apart from *Adventure Story* and possibly *Cause Célèbre*. But to write a successful play was, and always has been, his special object. Just as Napoleon regarded good luck as a mark of personal merit in his generals, Terry thought of success as a positive asset, and sought it consciously.

The Winslow Boy is definitely not a 'big' play. It is the story of a family assailed by a misfortune that they have themselves inaugurated, and Terry never suggests that the case of 'Ronnie versus Rex' (the awful title that Chips Channon suggested for it) is in any way symbolic of greater things. 'The drama of injustice and of a little man's dedication to setting things right,' Terry told an interviewer, 'seemed to have more pathos and validity just because it involved an inconsequential individual.'

But the critics, and especially the American critics, could not forgive Terry for putting the big scene in the mouths of witnesses instead of spreading them before the audience. How could one write a play that included an exciting debate in the House of Commons and an emotional judgment in the courts, and present one of them through a telephone call from a clerk and the other by a hysterical report by an uneducated woman? Here was a play that was 'about something'; yet it was treated in a purely dramatic, almost romantic, way, and no attempt was made to revel in the victory of this 'inconsequential individual' over bureaucratic oppression.

The truth is that what the play is 'about' is encapsulated in that ringing phrase, 'Let Right be done', and it concerns a single instance, not a universal principle. Philip Hope-Wallace hit the right note in his notice in *Time and Tide*, that the victory concerned not the world, not the British nation, nor even very closely the subject of the case, Cadet Winslow, who took little interest in the struggles on his behalf. It concerned Arthur Winslow with his obsession for truth, demonstrated in his first examination of his son; with Dickie, who doesn't think that pinching a postal order is all that serious (or that his little brother is all that innocent), but must give up the university; and most of all with Catherine, deeply in love with a man who has no sympathy with her radical beliefs but was prepared to live with them until he saw where they would lead her.

The play is deliberately romantic in ways that critics looking for evidence of a great writer would not approve of. Desmond Curry, the tedious lawyer who lives on recollections of former cricketing glory, has to be there as a link between the Winslows and Sir Robert Morton, but he doesn't have to sit at the corner of a very scalene triangle and propose to Catherine in the last act, after her ex-fiancé John has directed his affection elsewhere. He could fulfil his functions, legal and social, as a happily married man with a family. The break with John is melodramatically handled; he always contrives to be on hand at the moments that tell most strongly against him.

And on three separate occasions, Terry leads us towards an unhappy decision and substitutes a happy one at the last moment – in Morton's cross-examination of Ronnie; in the Parliamentary debate that is miraculously saved by the intervention of F. E. Smith; and in the final court proceedings. Purists may find such easy point-making inartistic; but Terry was writing a play aimed at popular success. That was what it had – 476 performances in London, 218 in New York.

It is tempting to think that some of the political and the legal background may owe its detail to the help of Chips Channon, whose friendship with Rattigan was at its zenith. Channon wrote in his diary that he made 'many comments, suggestions and criticisms', when Terry read his newly complete play to him. But it seems more likely that Terry was doing his own research. The play is first mentioned in Channon's diaries on 19 August 1945: 'Terry read me out the first act of his new play about the Archer-Shee case.' A month later, 'We discussed his play, which he has at last finished. . . . He has completed it in six and a half weeks.' It was the following day that we hear about the 'suggestions and criticisms', which we may believe Terry accepted courteously but probably did not use – though Channon takes the credit for having persuaded him to alter the name from *The Hamilton Boy* to *The Winslow Boy*.

When the play was published, it bore the dedication to Chips Channon's son: 'For Paul Channon, in the hope that he will live to see a world in which this play will point no moral.'

The play opened in New York a year after its London opening, at the Empire Theatre. Arthur Winslow was played by Alan Webb; Valerie White was Catherine; Frank Allenby played Sir Robert Morton. The New York critics agreed that it was a pity that, with all its merits, it wasn't a 'big' play. One who believed that the play was neither good nor big was Louis Kronenberger in *PM*. He reckoned it displayed Rattigan's 'incurably trashy mind'. The people came, all the same. And the following year, the film, which Terry had scripted with Anatole de Grunwald and which Puffin Asquith had directed, was released.

Seven

The Browning Version
and Harlequinade

Various theories have been put forward to explain why, after the success of *The Winslow Boy*, Terry should have turned to writing one-act plays. An explanation is hardly necessary; as a devotee of the theatre since his boyhood, he would have encountered one-act plays very frequently. No end-of-term performance can have happened for decades where *The Monkey's Paw* or *The Dear Departed* was not considered. It is true that one-act pieces were for amateur use as a rule; but in the nineteen-thirties Noël Coward had offered evenings of his one-act works in *Tonight at 8.30*, and Olivier himself had played in a double bill of *Oedipus* and *The Critic*. Terry, who had known nothing but a huge success with anything he had written since *Flare Path*, was surely justified in believing that an evening of one-act plays by Terence Rattigan would appeal to the public.

Moreover, he believed that there was a particular quality in the one-act piece that was hard to achieve with plays as conventionally presented in the theatre. Once or twice in the evening, the curtain came down, preferably on a 'curtain line' devised to maintain interest throughout the interval, and the audience went out into the bar and concerned themselves with other things, or – even worse – discussed what ought to happen in the next act, or what was wrong with what happened in the last act. With the one-act play, this broken attention did not happen. One of Terry's supreme abilities was the creation of long, developing scenes of the type that playwrights of our own day

71

seem to find so hard to write. He would no doubt have liked to fill the entire evening with a scene that developed over a couple of hours, and indeed there is no reason why, in another world, plays should not exist on that scale. Audiences are prepared to sit through two hours or more at a time for Wagner's operas. Peter Hall's first production of *Hamlet* for the Royal Shakespeare Company played two hours and a half before the interval, and more than an hour after.

The Royal Shakespeare Company has always been a law unto itself, though, and the commercial theatre preferred to allow audiences out after roughly an hour. In a piece that he wrote for the *New York Times*, Terry foretold that the day was coming when plays would last for sixty to eighty minutes – a forecast that has proved very largely correct. Meantime, in the belief that managements would be likely to bend in his direction, he let it be known that he was writing four one-act plays and that John Gielgud would play the lead in them.

Gielgud was in New York, working with Komisarjevsky on Rodney Ackland's version of *Crime and Punishment*, and Terry sent him the scripts of two pieces, *The Browning Version* and *Harlequinade*. He went to New York to ask him how he had liked them, and Gielgud hurt him deeply by his refusal. 'I have to be careful what I play now,' he is reported, in one version, to have said. A fuller version runs, 'They've seen me in so much first-rate stuff, do you think they will like me in second-class stuff?' This is how Rattigan reported it; but he had a way of elaborating other people's dialogue occasionally, and perhaps that was his interpretation rather than a verbatim report.

First rate or second class, Binkie Beaumont didn't want any part of it for H. M. Tennent either. He was convinced that the public would not come to an evening of one-act plays. Terry took it to Stephen Mitchell, who had no such belief. The two plays were to be done under the title *Playbill*, and the leads were to be played by Eric Portman. *Playbill* opened at the Phoenix on 8 September 1948, and ran for a modest 245 performances – perhaps a slight justification for Tennent's decree, since this was many fewer than *Flare Path*, *While the Sun Shines* and *The Winslow Boy*.

The Browning Version opened the evening. This has now become one of the most popular one-act plays in the repertoire, and deservedly so. It has the characteristic Rattigan theme of the power of the weak over the strong, the power of the good-natured schoolboy Taplow over the dry, unpopular disciplinarian Crocker-Harris, once a brilliant Greek scholar, now merely the teacher of classics to the Lower Fifth.

Andrew Crocker-Harris is avowedly modelled on Rattigan's own classics master, Coke Norris, an Oxford double first, who was still living when the play and the subsequent film appeared. Terry has given him a wife, younger and brighter than himself, who is carrying on an affair with another master. Although this plot appears to be the major element of the drama, it is really only a big subplot. (When I saw a fine production of the play in January 1976, I wrote in my notice that the writing for some of the supporting characters seemed sometimes a little flat. Dining with Terry subsequently, I mentioned this. 'That's done on purpose,' he said. 'You don't want people to be so interested in them that they lose interest in the main characters.' The main characters, he said, were Crocker-Harris, Taplow, Crocker-Harris's wife and perhaps Frank Hunter, the other master.)

The play has a wonderful double climax. Taplow of the Lower Fifth is worried about his prospects of a remove. He is doing extra work with Crocker-Harris, in whom he, almost uniquely, finds something to like. Crocker-Harris is due to leave at the end of the term (the following day) on account of a bad heart, and Taplow gives him a copy of Browning's version of the *Agamemnon* as a leaving present. Crocker-Harris finds this so affecting that he breaks down in front of the boy. That is the first climax.

When his unloving wife hears about the boy's gesture, she sneers at it. 'The artful little beast. . . . I came into this room this afternoon to find him giving an imitation of you to Frank here. Obviously he was scared stiff I was going to tell you, and you'd ditch his remove or something. I don't blame him for trying a few bobs' worth of appeasement.' The effect of this speech in the theatre is deadly.

Terry claims that Taplow is to some degree a recollection of himself at school. We are even given, in disguise, the French master's view of Rattigan's theatrical promise:

TAPLOW: Utter such a boastful speech – over – (*in a sudden rush of inspiration*) – the bloody corpse of the husband you have slain —

ANDREW: Taplow – I presume you are using a different text from mine —

TAPLOW: No, sir.

ANDREW: That is strange for the line as I have it reads: ἥτις τοιόνδ' ἐπ' ανδρὶ κομπαζεις λογον. However diligently I search I can discover no 'bloody' – no 'corpse' – no 'you have slain'. Simply 'husband' —

TAPLOW: Yes, sir. That's right.

ANDREW: Then why do you invent words that simply are not there?

73

TAPLOW: I thought they sounded better, sir. More exciting. After all she did kill her husband, sir. (*With relish.*) She's just been revealed with his dead body and Cassandra's weltering in gore —

ANDREW: I am delighted at this evidence, Taplow, of your interest in the rather more lurid aspects of dramaturgy, but I feel I must remind you that you are supposed to be construing Greek, not collaborating with Aeschylus.

Whoever Taplow may be, the school is certainly Harrow. Richard Price, a former master at Dulwich, made some notes on what seemed to him some eccentricities in the teaching methods and published them in *Punch*:

> Crocker-Harris had gained every possible prize and scholarship at Oxford and is described by the Headmaster as the most brilliant scholar on the staff. Normally he would have got a Fellowship, or at least a Sixth Form, yet he takes only the Lower Fifth. More curious still, his successor expresses delighted surprise at being given so high a form. Here the clue is given by the repeated references to the Upper Fifth studying science. Crocker-Harris has a private pupil who longs to take up science but cannot do so until he has obtained his promotion, and this he can only do by mastering Aeschylus. No Aeschylus, no Chemistry. Aeschylus is, in any case, not a beginner's writer, and the only satisfactory explanation is that the Lower Fifth was the top form on the Classical Side – in this school Sides being not parallel as elsewhere but successive. The Upper Fifth would be the beginning of the Science Side. Hence, to be appointed to the Lower Fifth was to be appointed to the senior Classical post.

My inquiries at Harrow proved that this was not quite such a bizarre arrangement as Richard Price imagined. James Morwood, the Librarian, explained with great courtesy the relationship of Harrow to the school in *The Browning Version*. At Harrow, the Lower Fifth was regarded as a colt stable for the brightest young classics, and to be appointed to it would be a really plum job. Moreover, Coke Norris, and so Crocker-Harris, would teach elsewhere as well. Science would be taught in the Upper Fifth and upwards.

The matters of Crocker-Harris's pension and the farewell speech that he at first agreed to concede to a more popular master but subsequently, invigorated by the unaccustomed experience of goodwill, however transient, insisted on making at the moment he considered right, have no place in Harrovian custom. Like the bloody corpse in the *Agamemnon*, they are dramatic license. One other detail, however, was confirmed by the Librarian as authentic. In his final speech Crocker-Harris talks knowingly about the school time table; and Coke Norris was indeed Organization Master between 1924 and 1926, when the time table would have been his responsibility.

Crocker-Harris's personality as a fictional character is summed up by himself in his conversation with the young master who is to replace him:

'I can only teach you from my own experience. For two or three years I tried very hard to communicate to the boys some of my own joy in the great literature of the past. Of course, I failed, as you will fail, nine hundred and ninety-nine times out of a thousand.' And he goes on, 'I discovered an easy substitute for popularity. I had, of course, acquired – we all do – many little mannerisms and tricks of speech, and I found that the boys were beginning to laugh at me. I was very happy at that, and encouraged the boys' laughter by playing up to it. It made our relationship so very much easier. They didn't like me as a man, but they found me funny as a character.' And then, 'I knew, of course, that I was no longer not liked, but now positively disliked . . . I don't know why they no longer found me a joke. Perhaps it was my illness. No, I don't think it was that. Something deeper than that. Not a sickness of the body, but a sickness of the soul.'

His relations with maturer people were no warmer. His wife deceived him with other masters, and told him whenever it happened. 'Hurt? Andrew hurt?' says his wife Millie to her current lover, the popular young master Frank Hunter. 'You can't hurt Andrew. He's dead.' He is quite ready to believe her tale that Taplow only gave him a present to keep himself out of trouble. Frank Hunter, when all the cards are on the table, tries hard to establish some kind of friendly relationship, but Crocker-Harris tells him, 'If you think, by this expression of kindness, Hunter, that you can get me to repeat the shameful exhibition of emotion I made to Taplow a moment ago, I must tell you that you have no chance.'

Yet when the curtain falls on a characteristically uncertain conclusion – Crocker-Harris destined for a second-class life at a crammer's, Millie resolved to leave him, but now disappointed of her hope of marrying Frank, Frank determined to build up an intimacy that Crocker-Harris discourages – it is Crocker-Harris that engages the sympathies. The play is a masterpiece of dramatic magic.

The second piece in *Playbill* is as autobiographical as *The Browning Version*, but relies much more on Rattigan's own invention. *Harle-*

quinade is a farce, and as A. B. Walkley wisely said, to narrate the plot of a farce is, at the best, to decant champagne. What the play shows is the dress rehearsal of a production by the celebrated theatrical duo Arthur Gosport and Edna Selby of *Romeo and Juliet*.

The Gosports are broadly derived from Alfred Lunt and Lynn Fontanne, but Terry never saw the Lunts in Shakespeare, and the choice of *Romeo and Juliet* let him introduce his memories of the OUDS production of that play in which he was directed by John Gielgud. Indeed, he has a joke about the line which caused him so much trouble in his own performance, 'Faith, we may put up our pipes and be gone.' In *Harlequinade*, the line is originally given to an old actor who walks out after being insulted, and is then transferred to a young man playing the part of a halberdier, and the young man tries it over and over, as Rattigan did, with the accents falling on this word or that.

A merciless look at the problems to be met by a troupe of actors in their labours to provide acceptable entertainment for their audience and at the same time to satisfy their own artistic requirements is a never failing theme for comedy. But, as always, Terry has relied on personalities to chart the course of the action. We are not only concerned with the acceptability of Arthur Gosport's little jump onto a garden stool at 'Shall I hear more, or shall I speak at this?' but at his relationship with a strange girl who announces herself as his daughter by a previous marriage that he had blithely imagined to have been concluded by a solicitor and a lot of documents to sign. If it has not been concluded, his much publicized marriage to his leading lady Edna Selby will be bigamous. Another difficulty arises when the stage manager's fiancée is accidentally engaged for *The Winter's Tale*.

The small talk among the players reflects the talk of the theatre people that Rattigan moved among, and might be expected to contain at least some hint of his current views. And indeed it does, though only of his current views about the theatre, where there are some rather dismissive lines about official sponsorship of the arts. Edna is talking to Dame Maud Gosport, Arthur's aunt:

EDNA: The theatre's gone through a revolution since 1900.

DAME MAUD: It was 1914 I played Juliet, dear. I remember the date well, because the declaration of war damaged our business so terribly.

EDNA: There's been another war since then, Auntie Maud, and I don't think you quite understand the immense change that has come over the theatre in the last few years. You see, dear – I know it's difficult for you to grasp, but the theatre of today has at last acquired a social conscience, and a social purpose. Why else do you think we're opening at this rat-hole of a theatre instead of the Opera House, Manchester?

DAME MAUD: Oh, I didn't know it was social purpose that brought us here. I thought it was CEMA.

EDNA: CEMA is social purpose.

CEMA, the Council for the Encouragement of Music and the Arts, was the forerunner of the Arts Council, a body whose patronage Terry never needed. It was not taken very seriously in the profession at that time. Terry gives a glimpse of what he thought of his activities a little later. (*Harlequinade* is an extremely conservative play; the new vogue for verse plays is written off with a reference to 'a modern play in verse called *Follow the Leviathan to My Father's Grave*'.) Jack, the stage manager, is talking with Mr Burton, the theatre manager:

BURTON: Funny for them to choose to open up here, I must say.

JACK: Social purpose, Mr Burton.

BURTON: Social purpose? Now what the blazes is that when it's at home?

JACK: As far as I can see, it means playing Shakespeare to audiences who'd rather go to the films; while audiences who'd rather go to Shakespeare are driven to the films because they haven't got Shakespeare to go to. It's all got something to do with the new Britain and apparently it's an absolutely splendid idea.

Short as the run at the Phoenix was by Rattigan standards, the plays raised Terry's reputation higher than ever. The plays were awarded the Ellen Terry Award for best new play of the year (as *The Winslow Boy* had been in the previous year), and Eric Portman had the award for best actor of the year. The plays are dedicated to their director, Peter Glenville – 'in gratitude.'

A production at the Coronet Theatre in New York the following year did not duplicate the London success. The New York critics did not seem to know what to make of the plays. It is easy to say that they could not enter into the thoroughly English environment of *The Browning Version*; it is unlikely that anything like the relationship between the English schoolmaster and his pupil would exist in any American educational establishment. But the backstage view of the Gosport company at rehearsal must at least have struck a chord with Americans familiar with the work of the Lunts. Nevertheless the reviews were bad, and the bill ran for only 62 performances.

Terry attributed this to what he called the 'sea change problem', a phenomenon he had experienced before. He examined it in an article in the *New York Times* (a paper that was always glad to welcome him in its pages). The problem, he reckoned, was one of recognition:

> ... plays of character, be they Russian, American, English or French, really demand a contribution from the audience which, when that audience is foreign and unversed in the customs, idiom and idiosyncrasies of the dramatist's native country, cannot readily be given. The portrait, however meticulously drawn, becomes blurred and coarsened and emerges as a type, confused in this audience's mind with a hundred other such Russians or Americans, or Englishmen or Frenchmen, all very like each other and totally unlike anyone else.

To show that the phenomenon worked both ways, he instanced *A Streetcar Named Desire*, which, he said, was regarded by some of the English critics as a picture of tenement life in New Orleans rather than a portrait, of 'roundness and extraordinary theatricality', of Blanche du Bois. The point had been better made by Brooks Atkinson in the *New York Times*, choosing an American example that really had been underrated in London:

> Some English critics have dismissed Willy Loman in *Death of a Salesman* as pure sentimentality, although most of us look on him as a tragic figure. There is no accounting for this difference in attitudes, but it certainly exists, for to me Mr Rattigan's schoolmaster is pure sentimentality and I cannot grieve over his misfortune.

There is indeed no accounting for the 'sea change', for it does not apply if the sea is the English Channel or the North Sea. English audiences have no difficulty in appreciating the character in Anouilh's plays or Ibsen's or Chekhov's, whereas Neil Simon's comedies cross the Atlantic eastbound as reluctantly as Alan Ayckbourn's westbound. Lest anyone should try and extract some rule from these contrasts of national taste, it should be recorded that *The Browning Version* was highly praised in Copenhagen, where schools resembling Harrow don't exist.

The predominantly enthusiastic notices from the London critics for a bill that H. M. Tennent had deprecated could not fail to encourage Terry to continue in his belief that what he was writing for the theatre was what the theatre wanted. 'There is not much need at this point to praise Mr Rattigan's skill,' T. C. Worsley wrote in the *New Statesman*; 'that we may now take for granted.' It was the technique – the component that the ordinary theatregoer can only detect by his inner feeling of satisfaction – that was most highly praised. W. A. Darlington in the *Daily Telegraph* dropped in a peculiarly satisfying reference. 'Not only the superb craftsmanship which is the secret of his monotonous success in the lighter pieces but also that sure grasp of character which has been seen before in *After the Dance*, in parts of *Flare Path* and in *The Winslow Boy*,' he wrote. *After the Dance*! It was a long time since anyone had ventured to recall that ill-fated but by no means ill-written piece.

Another interesting point was made by Harold Hobson in the *Sunday Times*:

> As one listens wearily night after night to the banal, clipped, naturalistic dialogue of the modern drama, one's heart cries out for writing of courage and colour, for the evocative word and the bannered phrase. But Mr Rattigan can make one doubt the necessity of that cry.
>
> In *The Browning Version* there is not a single sentence that in itself would raise the emotional level of a railway time-table . . . and when at the end Mr Portman utters into the telephone these apparently quite unexciting words, 'I am of the opinion that occasionally an anticlimax can be surprisingly effective,' [the audience's] heart responds as to the sound of a trumpet.

Terry was to write later of 'the thraldom of middle-class vernacular'. And indeed thraldom is the right word; in his next play it was the weapon that the critics took up against him. But the writer who is able to use middle-class vernacular to raise the heart as to the sound of a trumpet can hardly have believed that he was under any handicap.

On the well-established principle of 'send them out laughing', *Playbill* began with *The Browning Version* and gave *Harlequinade* after the interval. Later it was decided to reverse this order. A one-act play requires attention from the first line to the last, and Terry, who had at first not approved of the change, conceded that 'the latecomers no longer disturb the mood of *The Browning Version*, the comedy does not hurt as a curtain raiser, and it proved the value of theory in the theatre – it is of no value at all.' Later, when theatres out of the Broadway and Shaftesbury Avenue circuits found that they were able to lure audiences into eighty-minute evenings, *The Browning Version* has frequently been played on its own.

It was filmed three years later, with a film script by Terry that damaged the magic of the play a good deal. It is vital that the action should be confined to Crocker-Harris's enclosed surroundings. (A Danish critic compared it to Strindberg's *Dance of Death*.) To gratify the taste of cinema audiences, Terry and his director, the usually reliable Puffin Asquith, thought the film should be 'opened out'. School life was brought in as lavishly as if the story were *Goodbye, Mr. Chips*. Crocker-Harris (admirably played by Michael Redgrave) is seen at his school duties and in his associations with the rest of the staff. The author's principle, expressed years later, that too much interest in the supporting characters detracted from interest in the principal characters, was thrown out of the window. Worst of all, Crocker-Harris was allowed to make his farewell speech, and chose to apologize to his former pupils for his shortcomings – an attitude inconceivable in the dried-up pedagogue whose one relapse into emotion is the culmination of the play. The contrast between film and stage standards is emphasized by the fact that the script was recommended for an award.

And what about the rest of those four plays that were to be shown two at a time on alternate nights? Only one of them, *High Summer*, in the event appeared at all, and that was not in the theatre but as a television play, directed by Peter Duguid for Thames Television in 1972.

It is a very poor piece that seems as if it might have been meant to be in the style of Oscar Wilde – not *The Importance*, but the more serious works – but has somehow slipped into the world of Dornford Yates. It is set in the gardens of a stately home, White Manly, where a very distinguished party, including a German Crown Prince, is attending a cricket match against the town. The plot turns on the ownership and the sale of the estate.

The television production was decently cast, with Margaret Leighton and Christopher Gable in the leads and Roland Culver supporting. The author (who, on being reintroduced to his work a quarter of a century later, observed 'It's awful, isn't it?') was persuaded to make some alterations. Margaret Leighton had been alarmed by the prospect of the play's going out at all; but she was won over by such improvements as Terry wrote into it, and the play was duly broadcast to a satisfactory lack of publicity.

And here I have to say that Terry was not always scrupulous about his work. There can have been no pressing reason, financial or artistic, why he should have allowed *High Summer* to go out on the air. For a writer so confident in his opinions, to offer the public a play that he knew to be 'awful' is hard to forgive. The truth is that, once the enthusiasm of comparative youth had been eclipsed behind the professional certainty of vocational writing, he was not always above saying or doing what would immediately please whomever he was dealing with. His opinions in private were not always the same as his opinions in public. In the *Spectator* of 3 August 1985, John Osborne recalled that in his 'desultory, forlorn' correspondence with Terry, written during Terry's days in Bermuda, 'there was a great deal of regret for his past, confessions of professional dishonesty and avarice.'

Avarice is a vice that any professional writer may be forgiven, may even be encouraged to cultivate, since it increases the volume of work in which in due course the public may take pleasure. Professional dishonesty is another matter. It would be good to think that, if Terry had such a thing on his conscience, it concerned only his work for the films; for a film script ceases to be a writer's work the moment the producer and the director set to work on it. The mental agoraphobia of Crocker-Harris in *The Browning Version*, created with such masterly economy, is destroyed in the film where the story is 'opened out', where, especially, Crocker-Harris is actually seen to be making his leaving speech. Terry must have known this perfectly well. Puffin Asquith, the director, whose principles were based almost entirely on film work, would not have seen the point; the film had to be 'opened out' because that was how audiences liked their films. *The Browning Version* remained a good film, because the pluses so greatly outweighed the minuses.

I doubt if one could conscientiously say as much for the film of *French without Tears*, certainly not of *English without Tears*, a lightweight comedy about a well-born lady in love with her butler, which used a lot of what was left over from *While the Sun Shines*. Later film work, in such pieces as *The VIPs* and *The Yellow Rolls-Royce*, is fairly sparing in its use of the Rattigan talent. They were written as much to please his bank manager as the public, and there, at least, he was generally honest when discussing them with his friends.

Eight

Adventure Story

Terence Rattigan was thirty-seven when *Playbill* opened in September 1948, no longer the young genius. He had seen ten of his plays publicly performed, if you count the two halves of *Playbill* as two plays. Six of them were comedies, one was a farce, three were dramas of more serious intent. Of the comedies, two are not altogether safe from classification as farces, and one (*Flare Path*) must be rated as unserious, in spite of the serious things – war, death, etc. – that it deals with.

Terry did not see himself as a lifelong producer of comedies, like Ben Travers. He saw himself as a potential writer of serious, perhaps even historic, plays that 'would not be forgotten in fifty years', as he said. Fifty years sounds a modest claim, but there were not a lot of plays written in England in the previous half century that still kept a steady place on the stage. Shaw, of course, was *sui generis*. Galsworthy and Maugham were not commonly seen, though they might be remembered with respect; and once famous names like Drinkwater, H. M. Harwood, J. B. Fagan, A. A. Milne, were thought of, when they were, in other contexts. The time had come for Rattigan, nearing forty, to establish himself as a classic.

His disapproval of the 'play of ideas' proved a handicap. He would not write about current affairs, as Galsworthy had done in *Strife*, or Granville-Barker in *Waste*. Instead, he chose to harness the eminences of history. The character he selected for his hero was Alexander the Great, in whom he had been interested since he was a boy. Alexander's career, an amazing twelve-year sequence of conquests that began at twenty years old and ended with his death at thirty-two, had just the qualities that suited him.

The historical content of *Adventure Story*, the play with which he was to challenge the next fifty years, comes from Sir Thomas North's translation of Plutarch's *Lives*. Plutarch is perfect material for such treatment, full of anecdotes and picturesque detail. The life of Alexander (paired with Julius Caesar in the series of 'parallel lives') gives no more than the necessary outlines of the campaigns, but is full of character studies of Alexander's contemporaries. 'The fact is,' Plutarch said, 'that you often learn nothing by the study of campaigns of what kinds of men the leaders were. On the other hand you can sometimes learn more from an occasional remark than from the tremendous details of military successes.' The life of Alexander is full of dramatic detail; Rattigan's task was to decide how it was to be organized.

Shakespeare or Bulwer-Lytton or Brecht could have clothed it in verse and moulded history to their own needs. This was not Rattigan's way. Whatever the calling of his heroes, student, author, dictator, bomber pilot, cabinet minister, King's Counsel, all alike were united by the thraldom of middle-class behaviour, and so in his turn was Alexander of Macedon. It was not practical to set the play in a single living-room set; but it was possible to treat the participants as if they belonged to English middle-class society, the types with whom Terry was most at home. In speech and in thought, his Alexander is like a daring fighter pilot of World War Two.

The choice of incident is Plutarchian. Campaigns are discussed, but not shown on stage. The story is presented in terms of personal relationships, reasonably accurately borrowed from Plutarch. In making such an approach to his characters Rattigan was working on a Shakespearean principle. Shakespeare's Richard III or Henry V were not meant to be biographically exact, nor were their dramatic exploits closely matched with available history. Dates and ages were manipulated to suit dramatic needs. The plays were peopled with figures that would be familiar, and therefore easily comprehensible, to the audiences.

Terry used the same principle. If you are putting words into the mouth of some historical character, they must be words that the audience can understand.

Everyday speech and middle-class vernacular are however only the outward and visible signs of an inward and intellectual problem. Everyday thought and middle-class attitudes are also a part of the Rattigan armoury, and either he could not, or he would not, operate

83

without them. 'I've lost my copy of Homer,' Alexander complains as his forces pack up to begin their march into India. (Plutarch assures us that Alexander travelled everywhere with his *Iliad*.) Haven't we all seen Alexandrian characters, fighter pilots or squadron leaders of cavalry, in similar circumstances, even if only in films? Alexander's Homer in this context would have been a paperback, and why not? Shakespeare's Brutus takes a book from the pocket of his gown. 'Is not the leaf turned down where I left reading?' he muses, lest we should suspect his book to be a roll of papyrus. If speech is to be translated from one idiom to another, the speaker must be translated too.

Terry begins by setting us a problem.

The first scene of the play shows Alexander dying in his tent, the soldiers passing by in farewell, the senior officers debating amongst themselves who will be appointed to take command. Alexander, dying of fever, is only just able to speak, and he declines to name a successor. (Indeed, as we know, a succession dispute broke out a week after Alexander's death, with Perdiccus and Ptolemy on one side, and Meleager, who doesn't appear in the play, on the other.)

But we hear Alexander's thoughts on the matter, and in this Prelude he is still debating the matter in his mind. Worse, he is analysing the effects of the campaign. 'Where did it all go wrong?' is the problem that plagues him on his deathbed.

Adventure Story is a well-thought-out play, *durchkomponiert* as the musicians say, and the answer to Alexander's query is implicit in the first scene before it is acted out in the following ten. Alexander has gone to Delphi to consult the oracle on the chances of his success. The Pythia declines to see him, so he breaks into the temple by climbing the great statue of Apollo that stands outside, and demands that she give him an answer.

The Pythia involuntarily gives him the answer he wants when she thoughtlessly calls him 'invincible' in his determination – not to conquer Darius, but to have his question answered. Whatever she may say afterwards, Alexander is confident that the god had put that word into her mouth. What he refuses to recognize is that military invincibility is one factor only in his campaign, and he is not very clear about what he is to do with it:

PYTHIA: After you've killed Darius, what will you do?

ALEXANDER: Found a new order in Asia.

PYTHIA: With yourself at the head?

ALEXANDER: Yes, I suppose so. I hadn't thought.

84

Alexander's principal motive in embarking on his campaign was 'to make good my boast' – the boast, made to counter his father's disparagement, that 'Greece will have cause one day to rejoice when the Captaincy-General falls to his legitimate heir'. What he was to do with his new order was still vague. 'If there's a worthier man than myself to rule this new state, let him do so. Only he must be a Greek, of course . . . national sovereignties will have to be given up – but that's a small price to pay for a world state and universal peace.'

The Pythia perceives the weakness. 'Before any others, there's one conquest you will have to make first . . . yourself.' 'I know myself, Pythia,' Alexander assures her. 'Do you, Alexander? Are you sure?' 'Quite, quite sure.'

In the next five scenes, Terry charts Alexander's rise to what was as near to world domination as the Greeks of the time could have visualized. There are, wisely, no battle scenes. 'The purpose of the play,' Terry said at the time, 'is to explain the deeds by the man, and not the man by the deeds.' The action of the play is left in the hands of men and women of power. Terry uses the formula followed by Marlowe in *Tamburlaine*. There are scenes discussing preparations for battle, there are scenes discussing the consequences of battle. The battles themselves may be assumed to have taken place in between. As Terry very well knew, modern audiences of which a fair proportion will have been in battles themselves are inclined to think stage battles foolish, especially when they are executed by the modest numbers generally available to present day managers.

The climax of the campaign against the Persians comes in the first scene of the second act. The body of King Darius lies in a farm cart. Alexander is the master of the world. But the cart reminds him of another cart, in the citadel at Gordium, where he had solved the problem of loosing the Gordian knot by cutting it with his sword. 'I never did solve that puzzle, did I?' he says to Hephaestion. 'How can one solve a puzzle with a sword?'

Now we see that solving puzzles any other way is beyond Alexander's capacity. In a single act, he condemns to death Bessus, Darius's general who has promoted himself King Artaxerxes IV. He sends a punitive expedition against Oxyartes, a local chief. He reluctantly condemns his friend Philotas, who has been charged with plotting to kill him; and to make sure this leads to no further trouble, he sends Hephaestion to kill Philotas's father, the faithful Parmenion. The establishment of a world state and universal peace begins with a plan to march on Samarkand and invade India. It is hardly surprising that he finds his hands shaking uncontrollably. Every puzzle he is confronted with has to be solved with a sword.

'We began as the Companions of a Macedonian adventurer,' Philotas said rashly. 'We've ended as the slaves of an Oriental despot.' The rest of the play shows how right Philotas was. When his old companion Cleitas refuses to makes obeisance to the new queen – Roxana, the little girl whom Alexander is marrying to keep her tribe friendly – Alexander kills him in a quarrel. He insists that the Greeks must treat the Persian 'barbarians' as their equals. 'Despot I am,' he says, 'because I must be.' Darius's splendid finery, which he had had removed at the time of conquest, has all found its way back.

But when the army is being prepared for the advance into India, Alexander orders that his twenty cartloads of loot should be piled up into a bonfire and burnt, with Darius's splendid tent and his travelling throne on top of it. 'I should like to see that throne on a bonfire,' Hephaestion observes, exercising his critical privilege as Alexander's most intimate friend. If there is to be serious campaigning, it is obviously as well that the Oriental despot, with his high talk of Persian ancestors, should be sent on leave, and the simple Greek soldier resume command.

As we learn in the final scene, however, when the Indian campaign is over and Alexander is lying near to death in a courtyard in Babylon, the throne refused to burn. (Indeed, the throne was the focus of the disputes over the Asian succession years after.) 'You can't burn a conquered throne,' Alexander reflects, as we hear his thoughts. In this scene, his thoughts are all he can communicate. Perdiccus and Ptolemy wait anxiously for him to name his successor, but he will not. 'Who is to be the Master of the World?' he asks himself. 'Who shall I condemn to death? No one. This will be my last act of mercy. Let them fight it out for themselves.'

The conclusion is dramatically elegant, but it does little to round off the problem of where did it all go wrong. Terry, like Alexander, has solved his problem with a sword. Where it went wrong, as we have seen, was in Alexander's failure to know himself, to sort out the despot from the general. But his concluding words, effective as they sound, do not very much illuminate the situation. Historically, in so far as we may trust the sources, the scene is more or less truthful; Alexander did indeed decline to name a successor, is said to have left his power to 'the strongest'. But there was nothing in the history of his campaigns, or in the contemporary situation, to suggest that he would be condemning his successor to death. If he were aware of the jealousy of Perdiccus and Ptolemy and Meleager, he would know that it was vital to have a strong man at the head of things, with his own authority.

The fact is that, if Terry's Alexander may be said to have learnt to know himself, Terry didn't learn to know him. Which was right, the despot or the soldier? Only the bonfire of the captured loot suggests that

Alexander had any second thoughts about his status as Master of the World. By the standards of his own day, Alexander was a great hero and nothing less. But the shadow of Adolf Hitler lies uncomfortably across the play. It would not be possible to write of a great imperialist conqueror in 1949 without remembering that a great conqueror had subdued the whole of Europe between 1938 and 1945. To turn the Macedonian Hitler into a shining English fighter pilot was asking too much, especially as Terry never seemed entirely certain whether Alexander's ideals should be admired or not.

'I was afraid of the obvious cliché,' he told an interviewer in 1974, 'that all conquerors are necessarily dictators, which I don't think is necessarily true . . . I suppose I was trying to say that it depends on who has the ideal. I think what I meant was that if Alexander failed, then everyone would. It would seem to me to make the most sense, because Alexander was a very special person.'

He was even more frank in another interview two years later. 'I'm bound to acknowledge that it didn't work,' he said. 'I wasn't ready.'

There he was not being quite fair on himself. It *did* work – dramatically. If the audience left the theatre uncertain what they should think, this suggests a quality in the play that Terry used deliberately in several of his plays. He liked people to go away with their minds full of argument. But it is certainly true that the characters in *Adventure Story* are built on less than a heroic scale. Terry has defended his use of middle-class English for all purposes, but it is possible to write middle-class English less ordinary than the dialogue in this play. 'It seems to me idle to pretend,' wrote Alan Dent in the *News Chronicle*, 'that the general level of Mr Rattigan's dialogue is high enough for the dignity of the subject. Nor is it witty enough for the opportunities that this theme of world-aggrandizement affords.' The truth is that Terry's 'thraldom' to middle-class English was a thraldom indeed, that he was unable to make his English sound better than drawing-room chatter, as Evelyn Waugh could, and Graham Greene.

So it is not easy to associate this pleasant young man – and in Paul Scofield's hands, Alexander was never less than pleasant – with some of the things he has to do. It is easy to accept the courtesy of the scenes with the Persian Queen Mother, though Ivor Brown wrote in the *Observer* that he could not believe in this 'Alexander, shadowed o'er with the pale cast of Freud and always aching to lay his head on mother's knee'. History confirms that an affection sprang up between Alexander and Queen Sisygambis, and when he died she fasted to death within five days. The *sang froid* with which he accepts a drink from her, after being warned that she may try to poison him, is in character, and indeed is borrowed from Plutarch, though Plutarch had one of the Queen's suite, rather than the Queen herself, proffer the cup. The playful manner in which Alexander gives the innocent child Roxana the choice between death and marriage – a ring in one of his concealed hands, a dagger in the other, the choice offered without benefit of explanation – will pass, though I cannot imagine the fatal choice, if it had happened, being followed up fatally. This episode is purely a Rattigan invention.

Alexander's acts of wilful cruelty do not conform so nicely to the pattern. To refuse the Persian general Bessus a military execution after he has pleaded for one in terms that sound a little like the dialogue of *The Mikado* is nearer to the Alexander Terry should have drawn than the Alexander he did; and if the subsequent explanation brings him back into the dramatic sphere, that the refusal was not harshness to a defeated enemy but the proper sentence on the killer of Darius according to the laws of the Medes and Persians, he remains a bit cold-blooded. The scene then goes on to the sentencing of Philotas and the despatch of Hephaestion to contrive the death of Parmenion. These are acts that sit less comfortably on the shoulders of the decent young man we have met hitherto. Perhaps 'it has all gone wrong' already.

With characters so lightly drawn, what we have is not much more than a pageant in which the contestants in the struggle to be the Master of the World are played by public-school boys. The play was not very well received when it opened at the St James's on 17 November 1949. Tennent's gave it a lustrous production, directed by Peter Glenville. There were handsome sets designed by Georges Wakhevitch. (Terry told Harold Hobson that he had never enjoyed anything so much as writing 'Scene 2. The hanging gardens of Babylon'.) There was music by Benjamin Frankel. Paul Scofield was supported by a fine cast, whose merits may be assessed when you hear that Richard Burton, who was to play Hephaestion, was sacked during rehearsals. He was replaced by Julian Dallas.

The press was hardly fair. If neither Shakespeare nor Shaw had tried his hand at Alexander, what right had a boulevard writer like Rattigan to do so? (Handel had not done so badly, but you wouldn't expect a drama critic to know that.) Moreover, weren't we tired of examining the motives of world-challenging dictators? At least, some critics paid their tribute to the poetic nature of the scenes with the Queen Mother and the dangerous little game with the innocent Roxana; but if Rattigan were pleased with such praise, he was betraying himself, for they are popular romantic material of a kind that he was trying to avoid.

The reviews were succinctly summarized, in Terry's own words, that the play 'lacked the language of the poet and the perception of the philosopher.' One thing that we can see now, and that would not be generally perceptible then, is the autobiographical nature of the story. Terry had a Hephaestion of his own at the time, a young actor named Kenneth Morgan. The affection of Alexander for the Persian Queen Mother was the affection of Terence Rattigan for his mother, an emotion that remained strong all his life. Less admirable was the display of Alexander's dislike of his father, Philip. It was Philip's contempt for his 'weak, effeminate coward' of a son that set Alexander on his campaign. Frank Rattigan had disapproved of his son's choice to live as a playwright. If *Adventure Story* had been the neo-Shakespearean triumph its author imagined, Terry would have been able to say to him 'Let him see me now – in Darius's tent, wearing Darius's mantle.' His next play was a more direct barb, and ran three times as long.

Nine

Who Is Sylvia?

It would have been typical of Terry if he had begun the consideration of his next play once *Adventure Story* had been safely launched. In fact, of course, it was not safely launched. The reviews, as we have seen, were less than generous, and the play closed in July 1949 after a modest run. Terry was indeed considering a new piece, but not the next piece he wrote. 'The play will open with the body discovered in front of the gas fire,' he said unexpectedly to Peter Glenville as they were leaving their hotel in Liverpool in the final week of *Adventure Story*'s tour.

Certainly this was a characteristic example of Rattigan's working method, for a body had indeed been discovered in front of a gas fire. It was the body of Kenneth Morgan, to whom he had been devoted. The devotion was less absolute from the other side, and Kenneth Morgan had broken his liaison with Rattigan to go and live with someone else. The new connection had not proved solid enough to fill the gap that he had created in his life. He swallowed an overdose of sleeping pills, then lay down in front of his gas fire to ensure the onset of his eternal sleep.

The news had been sent to Terry in Liverpool. He was heartbroken. Yet instantly he must have decided that the way to commemorate his great friendship should be in the form of a play.

This is perhaps the moment to speak of Terry's homosexuality, to which so much has been attributed that it is not responsible for. Fundamentally it was another example of his inability, or unwillingness, to grow up. Both Kenneth Morgan and a later friend, Michael

Franklin, had notably boyish faces, and Terry's relations with them, *mutatis mutandis*, were the relations of a senior schoolboy with a younger. 'His homosexuality, of which he made no particular secret, probably unswerving, was not at all obvious on the surface,' Anthony Powell reported. We need make no more of it, and no less, than he did himself. He sometimes told people that he regretted the circumstance, even that he felt ashamed of it, but he never made any effort to reorient his outlook. Anthony Powell's judgment would have remained valid all his life. He was not ashamed of his homosexual friends, though he was tactful enough not to mix the younger ones with more serious acquaintances who might have found them antipathetic, and indeed *vice versa*. Of course there were occasional episodes, but they are of no more importance than the little romances indulged in by more normally sexed people. Compared with the often-married figures in the film and theatre worlds around him, Terry might almost be set down as chaste. There were only two importantly long-standing romantic friendships in his adult life.

It has been argued that the stories of some of his plays, *Variation on a Theme*, for example, would be more easily assimilable if they dealt, not with transactions between men and women, but between men and men. It seems to me likely that such suggestions would not have been made if it had not been fairly widely known that Terry was himself homosexual. *Variation on a Theme* may not be a very good play, but there is nothing intrinsically improbable about the plot as it stands. The one example where a sex change has clearly taken place is 'Table Number Seven' in *Separate Tables*, where the bogus major has been up in Court for interfering with women at the cinema. In the high and palmy days of the *News of the World*, interfering with boys at the cinema was an offence that flavoured many a spicy paragraph, whereas interfering with women was seldom worth the editorial space unless a rape followed.

The sex change was competently executed by a master surgeon, and it left the play halfway between two harmonies. Sophisticated audiences agreed among themselves that what the major had done was grope young boys. But when for an American production, where there was no censorship, the play was rewritten with the major's offence switched from women to boys, it was generally agreed that, so completely had the women been written into the argument, the play was better in its pristine orientation.

The truth is that the emotions felt between romantic couples are fairly standard, however the genders are sorted out. When the censorship was lifted from the British theatre, and plays began to appear in which homosexual affairs might be frankly represented, their

91

plots looked too often as if they dealt with conventional affairs in which a woman had arbitrarily been turned into a man. Terry was an efficient, pragmatic writer, who thought up stories that he reckoned the theatre-going public would like to see. Naturally the emotional adventures of his own experience would provide the visible patterns on which to mould the emotional adventures of his characters, male or female. Love, loyalty, generosity, jealousy and the other outward signs of a twofold affection are much the same whoever the two may be, in the theatre at any rate. Terry was not the man to make unprovoked attacks on the social conventions in which he had been brought up and from which he earned his living. There were cause mongers only too anxious to write plays 'about things' while he wrote 'about people'. If his stories paralleled the events of his own life, this is simply a demonstration of the universal nature of romantic love.

There was, though, one quality in Terry's own life that often coloured his plots, and this was the desire to be wanted – not physically but emotionally. He was less concerned that the object of his affection should return that affection than that he, Terry, should be regarded as a necessary factor in the other's life. He was prepared to undergo tiresome embarrassments at the hands of his friends, and this is a theme that often shows in his plays, especially the later plays. Mastery of the strong by the weak became his trademark.

It seems likely that such a feeling had been with him for a good deal of his life. When he wrote his radio play *Cause Célèbre* in 1975, he confessed that he had wanted to write about the case of Mrs Rattenbury and George Wood (with which it deals) ever since he read about it in the newspapers in 1934, when he was twenty-four years old. In the event, he did not write about it until forty years later, and it is important in any consideration of Rattigan's life to note the lifelong interest that he had in the power of the weak over the strong. I doubt if Terry's is basically connected with his inversion. Men perform the most absurd stupidities because the lady likes Milk Tray. Great men have lost reputations, thrones even, out of unwise devotions.

This theme is constantly repeated. It is in *The Browning Version*, where a schoolboy's kindly gesture towards an unpopular master breaks the master's rigid self-control. It is the mainspring of *The Deep Blue Sea*, which shows the helpless infatuation of a respectable woman for a more or less worthless man. It is the whole basis of *Variation on a Theme*, the account of a successful demi-mondaine's sacrifice to a young dancer who has caught her fancy. It occurs in both halves of *Separate Tables*. It is detectable in *Man and Boy*, though not as the title might suggest, and in *Bequest to the Nation*, where it is introduced as a sub-plot. It is presented nakedly in *Cause Célèbre*. T. C. Worsley, reviewing *Man and Boy* in the *Financial Times*, distilled the essence of the matter: 'Its subject is humiliation, which has indeed been the subject of all Mr Rattigan's plays . . . the weak have a terrible clinging strength . . . they will always come back to haunt and weaken the strong with their misguided devotion.' In *Cause Célèbre* this kind of relationship is freely admitted. Alma Rattenbury, on trial with her 18-year-old boyfriend for the murder of her husband, is addressed by the judge:

JUDGE: Now I am not sure that I have followed this. You say you tried to break the affair with Wood but were unable to – one of the reasons being the difference in your ages. Surely that very thing would make it easier?

ALMA: No, my lord. Sorry, but it makes it harder.

JUDGE: But surely the older party must be the dominant party?

ALMA: Excuse me, my lord, but to me it's the other way round. Anyway it was with me and George. I think it must be with many people.

That's how it was with Terence Rattigan. The homosexual element is evident in his plays, no doubt, to psychiatrists, but it is no more important than it is in Marlowe or Maugham or Wilde.

Terry's next play, *Who Is Sylvia?*, was originally announced as being 'a serious comedy', though in the event it turned out to be as frivolous a comedy as you could imagine, no matter how serious you may consider such a venal sin as deceiving your wife. Only a determined analyst could find homosexuality in it. Terry took longer than usual working on it, and allowed himself time off for non-dramatic composition.

He accepted a BBC commission to write a play for the Festival of Britain in 1951. He contributed a piece to an occasional anthology, *Diversion*, edited by John Sutro for Max Parrish; *A Magnificent Play for Camels* was a plea for more recognition of script writers in the cinema, where their work was treated only as raw material for directors and cameramen. The estimation of writers was always important to him, particularly at that time, when a play that was original in concept, and had been received with tolerably friendly notices, had failed to draw the public. *Adventure Story* closed in July 1949 after just over a hundred performances. Weighed down by both his professional and his private distress, Terry drove through Germany to Denmark, with the excuse that he could discuss a forthcoming production of *The Browning Version* in Copenhagen. In London there was a revival of *French without Tears*. In New York he went to oversee the production of *Playbill* at the

Morosco. It was not well received, and ran for only sixty-one performances.

Terry began to wonder why this apparent gulf between himself and his public had opened, and when he came home he put his ideas into an essay which he sent to the *New Statesman*, where the drama critic, Cuthbert Worsley, was a friend. He called it 'Concerning the Play of Ideas', and it took up once more the argument, first flown in 1937 in New York, that plays should be about people, the plot should develop from character rather than dogma, principles or current affairs.

He traced this heresy that was poisoning the drama with ideas back to Bernard Shaw, who had begun it in his *Saturday Review* writing in the 1890s; he held that those who had maintained the Shavian principles since then, as though there were no conceivable alternative, were holding back the possibility of progress in the theatre. If painters were not encouraged to paint like Burne-Jones, he argued, or poets to write like Swinburne, why should playwrights be expected to write like Bernard Shaw?

Shaw was not the only villain of the piece. He was joined by Ibsen, whose drama Shaw had praised as 'theatre as a factory of thought, a prompter of conscience and an elucidator of social conduct'. But Terry could not write off Ibsen as he wrote off Shaw; instead, he argued that Shaw had misread Ibsen, who, he held, cared more about his characters than about the situations he put them in. Broadening his assault, he said roundly that 'from Aeschylus to Tennessee Williams, the only theatre that has ever mattered is the theatre of character and narrative'. The trouble with the current theatre, he thought, was 'not that so few writers refuse to look the facts of the present world in the face but that so many refuse to look at anything else'.

The essay was not a very good one. He wrote off the 'play of ideas' in a wholesale fashion, but never made it clear what he meant by that definition. If there ever was a play of ideas, *The Second Mrs Tanqueray* is one, yet Rattigan specifies Pinero as a main target of the 'ideologists', who used his name only as a term of reproach. But good or bad, there was no question that such opinions would raise the hackles of the other contemporary playwrights, and indeed they charged in with every ideological gun firing. The order of battle ran: James Bridie, Benn Levy, Peter Ustinov, Sean O'Casey, Ted Willis, Christopher Fry and, in a grand culmination, George Bernard Shaw.

Shaw was ninety-four years old at the time (he died later in the year), and it is not surprising that he failed to reach the critical standards of the *Saturday Review* in 1895. He made the correct deduction that Rattigan disapproved of Shaw's plays because he did not enjoy them. He did not go so far as to say that he enjoyed Rattigan's plays, but he was generous and polite. 'His head is a bright one,' he conceded, 'and the things that come into it, reasonable or not, are all entertaining, and often penetrating and true.' On the other hand, 'The difference between his practice and mine is that I reason out every sentence I write to the utmost of my capacity before I commit it to print, whereas he slams down everything that comes into his head without reasoning about it at all.' In his earlier reaction to Terry's articles James Bridie said, 'It is difficult to believe that he has ever read or seen a play by Shaw.' Shaw went further than that. None of the correspondents showed 'any convincing evidence that the writers have ever seen, written or produced a play.'

Terry wrote a winding-up answer to all his critics, but without offering any powerful blows in reply to their several onslaughts. The whole correspondence seems today something of a storm in a teacup, but the theatre of that time was in a state of instability, as indeed the country was. There were characters, such as George Devine, Joan Littlewood and Oscar Lewenstein, hovering in the wings. Terry was still under forty, and no doubt looked forward to a long lifetime in the theatre. He must have known what was going on on the theatrical left (George Devine was a friend of his, they had played in OUDS together), but if he did, he declined to take it seriously.

The Final Test, Terry's first play for television, was a great success. It was, though no doubt he was quite unaware of it, a play of ideas, even if the ideas were not political.

As a festival play, he wanted to wrap it around some popular event, and with the facilities of the television screen available to him, he chose a Test Match against Australia. Cricket had always been one of his enthusiasms, and he could write about it with inside knowledge. His hero, Reggie Palmer, was the son of the great English batsman Sam Palmer, due to make his last appearance in the English side. Reggie, however, was not an open-air boy but a poet; Paul Dehn contributed the lines he was supposed to have composed, lines that suggested an unsympathetic look at Ronald Duncan. On the day of Sam Palmer's final innings, Reggie has contracted to pay a visit to a famous verse playwright. When the playwright learns that his protégé is the son of Sam Palmer and is not attending the match although he has a couple of tickets in his wallet, he is appalled. The boy complains that he finds cricket dull, and is rewarded by a very funny, and wise, speech explaining why its dullness is one of cricket's great merits. All further poetic discussion set aside, they jump into a car and make for the Oval.

There they arrive in time to see Sam's innings. He is out at the third ball, but the crowd give him a hero's reception as he goes back to the pavilion. In an epilogue that is characteristic of Terry's style in its reluctance to end on an actual full-stop, poet and cricketer dine together, both of them politely diffident about the other's renown.

Terry's instinctive grasp of the possibilities of television was derived from his experience of films, but his decision to incorporate real shots of the Test was a clever feat of imagination. I have broken with chronology to describe it here, though it was not broadcast until the summer of 1951, the year of the Festival of Britain, because it displays Terry's fatal weakness for writing a play of ideas when he thought he was only writing a play of character. *The Final Test* is no less a play of ideas than, for example, Shaw's *Fanny's First Play*. Before C. P. Snow ever brought up his thoughts about the 'two cultures', there had always been the conflict between the aesthete and the hearty, which indeed concerns, or anyway used to concern in the days before education had grabbed the front-page headlines, students more potently than politics. *The Final Test* is a simple case of aesthete versus hearty, and although Terry cheated by turning his aesthete into an undercover hearty, he brought the argument into the open in a way where it is bound to attract supporters for either side, Test Matches being affairs of national importance even to the most unpolitical classes.

Of course Terry would have held that such an argument is not important enough to matter, and this unwillingness to recognize importance in any but political or sociological contentions is one of the weaknesses in his diatribe against the play of ideas. Certainly there is no trace of ideology in *Who Is Sylvia?*

It is, all the same, full of reflections of his own life and thought. The story is very simple. Lord St Neots, a young man in the Diplomatic, is obsessed with the recollection of a girl whom he kissed when he was seventeen. An amateur sculptor, the heads that he makes are all portraits of Sylvia. A tireless amorist, the quality he looks for in the girls he chooses is that they must look like Sylvia, no matter how worthless in other respects. He picks up Sylvias as persistently as any hero in Feydeau. There is only one disadvantage in his happy and generously endowed existence. He is married, and Lady St Neots, contented as they are together, is not a Sylvia.

The first act is set in the year 1917. The domestic circumstances are set in the classic manner of farce with conversation on the telephone. Mark St Neots gives a generous autobiography to the duty secretary at the Foreign Office in order to establish his identity. He needs to speak to the Middle East department, where he works, to ensure that if his wife calls, she can be told that he will be late home. If any complications ensue, he may be found in his friend Oscar Philipson's flat in Chelsea. Seldom is so much information given in a single speech.

Who Is Sylvia?

The Sylvia he is waiting for in his friend's flat is Daphne Prentice, an office girl he has picked up on a bus. She is accustomed to evenings of this kind, apparently, even though she doesn't know the name of her host. In fact she never does, for he tells her he is called Wright. A series of interruptions punctuate their evening. First, Daphne's little brother Sidney arrives (and how he knew where to find his sister we are not told). Mum has sent him to bring her home. Mark sends him out to find a taxi, and before he returns, Ethel lets herself in with her own latchkey. Ethel is Oscar Philipson's current girlfriend, and she is soon followed by Oscar Philipson himself, unexpectedly home on leave from France. Oscar, a more experienced seducer than Mark, bribes Sidney to go home and say there was no answer when he rang the bell, and organizes a *partie carrée* at the Savoy. Before it can swing into action, however, alarm whistles signal a Zeppelin raid and Mark, family duty triumphing over romance, insists that he must go home to look after his little son Denis.

In the next act, Mark has aged from thirty-two to forty-four. The date is 1929, Mark has just been appointed Minister in La Paz. Oscar, a colonel in the Grenadiers, is on leave from Egypt. Mark has also inherited his father's title, and is now the Earl of Binfield. (Rattigan kept rooms in the Stag and Hounds pub in Binfield, where he retired to write out of reach of his friends. *The Deep Blue Sea* is dedicated to the landlords, Mr and Mrs Norton.) Mark's son Denis, the new Viscount St Neots, should be at a French crammer's preparing to join the Diplomatic, but in fact, having perhaps seen *French without Tears*, has come home to become an actor. Mark has added a studio to Oscar's flat (which he is renting, furnished, complete with servant) and a party is going on there.

The current Sylvia is actress Nora Patterson, and Mark is so much devoted to her that he is proposing to decline the posting to La Paz and give up the Diplomatic altogether. Nora is looking after the guests at the party, while Mark stays upstairs gossiping with Oscar; they can't join the rest because there is someone there who knows them and will give away their double lives. But worse, Denis turns up with his current girlfriend, who is playing a lead part in the same play as Nora. Mark is exposed as being Lord Binfield, forty-four years old and the father of a presentable son. Another Sylvia has to be written off.

The third act brings the date to 1950. Mark is the Ambassador in Paris, Oscar is a general, Denis playing Mark Anthony at the Old Vic and Sylvia is a model, Doris, who knows quite well that her sugar-daddy is 'an earl and an ambassador and all that', but is prepared to pretend that he is only Mark Wright. Doris and her friend Chloe are going to the Old Vic with Mark and Oscar, a complex plot having been thought up that will enable them to sit together when Mark's original guests were to have been his wife, who is in bed with a cold, and an extraneous character, Charlie Bayswater, who in fact is going with the War Minister.

While they are taking a little *bonne bouche* of oysters and champagne, Mark's wife Caroline telephones, and though Mark assumes an immediate Cockney accent, she recognizes his voice. This would not have surprised her, for she knew all along about the theatre party, Doris, an old acquaintance from her dressmakers', having revealed all. Caroline, in fact, has decided to put an end to Mark's tiresome double life. She arrives at the flat and assures her husband that she has known about the whole thing since the days of Daphne Prentice, but has enjoyed following the various encounters, has even ensured that Mark will never get into trouble. The act is prettily adorned with references to what we will remember from the earlier acts but imagined Lady Binfield knew nothing about. Moreover, the original Sylvia has not disappeared in South Africa, but lives in Chester Square and plays bridge with her.

All four of them leave together for the theatre, Oscar's Chloe having left to help her mum with the washing. If there is a moral (and Rattigan would have been horrified by the suggestion) it is contained in the last exchange between the two old men.

OSCAR: What does it feel like to grow from seventeen to sixty-four in five minutes? Having your cake and eating it, eh?

MARK: Well – all I can say is this. I have jolly well had my cake and I have jolly well eaten it – and that's more than can jolly well be said for most people, including yourself, so yah!

OSCAR: A little prep school, wasn't it, for an ambassador?

MARK: That wasn't an ambassador speaking. That was the last recorded utterance of Mr Mark Wright.

Now it is no secret, and it wasn't much of a secret in October 1950, when the play opened at the Criterion, that Mark is a caricature of Frank Rattigan. It cannot even have been a secret from Frank Rattigan, for, as he always did, his son read the play to his parents as soon as it was finished. It is dedicated to 'My Father, with love, with gratitude, and in apology.'

'Love' and 'gratitude' are perhaps unexpected, because Terry seldom expressed such feelings about his father. Indeed he was often embarrassed by 'the Major's' appearance at his plays with a series of

Sylvias. But the basic relationship between Frank and Vera Rattigan is reflected to this extent in the play, that Vera Rattigan knew very well about her husband's antics, but remained generously tolerant of them. Her son was very close to her all his life. He was, on the other hand, less than loving and grateful to his father. (He used the same combination in his dedication of *Cause Célèbre* to 'Pegs' – Mrs Harold French – who for years was his hostess, housekeeper and confidante, and to whom he was devoted.) It was to his mother that he dedicated his first published play, *French without Tears*, and in later years he dedicated *Separate Tables* to her, when she was living in just such a hotel as he depicts in those plays. She was known, somewhat cryptically, as 'Old Blighty'.

If the relationship between Mark and his wife is truly a reflection of the relationship between Frank and Vera Rattigan, then homosexuality creeps into the picture. It is widely believed that homosexuality in boys occurs when they are exposed more to their mothers than to their fathers, and indeed experience goes to confirm this. It is for experts to explain this phenomenon; but if we accept it as valid, we may well say that the child of the home Terry has suggested, offstage, for the Binfields would at least be at risk. The life of Denis in the play is similar to the life of his creator, at home with his mother during the war while his father is away on duty, even if some of that duty is bogus; studying unwillingly at a crammer's with an eye on the Diplomatic, and leaving his studies to go into the theatre; a theatrical success in middle life. If the Binfields represent Frank and Vera, there is no alternative to regarding Denis as Terence. Denis has a crush on Ursula Culpepper, a famous actress, in Act Two; but who has not had a crush on a famous actress at eighteen? He puts her off readily enough when something more immediately in his own interest turns up. The passage in which he beseeches his father not to leave the Diplomatic, and at the same time not to insist on his joining it, must have been full of domestic reflections. Whether adult thespian Denis has found a famous actress to share his life, we don't know, though he chucks his first-night party quickly enough for the alternative of supper with the family.

But however close Denis may be to Terry, ironically there is no doubt that Mark Binfield contains as much Terry as Frank. His younger friends tended to conform to a steady pattern, a pattern that might well have been established at school or at Oxford. 'You're an emotional Peter Pan,' Oscar says to Mark. 'Well, what's wrong with that?' Mark says. 'I prefer to keep my emotions adolescent. They're far more enjoyable than adult ones.' This was Rattigan talking about himself.

Mark was written to be played by Rex Harrison, an emotional Peter Pan if ever there was one. Rex Harrison is said to have declined it because he thought the part of Oscar outweighed it, and the truth is there is nothing much in it beyond the simple situation of the two existences rubbing against one another, repeated with variations. Robert Flemyng and Roland Culver, two experienced Rattigan players, kept the evening happily alive with the bounty of good lines; but neither the parts nor the play itself have any depth to them. 'A serious comedy', Rattigan had called it when he embarked on it, and some of the reviews found seriousness still struggling to make itself felt. The *Times* wrote:

> If this theme were treated seriously, and the first act is scattered with what seem to be the bits and pieces of a serious attention, the repetitiveness of the story would be its theatrical strength; but treated as a light comedy the story, entertainingly as it is told, divides itself into three short plays with too many points of resemblance.

What the critics could not know was that a serious play about the life of Frank and Vera Rattigan would have deeply offended them and their friends, and in any case was unthinkable from a man of such generous nature as Terry. So an unserious comedy it had to be, and Terry was lucky that, despite the moderate reviews it got, it ran for 381 performances. It has had some success in the Scandinavian countries, too, but it was never played in New York, has never been revived in London.

Ten
The Deep Blue Sea

The opening of *Who Is Sylvia?* was the last occasion when Frank Rattigan was able to attend one of his son's first nights. When *The Deep Blue Sea* was in rehearsal, a year and a half later, he died, and his death triggered something of a change of life in his son.

Terry gave up his chambers in Albany and took a flat in Eaton Square. He also bought a house in Sunningdale with a garden backing on the golf course where he so often played. His mother was not anxious to live on her own out of London, or to set up housekeeping in some new home. She took rooms in the Stanhope Court Hotel in South Kensington. She was still a beautiful woman and, now in her sixties, retained great dignity and charm. Terry took her out as often as he could, and lunched or dined with her at her 'separate table' in the hotel dining room, later to become dramatically famous.

The Eaton Square flat had a fine outlook over the tree-lined square, through a vast window leading to a balcony lined with window boxes where flowers were scrupulously tended. On the opposite wall, a photo-mural of a forest scene reflected the open-air feeling. Photo-murals lined the walls of the dining room too, views of old London covering all four. Besides these two handsome rooms, there was a small study where Terry's secretary, Mary Herring, dealt with his letters, his appointments and his manuscripts.

His working day began at about 10.30 and continued until the middle of the afternoon, with a break for a light lunch. There would be

101

a walk for exercise, or a round of golf, then work would resume until 8 p.m. or so. At this time of his life, he always looked faultless in health and in turnout, and younger than his forty years.

Weekends would be spent at Little Court, the Sunningdale house. It stood back from the road, from which trees concealed it. On the other side, a comparatively small garden led to the golf course. There were a tennis court (though I never saw anyone playing on it) and a croquet lawn. The house was modest enough to enable a married couple to cope with cooking and housework, but the serious business of managing and organizing the household and all the entertaining was entrusted to Harold French's wife Peggy, or Pegs – patient, efficient and everyone's friend, capable of dealing with any kind of emergency.

And at Little Court anything might happen. One Saturday, Rex Harrison and his wife Kay Kendall arrived for the weekend in a beautiful grey Rolls Royce convertible. By teatime, Rex was in bed with a temperature, his wife said, of 100°, and the doctor was sent for. It was all the fault of the car, in Kay's opinion. 'I always said it was unlucky.'

Late next morning, the Harrisons came down, none the worse for their plague. But there was no question of driving back in their unlucky car. 'It will be absolutely packed with germs,' Kay Kendall pronounced. So a hired car had to be provided, and the Rolls was left in the drive until a driver could be found to return it.

The Deep Blue Sea had a troubled birth. It had been in development for a long time; Terry's sibylline observation to Peter Glenville at Liverpool clearly marks the moment of its invention. It suggests that the play Terry had in mind was to have been directly stimulated by the circumstances of Kenneth Morgan's death, and in fact this was exactly the play that turned up, an account of the tragic end of a homosexual affair. It would not be the first time that Terry had translated his own experiences into drama; indeed, *Who Is Sylvia?* and *French without Tears* did just that, with a little help from the imagination.

But the British theatre still laboured under the confinements of the censorship, and there was no prospect that such a play could ever be performed in a West End theatre. It is true that, almost two decades before, a play about a homosexual attachment, Mordaunt Shairp's *The Green Bay Tree*, had played at the St Martin's without let or hindrance for six months. That was a play, though, in which the affair was seen in retrospect after the younger member had freed himself from the affinity, and nothing more sexually suggestive occurred than the playing of a gramophone record of a boy soprano. Hugh Beaumont persuaded Terry that he must take his story and cast it in a more acceptable form if he wanted it produced by H. M. Tennent.

So the tale of Ken Morgan's death was put aside and transmuted into something that to the uninitiated would seem absolutely different. The work cost Rattigan a great deal of time and trouble and spiritual sorrow, and a great deal of argument with Beaumont. Moreover it was disturbed by two events. The first was a commission to write the film script of *The Sound Barrier* for Alexander Korda. The second was the advent of Michael Franklin.

Michael Franklin was the ideal companion of the moment. He was young and cheerful and good-looking, and anxious to be looked after. (He had lately tried to inveigle Benjamin Britten into asking him for designs for an opera.) Terry needed someone of that precise character. In his newly collected persona, he was wise enough not to suggest that they should live together; what he wanted was a character who would always come to him, like a child to his mother, when there was anything he wanted. There is a line in *The Sound Barrier* about an engineer in dispute about some point. The engineer is called Franklin. 'Mr Franklin is very anxious to keep his job,' his superior says meaningfully.

It was, incidentally, partly through Michael Franklin that my own acquaintance with Terry ripened from casual acquaintance into friendship. I had known Michael before he met Terry, when he was a neighbour of mine in Chelsea. Terry sometimes used to use me as a responsible agent when he was away. One day in the spring of 1953, for instance, I received an unexpected telegram: 'Please see to Michael's requirements which do not include a Jaguar. Love Terry.' I found Michael's requirements were generally easy to cope with. Terry, on the other hand, sometimes had difficulties that distressed him. Only a few weeks after that confiding telegram, he invited me to call and discuss with him how to settle a quarrel which looked likely to cause a final break.

That evening I met Michael for dinner and heard his side of the story. It corresponded nearly enough with Terry's. The end of a beautiful friendship was in the air. I gave such advice as I could, and left for a fortnight's holiday in Monte Carlo. Normal relations had been restored by the time I came back. This was more or less the pattern of their friendship until the end of Terry's life.

The Sound Barrier was an unexpected bonus that distracted Rattigan's attention from work on the play, but gave him something to think about which was unconnected with the death of a friend. The film was conceived by David Lean, the director, as dealing with the question – financial, social, philosophical – whether it was right to devote great quantities of money and research and labour to building an aircraft that would fly faster than the speed of sound (about 760 mph at ground level). Terry was not interested in aeroplanes any more, particularly in an engineering context. But Alex Korda and David Lean were keen to have him. They took him to Farnborough to see aircraft potentially able to 'break the sound barrier'. But characteristically, it was not the aeroplanes that fired his imagination; it was the men that flew them.

So the script that he wrote was not a 'play of ideas' but a play of personalities. There is a certain familiarity about Sir John Ridgefield, the ambitious aircraft builder. He is a man who wants to be wanted, and determined to see his son do well, if it costs him his life – Frank Rattigan and Terence Rattigan rolled into one, with a touch of Alexander the Great, Arthur Winslow, *et hoc genus omne*. The plot is not about aircraft engineering. It is about Ridgefield's son determined to fly to please his father, though he is killed on his first solo; and it is about the love between Ridgefield's daughter and the chief test pilot. The test pilot is killed too, but not before he has broken the sound barrier. You can no more fail to make an attractive film with aeroplanes than you can with horses. *The Sound Barrier* was a success, and Terry's script was nominated for an Oscar.

The Deep Blue Sea was finished, in so far as it was ever finished, in the summer of 1951. It had been through more than one mutation since it flashed into Rattigan's mind on the day of his friend's death, but at least it had now reached a practical form. Rattigan's agent sent copies to Tennent and to the American actress Margaret Sullavan, who was looking for a vehicle for a return to the New York stage. Margaret Sullavan was keen to play it; but it seemed to Terry that a New York opening ought to be accompanied by some good reports of a London production, and he asked her to wait and see how it went in London.

He was still uncertain of its worth. It was not at all the play he had had in mind to write about Ken Morgan. Even after he had agreed to throw out the male friendship, he had made innumerable changes, sometimes to satisfy himself, sometimes after discussion with Beaumont, who was anxious to present it. When he took a copy to Peggy Ashcroft, whom he wanted as his heroine, she told him that she was not keen to do it. (She had been hoping for a comedy.)

Terry and Binkie Beaumont were both determined that she should play the lead part of Hester Collyer. She found the character uninteresting; but she agreed to take the part. Only after rehearsals had begun did she perceive that the characteristics she had taken against in Hester Collyer were positive qualities: approve them or not, they were attributes capable of arousing attention. There were no reservations in her final interpretation of the part.

The Deep Blue Sea must be unique as the only play centring on a conflict of two men over a woman in which love, as a sentimental emotion, is hardly considered. At the three corners of the traditional triangle are Hester Collyer, the wife of a High Court judge; Freddie Page, a wartime pilot in the RAF; and the judge himself, Sir William Collyer. Sir William, a decent public man, has a wife in the way that he has a house and a collection of pictures and a motor car. They are what is called 'happily married'; they go to theatres together, they dine together, they play golf together. Whether they sleep together is a factor not discussed, but they have no children, though Hester is still in her thirties and they have been married for seven years. No passion there: only affection.

Hester has lived this life without a hint of complaint, when, like a thunderclap, she is overcome by desire for Freddie, whom she had met several times at Sunningdale but never paid much attention to. They sat and talked while they waited for Sir William to finish his game. Then this happened, as Hester tells her husband:

HESTER: For some reason he talked very honestly and touchingly about himself – how worried he was about his future, how his life seemed to have no direction or purpose, how he envied you – the brilliant lawyer —

COLLYER: That was good of him.

HESTER: He meant it sincerely. Then quite suddenly he put his hand on my arm and murmured something very conventional, about envying you for other reasons besides your career. I laughed at him and he laughed back, like a guilty small boy. He said, 'I really do, you know, it's not just a line. I really think you're the most attractive girl I've ever met.' Something like that. I didn't really listen to the words, because anyway I knew then in that tiny moment when we were laughing together so close that I had no hope. No hope at all.

Hester left her husband and went with Freddie to Canada, where he had hopes of finding a job, though he muffed it. No love there: only passion.

To Freddie, this had begun as an ordinary pick up, but now it had run out of control. Terry has put in a scene where Freddie describes his predicament to a fellow spirit, Jackie.

JACKIE: There must have been some rows.

FREDDIE: Very minor ones. Nothing like the real flamers we had when we first started.

JACKIE: What were they about?

FREDDIE: Usual things. Damn it, Jackie, you know me. I can't be a ruddy Romeo all the time.

JACKIE: Who can?

FREDDIE: According to her, the whole damn human race – male part of it, anyway.

JACKIE: What does she know about it?

FREDDIE: Damn all. A clergyman's daughter, living in Oxford, marries the first man who asks her and falls in love with the first man who gives her the eye. Hell, it's not that I'm not in love with her too, of course I am. Always have been and always will. But – well – moderation in all things – that's always been my motto.

No love there, whatever Freddie says: only recreation.

The action of the play conforms to the classic unities. It passes in a single day in a single scene, the sitting room of a dingy furnished flat in Ladbroke Grove. The play indeed opens with the body discovered in front of the gas fire. It is Hester, and all that has saved her from death is the lack of a shilling for the gas meter.

There is, in fact, comparatively little action. The situation is complete when the curtain rises. It only needs explanation, and the explanation is conducted with the subtlety of a good whodunit.

There are two problems to be solved. The first is, why did Hester try to kill herself? The second is, given the same circumstances, would she do it again?

The background is filled in item by item. Hester is living with Freddie Page, but is not his wife. Her landlady is the only one in the house who knows whose wife she is; and, faced with what looks like a potential emergency, she tells a young couple who have been tending her. The triangle is complete: the wife, the husband and the other man. And the suicide? The devoted Hester has laid on a dinner to celebrate her birthday, and the indifferent Freddie has forgotten about it and failed to show up. We'll have it tonight, Freddie proposes when he realizes what has happened. No more sulks. I've said I'm sorry. I can't say more, can I? No, says a resigned Hester, you can't say more. As the curtain falls, Freddie is reading Hester's suicide note, which she left in her dressing-gown pocket. There is the first he has heard about suicide.

The second act begins with the talk with Jackie quoted above. Jackie is no more than a confidant on Restoration-drama pattern, introduced only to hear information on the audience's behalf. At the end of their conversation, he goes, and Freddie, warned that Collyer is coming to see his wife, prepares to follow him. Here there is a line of the most telling brutality, a line of potency to match Sir Robert's 'The boy is clearly innocent' in *The Winslow Boy*. He meets Miller at the door. 'Can you lend me a shilling?' he asks him. He throws the coin down on the table. 'Just in case I'm late for dinner,' he tells Hester.

He is not late for dinner; indeed he returns before Collyer has left, but rather than talk to him, he disappears into the bedroom. When he comes out, he has changed into his best suit. He is off to meet a South American who has offered him a job as a test pilot – in South America. He has a rare burst of honesty:

FREDDIE: You've always said, haven't you, that I don't really love you? Well, I suppose, in your sense I don't. But what I do feel for you is a good deal stronger than I've ever felt for anybody else in my life, or ever will feel, I should think. That's why I went away with you in the first place, that's why I've stayed with you all this time, and that's why I must go away from you now. . . . It's asking too damn much to go on as if nothing had happened when he knows now for a fact that he's driving the only girl he's ever loved to suicide.

HESTER: Do you think your leaving me will drive me away from suicide?

FREDDIE: That's a risk I shall just have to take, isn't it. It's a risk both of us will have to face.

It is what the audience has to face throughout the third act. Despite the impassioned plea with which Hester follows the departing Freddie – 'Don't leave me alone tonight. . . . Not tonight . . .' – he has not come back for the postponed birthday dinner, nor has Hester prepared it. She sits, at eleven o'clock, in front of the telephone, and a procession of well-wishers comes to see if she is all right. Miller gives her some sleeping pills. Her husband invites her to go back to him. Young Philip Welch, the one who discovered the escape of gas that morning, comes to collect Freddie's suitcase for him. When he has gone, having accidentally revealed where Freddie wants it taken, Hester picks up Freddie's emergency shilling, stuffs the rug against the door, and takes out Miller's dope; but before she can take her preparations any further, Miller calls her through the door and insists on seeing her. 'If you put a rug down in front of a door,' he tells her, 'it's wiser to do it when the lights are out.'

When he is gone, an angel of salvation, Freddie himself arrives. He does what he can to wish her a civilized farewell, but by now Hester's emotions are played out. She responds to his kind intentions with a cool 'Good night'. When he has gone, she packs some of his clothes into a case, allowing herself a moment's hint of affection. Then she turns down the lights and goes to the gas fire. And lights it.

This final act caused Terry a lot of difficulty. He is said to have rewritten it seven times. The tension that has built up by the end of Act 2 must be sustained until the very last line of Act 3, for plotwise, without going into the philosophy, the whole point of this act is to keep the audience on the edge of their seats, wondering if Hester will gas herself or not, and the longer the tension can be maintained the better. No doubt about it, some of the incidents of the act can only be justified in that way, though Terry was too good a writer to bring a character on the stage without something to say. Ann Welch's quest for her husband Philip puts Hester on Freddie's track. Mrs Elton, who just thought she'd 'pop up and see how you were', revealed all the secrets of Miller, a former German refugee who had been a specialist in infantile paralysis until he was struck off the Register for some unrevealed offence. Collyer offers the opportunity of a reconciliation and is turned down. Only Philip exceeds his real function with his puerile advice about going away to somewhere like Italy or the South of France and trying to forget. But they all of them, even Miller in his second, more practical visit, when he prevents Hester from going back to the gas fire, are only machinery, very efficient machinery, to delay the conclusion.

What conclusion? The play ends in a characteristic Rattigan vagueness. The fact that Hester does not kill herself, but lights the symbolic flame of life, is not an issue that previous events have led up to. If the lights were to go down on Hester sitting expressionlessly in front of the gas fire, having made no gesture one way or another, the final act would not have ended very differently from the way in which it acts now. There is always another night, another shilling. We cannot be expected to take seriously the suggestion that Hester will embark on a new life painting pictures of Weymouth Pier.

However, there is nothing to be gained in trying to follow the course of a play once the curtain has come down on it. How did Fortinbras get on as King of Denmark? Was Malvolio ever revenged on the whole pack of them? *The Deep Blue Sea* ends when Hester lights the fire. The problem that remains is, how much is it still concerned with the death of Ken Morgan?

Deeply so, as I see it. We have here the classic Rattigan situation of the victory of the weak over the strong. But Terry has played his other classic card; he has taken an established circumstance and turned it on its head. Literally to correlate the dramatic characters with their archetypes, we should have to cast Terry as Hester, a woman of standing and affluence, interpreting a mild come-on as the cue for an insane elopement, and Kenneth Morgan as Freddie, happy with what he gets, but by no means anxious to prolong his fortune too long. In the perennial conflict, Hester represents the strong, Freddie the weak.

But in practice, it is not so. Freddie, for all his drinking and his idleness, is the stronger of the two. It must have been he, for example, who organized the flight to Canada – where, if he had not had too much whisky before a demonstration flight, he might still have been holding down a decent job as a test pilot, while Hester kept house for him. It was Freddie, moreover, who had the guts to break up the association when he knew that it was reaching its ultimate collapse.

Hester, on the other hand, no matter how imperious she is with lower-class characters like Mrs Elton the housekeeper, is consistently weak. It was weak of her to give in so immediately and so completely to Freddie's clubhouse flirtation; and during the whole of their association, it has been she who asks the favours and he who grants them. And she is the one who finally collapses when the strain is too much for her.

We cannot then, to my mind, imagine Hester and Freddie as filling the exact roles of the people whose misfortunes gave rise to their invention. Because Terry had to work so hard on the play, what was to be another page from his life became a true work of imagination. Hester is no one from Terry's life; she is a dramatic invention, a character better equipped with human qualities than anyone else in his work, because she is built up from scratch. Freddie too, though he is furnished with Terry's recollections of life in the RAF and with the attributes he saw in the airmen who were to inhabit *The Sound Barrier*, is also someone embellished with original invention until he is utterly independent of his mould.

Sir William Collyer is a ready-made successful professional out of stock. There was no reason why Terry's heart should have been involved in his invention, and the one characteristic that stands out more than any in his personality is his lack of emotional charge. After Hester and Freddie, the character in the play given the most interesting attributes is the doctor Miller.

His function in the play is comparatively small. He looks after Hester in Act 1 after her first suicide attempt. In Act 3, it is he who, noticing that what should have been a crack of light under Hester's door has been obliterated by a rug, dissuades her from making another attempt on her life, and gives her advice on how to face the future.

Now Terry was not given to decorating his minor characters with interesting characteristics. Indeed he believes that it is a mistake to do so, since it attracts attention away from characters who need it more than they. Yet Miller is given a complete and interesting personality. He speaks English with a slight German accent ('I've spoken no other language since 1938, except for a year in the Isle of Man'), so we know he was a refugee from the Nazis. He displays the knowledge and ability of a doctor, but insists that he should not be addressed as 'Doctor'. We learn why later; he has been struck off the Register. We are not told the reason. One critic assumed that he had been doing abortions. But in fact, Rattigan gives some good hints. 'To love with one's eyes open sometimes makes life very difficult,' he says when Hester has involved him in a talk about her relations with Freddie. More specifically, in a speech that was not used in the final version, Mrs Elton says, 'Some people are born different to others and it's no good pretending that that makes them wicked and striking them off registers just because of it.' It is clear that Rattigan meant him to be a homosexual. Mrs Elton, the landlady, says she remembers having read about the case in the papers, but she doesn't tell anyone.

Certainly Terry intends people to like him, for it is he who finally persuades Hester to come to terms with herself. What is more, although his daily work is no more exciting than a bookie's runner, he spends his evenings doing voluntary work at a hospital. Yet in spite of all these admirable qualities no one likes him. Mrs Welch labels him a phony almost at once. Her husband thinks he is a callous swine. Hester says he looks too much like a blackmailer to be one, though after his last ministrations she seems on the verge of beginning a friendly relationship with him, and even he with her.

Why did Terry take so much trouble over this one supporting character, when he left Mrs Elton and the Welches as recessive as his supporting characters usually are? It seems probable that he was left over from a former version of the play, in which his having been struck off the Register for having been 'born different' would have been relevant. But – still in the realm of deduction – Miller might have been a posthumous tribute to Keith Newman. Miller's first name was Kurt; Newman's, before he changed them, were Karl Odo. The Ken Morgan version of the play can no longer be found (its last recorded appearance was in 1962, when Rattigan showed it to Alvin Rakoff, the producer of his television play *Heart to Heart*). With such a theme, the presence of a doctor with special sympathies would be appropriate. In what might be called the penultimate version of December 1951, he is still sufficiently committed to be given the speech about being born different. By the final version he has become only the friendly neighbour with a dubious past, for there is no real value in him from the psychological angle. His recommendation that Hester should devote herself to painting is really not much cleverer than Philip Welch's recommendation that she should retire to Italy or the South of France.

The play opened at the Duchess, a comparatively small theatre, in March 1952, after a week in Brighton. Playing opposite Peggy Ashcroft was a young, not yet well-known actor, Kenneth More, who had been working at the Windmill before the war, and had served with the Royal Navy from 1939 to 1945. He returned to the theatre as soon as he was demobilized and found no difficulty in securing parts, though not parts that brought him much attention. The actor whom Terry and Beaumont had in mind for Freddie was Jimmy Hanley; but Roland Culver, who sometimes played golf with Kenneth More (and was already cast as Sir William Collyer), had a feeling that he would fit the part of Freddie peculiarly well, and mentioned him to Terry who passed the word to Beaumont.

Terry, Beaumont, Culver, Peggy Ashcroft and the director, Frith Banbury, attended the audition. They were not convinced that Kenneth More was the Freddie they were looking for. He was not reading in the carefree manner they wanted. As he said afterwards, 'They just told me I was a sexy young man with a respectable woman in love with me.' Frith Banbury was still in favour of Jimmy Hanley, and so was Binkie Beaumont. Terry, on the other hand, saw some quality there that he had put into the part, and he wanted to hear him read in more relaxed circumstances. A couple of weeks later he invited him to have another shot, this time in his chambers in Albany. Terry gave him a couple of stiff drinks before he began. This time there was no doubt about the choice.

There had been one week out of town, at Brighton, before the West End opening. Up to the last moment there were still doubts about the last act, and Terry had been kept busy rewriting and rewriting. There were doubts too in the minds of the critics who tended to qualify what were generally excellent notices with their misgivings about Hester.

What had led this respectable, unadventurous woman into such an extraordinary course? T. C. Worsley put her down as a victim of an obsession, as inexplicable as such obsessions often are. This is not an explanation of her behaviour, however; obsessions may be resisted. Peter Fleming in the *Spectator* labelled her as irresponsible and inconsiderate, both of which things she certainly was, the problem being why. Ivor Brown, in the *Observer*, having tried out various possible causes, took a view much like Fleming's – 'Perhaps she just

111

needs a good slap or a straight talk with a Marriage Guidance Expert.'
At a higher level, Hester was compared with Phèdre and Berenice and
Cho Cho San in *Madame Butterfly*.

Critical examination of her behaviour is to some extent beside the
point, however. She is more completely Terry's own invention than any
other character in his work up to that time. Obsessed, irresponsible,
inconsiderate, in need of rebuke or assistance, she is a complete
person. If her behaviour seems unusual, improbable if you like, that is
because Terry had chosen to write about such a woman. Even Peggy
Ashcroft, who had taken against her at first, was prepared to defend her
when she had got into the part, with the author at her elbow whenever
she had a problem to solve.

Critics who were puzzled about Hester were especially puzzled
about the way she chose to behave at the end of the play. Logically,
some said, she should have committed suicide, thus satisfying their tidy
minds but falsifying the long dramatic tension of the last act. There
were others who perceived the beauty and the rightness of the vague
ending. In an interview, Terry defended his choice (which had not
been everyone's). 'The play has the most tragic of all endings. The
pistol shot offstage is the sentimental ending. Nothing is easier than
suicide in a case of that kind.' Almost everyone agreed that the play was
exceptionally good – 'the best English play in the naturalistic manner in
a long time,' said Harold Hobson. Opposition came only from the
Daily Worker, on sociological rather than artistic ground; since Hester's
trouble was purely personal and not part of a social malaise, she was
impossible to identify with, they said. The play ran at the Duchess for
513 performances. Peggy Ashcroft passed on the part of Hester first to
Celia Johnson, then to Googie Withers, with whom it went on tour
when the London run was over.

Margaret Sullavan had her chance with the play when it opened at
the Morosco Theatre on 6 November, after it had been playing in
London just over six months; and who should be playing Freddie
opposite her but James Hanley. Frith Banbury again directed.

The New York press was less impressed than the London critics had
been. The feeling among the more influential writers was that the
feeling in the play was not sufficiently put to use. John Mason Brown in
the *Saturday Review* complained that Rattigan had only hinted at his
theme. Brooks Atkinson compared it unfavourably with a contemporary play, *The Time of the Cuckoo*, which had 'more spontaneity,
discrimination and spirit'. *Variety*, displaying an inadequate knowledge
of current English theatre, thought it suggestive of Pinero in 'its careful
knowing construction as a "well-made play"'. Walter Kerr and
Richard Watts were both dissatisfied with Margaret Sullavan's playing;

Watts labelled the play a soap opera. Never were the causes of the 'sea change' so clearly demonstrated.

The New York run lasted for 132 performances, Terry's longest there so far, apart from *O Mistress Mine*, the American production of *Love in Idleness*.

Eleven

The Sleeping Prince

Put not your trust in princes, nor in any child of the theatre. Here is Terence Rattigan in his contribution to *Olivier*, a *Festschrift* put together by Logan Gourlay in 1973: 'On 1 January 1953 I woke up with the customary blinding hangover and, later in the day, to the equally blinding thought that this was coronation year and I ought to do something about it. . . . On that grim New Year's morning I didn't even have a play to write. Not a glimmer. Not a notion.'

This time, something did come of nothing – a coronation play with a coronation theme. It was designed to be, in the author's words, 'a little nonsense for a great occasion. A non-star cast, a light production and a limited run.' The word must have got around in a distorted version. There was a telephone call from Laurence Olivier. 'I hear you're writing a play for the coronation that might suit Vivien and me.'

Terry assured him that he was doing no such thing. Yes, he was writing a play for the coronation, but it would not suit the Oliviers. Very well, they might have a glance at it when it was finished.

Other voices, other rooms. In the autobiography *Confessions of an Actor* (Weidenfeld and Nicolson, 1982), Lord Olivier records: 'A few nights later we met Terry Rattigan at a party. I remember taking him to one side and asking him if by any chance, he might have something in the oven for Puss and me and for this very special year. . . . He then said that, as a matter of fact, yes he did have something that might suit us very well indeed.'

It was somehow taken for granted that Terence Rattigan should write a play to mark the coronation. No one had commissioned him to do it; there was just this 'blinding thought' that this was coronation year and he ought to do something about it. He was not in the position of the Poet Laureate (who, as it happened, didn't write a word); but there was a spontaneous efflorescence of the arts. Walton composed a Coronation March (and one hopes it wasn't too discordant for Aunt Edna). Britten composed an opera for Covent Garden, about a previous Queen Elizabeth, and was rewarded with some pretty cool notices. Clearly the theatre would have to pay its tribute, and who should it call on? Ray Cooney? J. B. Priestley? William Douglas Home? Terry, in effect, commissioned himself.

His father had been involved in a coronation in his day, as Gold Staff Officer at the coronation of King George V. His mother had not been so closely involved, as she was busy giving birth to her son Terence, so here was a chance to let her see the kind of thing she had missed. Frank Rattigan's duties at the coronation had been to escort the former Grand Vizier of Morocco; so what more suitable than to devise some fun with the retinue of a similar visitor? The play was to be, in Terry's own chosen phrase, 'an occasional fairy tale', and in place of the Grand Vizier, he invented the King of Carpathia, a kingdom already celebrated in the romantic works of Anthony Hope. As the King was only sixteen years old, he also included the Prince Regent, the Grand Duke Charles.

The story has about it elements of two fairy stories, *The Sleeping Beauty* and *Cinderella*, the familiar tales being turned routinely upside-down. In the essay that Terry wrote for *Olivier* (one of the most complete analyses he left of any of his works) he apologizes for having decided on so lightweight a play for so auspicious an occasion. 'I knew I'd get hell from the critics if they thought I'd seriously meant this airy trifle to be the next step, after *The Deep Blue Sea*, in my development as a dramatist.' He was sensitive to the critics' opinions, more so than he should have been, and unfortunately there is some truth in this observation. It might well have been the case that some critics would condemn *The Sleeping Prince* simply for being a less portentous piece than *The Deep Blue Sea* or *The Browning Version*. It is not always realized, in this pinnacle conscious age, that as much skill may go into a small work as into a tremendous one. Beethoven did not hesitate to start work on his little Eighth Symphony because he had given his audiences the Fifth, Sixth and Seventh.

The Oliviers' entry into the project put it on a different footing. This would not only be Rattigan's contribution to the coronation festivities;

it would be that of Laurence Olivier and Vivien Leigh, the first lady and gentleman of the British theatre. At the very least, we should expect something on the level of *Love in Idleness*, with parts to exhibit the talents of the stars.

The parts Rattigan had in mind, however, were not designed to exhibit the talents of those particular stars. He was reluctant to have Olivier as the Grand Duke, whom he conceived as an unattractive man. 'How could Larry persuade an audience that he was "Prince Uncharming" when he had made even Richard III into one of the most sexually attractive characters ever to disgrace a stage?' He was still more reluctant to have Vivien Leigh, 'one of nature's grand duchesses if ever I saw one', as the Brooklyn-bred chorus girl who was to be his Cinderella. There must have been a momentary sense of relief when, just as rehearsals were about to begin, she became ill. Would it be possible —? But no, of course it wouldn't. The opening was put off until the autumn, and the Phoenix Theatre took in *Exit Charlie*, a backstage piece by a *Punch* writer, Alex Atkinson.

The Sleeping Prince, a bit late for the coronation, opened there on 5 November, to notices of restrained approval.

As with *Love in Idleness*, people thought the play's success due to the talents of the players, not the script. Considering Rattigan's reluctance to have those players in his play, such criticism must have hurt. 'The Oliviers have spoilt your play,' Noël Coward is said to have observed, 'just as the Lunts did mine.' Certainly there is no doubt that the Oliviers took over the play. 'Where I had expected my flimsy little confection to be burst asunder by the vastness of his talent,' Terry commented, 'it was in fact held firmly in shape by his quietly magisterial performance which, while remaining resolutely faithful to his author's frivolous intentions, succeeded in adding to the part those dimensions that one looks for from great acting.' 'Miss Leigh,' wrote the critic Cecil Wilson, 'is the most disarming little demon who ever upset a royal applecart.' He went on, with an apparent disregard of Miss Leigh's mental collapse, ended only six months before, 'It is the teasing sing-song accent of Blanche du Bois suddenly aware that all that neurotic nonsense was only a nightmare.' Whether it was he or Vivien Leigh who could not tell a New Orleans accent from Brooklyn is a small point in the circumstances.

The *Daily Express*, the *Sunday Express*, the *Observer*, the *Evening Standard* all made the point about the actors supporting the play. No doubt they felt confirmed in their views when the play opened in New York some years later with a new pair of leads – Michael Redgrave and Barbara Bel Geddes – and only managed a run of sixty performances.

A later British production at the Chichester Festival in 1983, that was taken to the Haymarket for a limited run, received somewhat condescending notices; but no one suggested that Omar Sharif and the virtually unknown Debby Arnold had carried the play on their shoulders.

The play's Cinderella is Mary Morgan, dancing under the name of Elaine Dagenham in *The Coconut Girl* (no doubt at the Gaiety) in 1911. The Sleeping Beauty has changed sex and discarded a principal characteristic to become the Grand Duke Charles, Regent of Carpathia. In a sense, the Prince Regent is also playing a London season, for this was the year of George V's coronation, and visiting eminences were given a lot to keep up with.

The Regent is a man to whom love is a medical rather than a social need. When he has to stay away from home, he arranges to have a chorus girl or similar creature brought to him to assuage his appetites. When they are assuaged, she is sent away with a present.

Mary Morgan – Morgan again! – doesn't take to this kind of casual treatment. The routines of love, especially love with a Balkan prince, require the decorations of romance, which she knows only from their representation on the stage. So Mary calls for 'turgid, intoxicating love talk'. There must be musicians playing Tzigane music outside the door. The Regent provides these things to the best of his ability; and if there have been any shortcomings in his treatment of his guest, she must remember what Shakespeare said, or what the Regent believes that Shakespeare said, 'It is hard to sleep well with a crown on your head.' The Regent also provides more vodka than Mary is accustomed to. She warns him that there is a danger of her falling genuinely in love with him. Instead, she passes out, and is respectably put to bed by a major domo.

In the morning, she is determined to carry on from the point where she left off the previous night. But there is more than romance in Carpathia. There is a revolution on the point of breaking out.

The King, whom the Regent tries to keep in his place with toys from Harrod's, is sympathetic to the revolutionaries. He speaks with some of the dissidents over the telephone. In Carpathia, they speak German. Mary, an unexpected eavesdropper, overhears his conversations and, by a convenient dramatic chance, she is able to understand German.

There is a lot of good comedy, and the minor characters are better inventions than Rattigan's minor characters usually are. Not young King Nicky; he is the teenage boy who is the hallmark of every Rattigan script since *French without Tears*, but he is a serious little

117

number with no function but his political activity. He is given a comedy scene with a young princess he is expected to marry, but even in this he is solemn and ill-tempered (and so is she).

But the Grand Duchess is good fun. She takes Mary for a great classical actress and adopts her as a lady-in-waiting, whisking her off to the coronation ceremony decked in the Order of Perseverance, second class. The attaché, Peter Northbrook, performing no doubt the kind of service Frank Rattigan performed in 1911, is comic, and good use is made of the vagaries of protocol, partly perhaps remembered from Frank Rattigan's accounts, partly extracted from the confidential papers distributed at the time, a set of which was provided by Roger Machell, Rattigan's publisher.

Mary's attentions succeed in awakening the Regent from his emotional sleep. Not only has he become fond of her, he has realized the advisability of a general amnesty at home and promised King Nicky a motorbike with unrestricted licence to ride it where he likes. It would have been embarrassing if Mary had followed him back to Carpathia when *The Coconut Girl* came off; but they decide, this being a fairy tale, that they have both enjoyed their brief encounter and will be satisfied with their memories of it.

A thin story, you may say – as thin as goldleaf. But there is more *imagination* in the characters than there is in any of the previous plays, apart from *The Deep Blue Sea* and *The Winslow Boy*. In both halves of *Playbill* he was drawing on his own life; the Greek campaigners of *Adventure Story* are British officers in fancy dress; *Who Is Sylvia?*, whether or not it has a hidden autobiographical content, is a caricature of his own circle.

But the Carpathian Court is full of genuinely imaginary, and imaginative, people. The Regent is a novelty in Rattigan's palette up to that time, a protagonist who is intended to be dull and unattractive. The Grand Duchess has something in common with Dame Maud Gosport in *Harlequinade*, but such a patrician old lady is again something new. Mary, of course, could have been derived from any young American actress of stage or screen. Later she actually became a young American actress – but not 'any' one.

It must have seemed odd to New York audiences when the play surfaced there three years after the coronation, with Michael Redgrave and Barbara Bel Geddes as the Regent and his chorus girl. In any event, it was a bad time to have presented it; as Redgrave pointed out in his book *In My Mind's Eye* (Weidenfeld and Nicolson, 1983),

Flying-Officer Rattigan in 1942, all pacifism dispelled.

Terence Rattigan at Oxford.

With his mother on board the *Queen Mary*.

French Without Tears at the Criterion Theatre.

Alfred Lunt and Lynn Fontanne in *Love in Idleness*, 1944.

Kenneth More and Peggy Ashcroft in *The Deep Blue Sea*, 1952.

At Little Court in Coronation Year, 1953.

With Vivien Leigh at a first night
(New Theatre, *The Summer of the Seventeenth Doll*, 1957).

Margaret Leighton and Jeremy Brett in *Variation on a Theme*, 1958.

At the door of his Bermuda house,
Spanish Grange.

Spanish Grange.

At his Albany chambers in 1974.

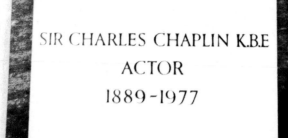

SIR TERENCE RATTIGAN, C.B.E.
Playwright
10 June 1911 – 30 November 1977

SIR NOËL COWARD
1899-1973
Author Composer and Actor

SIR CHARLES CHAPLIN K.B.E
ACTOR
1889-1977

Three great men commemorated at St. Paul's Church, Covent
Garden, "the actors' church"—Terence Rattigan, Noel Coward,
Charles Chaplin.

'the twin cries of Eden's Suez adventure and the Hungarian revolution were in full flood' (Redgrave's phrase). When the King, believing a *coup d'état* to be imminent at home, says, 'I will not have my country made the pawn of British imperialism and French greed,' the line drew what Redgrave called 'an audible *frisson*' from the audience. The *frisson* was repeated when the music behind the door was dismissed by the Regent as 'some Hungarian violinist'. The general opinion was that the play was dull, and it ran at the Coronet Theatre for only sixty performances.

The production was not put on purely to entertain New Yorkers, however. In the autumn of 1955, two years after the play had opened in London, Terry had a quite unexpected telephone call from William Wyler in Hollywood. Marilyn Monroe Productions were interested in filming it. What was more, they were interested in having Olivier to play the Regent and to direct the film. Could Rattigan fly over and have a talk?

The true course of events is not entirely clear. Terry was delighted to fly to Hollywood, especially as it would give him an excuse to see the Ryder Cup played at Palm Springs. He has said that he did not know whether approaches had already been made to Olivier or not, but it is hard to think that he would have gone without telephoning Olivier first.

Olivier's own account suggests that the first enquiries were made to Tennent's and they passed them on to him. It may be that this happened while Terry was in California, for there he found that Wyler was not ready to make a definite offer. Terry had in any case been ambushed by Marilyn Monroe herself, who sent a message as he was changing flights at Idlewild on the outward journey inviting him for cocktails that afternoon. It is hardly probable that she would have been so accessible at that special time if there had not been some previous discussion.

Terry told her he was on the way to talks with Wyler and promised that, if no agreement were reached, he would come back to her. In the event, no agreement was reached with Wyler, so Terry telephoned Monroe on his way home and told her that she could have the rights in the play.

Terry and Olivier then flew to New York for a meeting with Monroe and her business manager, Milton Greene, a stills photographer. Olivier claims to have fallen 'most shatteringly' in love with her at first sight (in spite of having been kept waiting for an hour while she decided what was the most suitable thing to wear). Terry gave her a more objective rating: 'She was like a shy exhibitionist,' he reported, 'a Garbo who likes to be photographed.' They drank a lot of champagne and got on terribly well together, and only as the party was about to

119

break up did Monroe shyly remind them that there had been no word about an agreement.

That was completed the next morning, at figures a good deal higher than had been mentioned by Wyler.

The film was made in England, at Pinewood Studios. The Monroe outfit rented Lord Drogheda's house in Englefield Green, convenient for the studios and only a short way from Terry's house Little Court in Sunningdale, where he gave an enormous party in her honour. After a couple of weeks settling in, work began.

The screenplay Terry had prepared was soon subjected to endless alteration. He had thought it rather a good script, and he was confirmed in his opinion by no less than Arthur Miller, who had lately married Monroe. It did not suit Milton Greene, though; nor Olivier. Monroe herself seems to have been less hard to please. Mary Morgan is given to exclaiming 'Gosh!' It is indeed her first word in the play.

'Would it be all right if I said "Golly!"?' Marilyn asked.

Rattigan demurred. He wanted her to say 'Gosh!'

'OK,' Monroe agreed. 'I'll think "Golly!" and I'll say "Gosh!"'

The filming of *The Prince and the Showgirl*, as the play was now rechristened in order to get the showgirl into the title, was not a happy affair. Marilyn Monroe had brought among her party Paula Strasberg, the wife of Lee Strasberg, who had been coaching Marilyn at his Actors' Studio according to his own Method. Paula Strasberg had achieved total dominance over her charge by subjecting her to endless flattery, and now every scene had to be gone over between the two of them. As Olivier reports in his autobiography, *Confessions of an Actor*, Marilyn Monroe became steadily less attentive to what he had to tell her. 'Whenever I patiently laboured to make her understand an indication for some reading, business or timing she would listen with ill-disguised impatience, and when I had finished she would turn to Paula and petulantly demand, "Wasseee mean?"'

Partly this was Olivier's own fault. Joshua Logan, who had directed her in *Bus Stop*, warned him that Monroe liked to have Paula Strasberg on the set with her, but added that, cooperative as Paula Strasberg had been, on the set was where she never should be allowed. Some time later, Logan visited Olivier on his set, where he was received with a furious enquiry: 'How dare you tell me to have Paula Strasberg on my set! She's a bloody nuisance.' Logan replied that what he had told him was that Paula Strasberg *never* appeared on the set. Suddenly, Olivier realized that he had misunderstood all that well-meant advice. All that suffering had been the result of a simple slip.

It was too late to do anything about correcting the misunderstanding, even if it could ever have been corrected. 'It was useless to get annoyed with her,' Douglas Wilmer said. 'One morning, Olivier finally stormed at her, "Why can't you get here on time for fuck's sake?" And Marilyn just replied, "Oh, do you have that word in England too?"'

Twelve
'Aunt Edna'

Terry never fulfilled the gift for writing novels and short stories that he had believed himself to have in his youth; but he liked to write when the opportunity occurred, and in the period of fairly affluent leisure that he enjoyed in the 1950s it sometimes occurred to him to try some non-theatrical, or marginally theatrical, writing. He was quite enthusiastic about trying a piece for *Punch*, which had just embarked on a new phase of life under Malcolm Muggeridge's editorship, and for which I was then working. We discussed a project he thought would be fun: suppose *King Lear*, a new tragedy by a contemporary playwright, had its first night in the West End, what would the reviews be like? 'I could do a Harold Hobson, comparing it with the French, and a Tynan, tearing it to pieces, and Ivor Brown and so on.' 'When can you let us see them?' 'I'll have a think about them.'

Nothing came of the reviews of *King Lear*, but one evening, when we were drinking late in the new Eaton Square flat, he said: 'I've written a couple of prefaces for my two volumes of collected plays.'

'Can we have those?'
'I'll let you know.'

Malcolm Muggeridge was delighted with the idea. He would often accept work without reading it if it were by somebody well known. I told Terry that we'd like to see them as soon as possible, and he replied sorry, he was afraid he couldn't let us have them now as Hamish Hamilton, his publisher, wouldn't let him. The two volumes of *Collected Plays* came out towards the end of the year, and there the two prefaces were, reading very much as if they had been written for *Punch*.

They are written in a light-hearted vein, and they must have done his reputation with the theatrical intelligentsia no end of harm. They almost give the feeling, in spite of the importance he attaches to technique, that he thought of himself as an amateur. (Some of the Restoration dramatists took the same attitude.)

The first preface opens the volume that contains *French without Tears*, *Flare Path*, *While the Sun Shines*, *Love in Idleness* and *The Winslow Boy*. Hamish Hamilton had published *After the Dance* in 1939, but it was decided not to include it in the collected edition. This was a pity, but its presence in the book would have deprived Terry of his first sentence: 'It will save a good deal of falsely modest circumlocution if I state at once that the five plays in this volume have all had very long runs.'

He then follows the line that 'by taking myself seriously as a dramatic author', he felt at a disadvantage compared with authors who were able to commend their plays on the ground that undiscriminating audiences had rejected them. No such ground enclosed him; he recalls an earnest young repertory manager who said to him, 'What's so nice about doing your plays in my theatre is that their profits pay for the good ones.' And this is where he makes his first pace towards an assessment of audiences, though he veers off at once in favour of critics, leaving his serious notions about audiences for the second preface.

The particular merit the critics had found in him, he observes with gratitude, is a 'sense of theatre'. This was exactly the merit that he observed in himself, had observed indeed ever since he wrote his first play at the age of eleven. 'I *have* a sense of theatre. I am not at all sure what it is, I admit, but I do know that I have it . . . and that, if I should ever lose it, I should also lose any hope I may have of achieving my ambition – and please do not jibe at it, for it is harmless – to write, before I die, one great play.'

Two more points are made in this first preface. The first is his indifference to beauty of speech. 'Writers like T. S. Eliot and Christopher Fry have rescued the theatre from the thraldom of middle-class vernacular in which it has been held, with rare intervals, since Tom Robertson' – this very proper opinion is torpedoed in the next paragraph:

'The thraldom of middle-class vernacular.' Such a phrase, from myself, must seem patently insincere. The merest glance at any of the five plays in this volume will show how very little I resent such

123

servitude. And yet the tribute to the poetic school is from the heart.'

Everyone, Rattigan argues, calling in Chekhov on his side, must write as he pleases to write. I have to say that Terry did not take much trouble even with his middle-class vernacular. The lines seem to come out exactly as they are first thought of, with no subsequent attempt to make them sound conversational, or current, or particularly suitable to a character, unless that character is a domestic servant. Terry was very patient with actors who wanted to make little alterations in his lines to enable them to speak more naturally, and he never stopped them as long as the sense he intended remained unchanged.

The second point is perhaps the most important that he has to make, the value of the implicit by the side of the expressed. 'It is a masterpiece of understatement,' Churchill said about *Flare Path* (secretly regretting, no doubt, that there were no flamboyant passages about loyalty and courage and patriotism); and it has been noticed in all his plays what a master Rattigan is of the unspoken. Here is Peter Kyle saying goodbye to Teddy Graham in *Flare Path*:

> TEDDY: OK, Kyle. Shoot. Give us the five-second burst. (*PETER does not reply.*) What have you got to say to me?
>
> PETER: Nothing.
>
> TEDDY: What do you mean – nothing?
>
> PETER: Nothing. Just goodbye. I'm leaving this morning.
>
> TEDDY: Oh, sorry to hear it. Percy told me it was something important.
>
> PETER: He must have got it wrong. It's quite unimportant.

There is a maelstrom of emotion surging around Peter Kyle's spirit at the moment. Pinero, to name a playwright with whom Terry is sometimes mistakenly compared, would have written a fine speech for Peter, and possibly a fine reply for Teddy. Terry writes 'Nothing. It's quite unimportant,' and proves, if Cordelia had not proved it before, how wrong Lear was to say that nothing would come of nothing.

The preface to Volume Two is about criticism. Not about the writing of the professional critics (in presenting his collected works, Rattigan had no argument to pursue with a body that had helped that collected work to come into being); but about the opinions of the audience. He begins by describing his juvenile addiction to the drama, both as creator and as recipient. This is where the tale of the French exercise comes from – worth repeating for the sake of the last half dozen words: 'French execrable, theatre sense first class.'

In explaining how this theatre sense had developed, Terry makes a significant point, that as he wrote his dialogue he imagined it *in performance*. From his childhood, he had watched plays whenever he could, and what he made up for the theatre he meant to be seen by himself. 'I was most conscious of being a member of my own audience, and of participating myself in the emotions that I, as author, had aroused in them.' This was, in the higher intellectual circle of the theatre at the time, not a universal sentiment. The fashionable catchphrases were 'director's theatre' and 'writer's theatre' and so on. Never 'audience's theatre'.

To illustrate his argument – to the point of critical suicide – he undertook to describe a characteristic member of the audience whom he imagined watching his plays. She needs a full description, for she is immortal:

> Let us invent a character, a nice, respectable, middle-class, middle-aged maiden lady, with time on her hands and the money to help her pass it. She enjoys pictures, books, music and the theatre, and though to none of these arts . . . does she bring much knowledge or discernment, at least, as she is apt to tell her cronies, she 'does know what she likes'. [There follow the fatal words.] Let us call her Aunt Edna.

Aunt Edna's artistic predilections are then reviewed. 'She does not appreciate Kafka – "so obscure, my dear, and why always look on the dark side of things?" – she is upset by Picasso – "those dreadful reds, my dear, and why three noses?" – and she is against Walton – "such appalling discords, my dear, and no melody at all."'

The argument is that whereas a novelist, a painter or a composer can survive without considering the demands of Aunt Edna or her appropriate sibling, a dramatist can't. Once a publisher has invested money in Kafka, once a gallery or a collector has bought a Picasso, once a concert promoter has scheduled a concerto by Walton, those things continue to exist. Perhaps no one buys *The Trial*, possibly no one ever looks at *Guernica*, there may be no audience at *Troilus and Cressida*, but these things, once created, have a kind of immortality that a play does not. A play must be presented before an audience. Until it is, it is no more than an idea looking for somewhere to perch. A play, therefore, must be tailored to a shape that Aunt Edna and her cronies will appreciate and go back to their hotels in South Kensington to tell the

125

others how much they have enjoyed themselves. Once a playwright has displeased the Aunt Edna gang, he is utterly lost.

This is not an argument that can stand up for a moment. Books have to be published, pictures exhibited, music played, always at someone's expense. If Aunt Edna's criteria were valid, and she were, as Terry describes her, averse to modern writing, modern painting and modern music, there would have been no writing since Trollope, no painting since Landseer, no music since Brahms. The fact is that Terry allied himself with Aunt Edna because Aunt Edna enjoyed seeing what he enjoyed writing – what, in fact, he enjoyed, by proxy, seeing.

Terry has indeed virtually described himself in describing her. Not a maiden lady, certainly, but middle-class, nice, respectable, with more time on his hands than he would have found in the Diplomatic and enough money to pass it. No great interest in books; fond of pictures but preferring to have someone to choose his tastes for him; unlikely to be found at the opera except as a social activity. True, he spent time, before his first big success, working as hard as he knew how and earning (or being allowed) less money than his life style demanded; but this was before Aunt Edna came into his life. He didn't write *French without Tears* for Aunt Edna, or those other miscellaneous dramas of the two previous years. He wrote whatever he thought a management might accept, whether it was light comedy or a turgid piece about tangled emotions. What is more, after Aunt Edna had signified her manifold approval of *French without Tears*, he didn't write *After the Dance* for her, or *Follow My Leader*. As he himself has put it, quoting from Chekhov's Trigorin in *The Seagull*, he wrote as he pleased, and as best he might.

By what seemed to him good fortune, this led him into Aunt Edna's territory. Once established there, he made his nest and settled comfortably until the events of the middle 1950s suggested to the managements that even in the West End there might be other bottoms on the seats than Rattigan's aunt's. Those events never shook Terry's belief in his notional aunt, but they made him alter her image fundamentally. The preface to the third volume of the *Collected Plays* was not published until 1964, during the seven-year silence that came between *Man and Boy* in 1963 and *A Bequest to the Nation* in 1970. It takes the form of a court hearing in which Terry is defending himself against a libel charge by Aunt Edna. Aunt Edna's case is based on Terry's use in the Volume Two preface of the phrase 'a hopeless lowbrow'. It is a difficult charge to defend, and it cannot be said that the defendant puts up much of a case for himself, though he makes some cogent points about the theatre of the time, most of which the judge regards as irrelevant.

What it reveals, of course, is no more than that Terry's own opinions had changed.

> It's only Aunt Edna's *emotions* that a playwright can hope to excite, because we know for sure that she does bring those to the theatre. But we can't hope to excite her intellect, because, if she has one at all, which is unlikely, she will almost certainly have left it behind in her rooms, or forgotten it on the bus, or checked it in at the theatre cloakroom. . . . Laughter, tears, excitement. That is all she demands. She is bored by propaganda, enraged at being 'alienated', loathes placards coming down and telling her what is going to happen next, hates a lot of philosophical talk on the stage with nothing happening at all, enjoys poetry only when it is dramatic and fine prose only when there is action to go with it. . . . She is unchanging and unchangeable, immortal and everlasting, and all she ever brings to the theatre is her undying love for it.

This might very well be a description of the original aunt, but in some earlier exchanges in the case Terry has slipped in some evidence that suggests a different person. This new Aunt Edna admits to enjoying Pinter, Beckett, Ionesco, Osborne, Wesker. ('She has a rejuvenation operation in 1955.') But did she really enjoy them? The seminal play in the new wave of the 1950s was John Osborne's *Look Back in Anger*. Terry disliked it so much that he would have left at the first interval if he had not been persuaded to stay by the critic T. C. Worsley. He later had a long conversation about it with George Devine, at whose theatre, the Royal Court, the play was showing. For two and a half hours, Irving Wardle records in *The Theatres of George Devine* (Jonathan Cape, 1978), he tried to persuade him that the play could not possibly be a success. '"Well it is," Devine kept repeating, "and it's going to make the Royal Court possible." "Then I know nothing about plays," Rattigan eventually answered. "You know everything about plays, but you don't know a fucking thing about *Look Back in Anger*."'

This hits the target squarely in the bull. Aunt Edna may indeed have gone to see the plays of the new dramatists; but if all she cared about was the laughter, tears and excitement she extracted from them, she knew little about them. She remained precisely the same middle-class, middle-aged maiden lady; the causes of her dislikes are in themselves significant. If she enjoyed Pinter and Beckett, how could she find Kafka obscure? What was particularly dreadful about Picasso's use of red? Where are the objectionable discords in (say) Walton's first symphony? The fact is (and it may only be a fact that was deliberately planted by her creator) that she is only repeating gossip she has heard from her friends in her South Kensington hotel, not offering original opinions of her own.

They are also, in an exaggerated way, the opinions of Terence Rattigan. Not necessarily his private opinions, but the opinions by which he believed drama ought to be judged – drama in general, that is, not solely his own. If his contemporaries were writing against the principles he advocated, they were wrong. 'Plays of ideas' are anathema. Alienation, and by extrapolation experimental techniques in general, will annoy the audience. Any kind of fine writing must be firmly subordinated to the demands of the plot.

He put these principles into action in his own work. Unless you count *Follow My Leader* he never wrote what he would have thought of as a play of ideas. The causes he espoused were already in the public domain, and had been settled one way or another – the Archer-Shee boy, the campaigns of Alexander the Great, the erotic problems of T. E. Lawrence, the marital infidelity of Lord Nelson, the trial of Mrs Rattenbury and George Stoner. Indeed, once he had outgrown the youthful socialism of his twenties, he didn't cultivate many ideas beyond what was necessary to live a civilized upper-middle-class life.

But what he retained to the end of his life were his strongly held ideas about the theatre. Until his last play, *Cause Célèbre*, he never used any device on the stage that would not have been familiar, *mutatis mutandis*, to Irving or Macready or Garrick. *Cause Célèbre* began life as a radio script, and its stage adaptation, made in consultation with the director, Robin Midgley, gave him a lot of trouble. He was already far into his final illness, and it's easy to see that, having already made three trial scripts before starting work with Midgley, he might easily accept the novelty of a single stage set representing the Central Criminal Court, a villa in Bournemouth and a drawing room in Kensington, according to the lighting.

Terry and his publishers both regretted the invention of Aunt Edna. Roger Machell, his editor, did not believe that it was meant to be taken seriously. Terry certainly meant it seriously, but reckoned that it had been misunderstood, even after he had tried to put matters right with the trial scene in the third preface. She was easy to misunderstand. The principles for which she stood were sufficiently valid to allow plays like *The Winslow Boy* and *The Deep Blue Sea* to be written without their violation.

Where it is easy to differ from Terry is in his belief that they are the only valid principles there are. It was obvious even at the time Aunt Edna was first dropped into the stalls that he was mistaken. *Look Back in Anger* proved a continuing success, even if it's not easy to say, as Terry observed at the time, just what it was we were to look back on so angrily.

It was followed soon after by *The Entertainer*, a play of ideas if ever there was one. Plays of ideas like Christopher Hampton's *Savages* and Trevor Griffiths's *Comedians* and Peter Nichols's *A Day in the Death of Joe Egg* have indeed found it as easy to please the middle-aged middle-class as the young and rebellious. Peter Brook's production of *A Midsummer Night's Dream* in a hollow white box drew crowds to the Royal Shakespeare Company for season after season, and not only because of the polished script by William Shakespeare.

Terry's mistake was to suggest that his own private canons were universal rules. Even after he had allowed, reluctantly, that they might be extended far enough to take in Pinter and Beckett and Wesker, anyone who had not left his intellect in his briefcase, or swopped it for his union card, or ruled it out of order, could see that they might be broken right and left, provided that mysterious power, craftsmanship, that magical gift, a sense of the theatre, was available. Those are the qualities that endeared Terry to his aunt, and sometimes at the same time reconciled him with the critics. His dealings with his aunt may be dismissed as light-hearted small talk, the curtain speeches that he never made. Perhaps it would have been better if they had been published in *Punch* after all.

Thirteen
Separate Tables

The first two volumes of Terry's collected plays were published in Novmeber 1953. The plays might speak for themselves; apart from *Adventure Story*, they had all been successful, and already it had become acceptable to say what a good play *Adventure Story* was. (When it was played on television, with Gary Bond as Alexander, it was generally admired.) But the prefaces called for fresh judgments. In the *Daily Express*, John Barber, who had been at Oxford with Rattigan, expressed his disapproval: 'To be so avid for more success and more success that it gets harder every morning to sit down in humble obedience to your own finest instincts' was his condemnation for Terry's thraldom to his Aunt Edna.

A more valid point was made by Kenneth Tynan, who referred to Terry as 'the bathtub baritone of the drama'. It was wrong, he maintained, to hold that the Aunt Ednas led popular taste in the theatre. They only followed it. They went to *Hamlet* because generations of playgoers had established it as something to go to. (In a few years' time that opinion would be confirmed, when a new wave of playwrights began to be heard, and Aunt Edna patronized them only with reluctance.) Only a few days after the publication of the prefaces, *The Sleeping Prince* made its belated appearance. '*The Sleeping Prince* demonstrates, once and for all, that he means what he says,' said Tynan.

Terry's next play, *Separate Tables*, opened in September 1954. It is acceptable to speak of *Separate Tables* as a single play, for, although in fact it consists of two one-act pieces, they are set in the same frame, a hotel in Bournemouth, and, although each play is given to a different pair of principals, these pairs are involved with the same community, the residents and staff of the hotel – the hotel, virtually, in which Vera Rattigan was then living, though her son took the precaution of transferring it from Kensington to the coast. The setting and the characters are handcrafted for the delight of Aunt Edna, who, middle-aged, middle-class and comfortably off as she is, almost certainly stays in a hotel of this kind. Terry has, in fact, confessed that his fictional hotel was based on his mother's abode, but none of the residents was modelled on his mother.

Stephen Mitchell, who had shown his faith in one-act plays when he presented *Playbill*, renewed his faith with *Separate Tables*. The same players were to take the leading parts in the two plays, though the characters were not at all alike. The men, a left-wing politician and a *soi-disant* retired major, were to be played by Eric Portman, who had demonstrated his value in *Playbill*. The women were initially intended to be taken by Kay Walsh, but there was a change of heart, and the parts were taken over by Margaret Leighton, so beginning a relationship with Rattigan that proved very durable.

These are the unchanging residents in the two plays.

Mrs Railton-Bell, dressed with more distinction than the ladies around her, has an air of being superior to them and in some way 'in charge'. We see her daughter only in the second play. Two other middle-aged women are the spinster Miss Meacham, who reads racing papers and allows a racy element in her attire, and Lady Matheson, who dresses with the neatness proper to a senior Civil Servant's widow but has to live on the modest pension proper to a senior Civil Servant. Mr Fowler is a retired schoolmaster permanently under the delusion that his former pupils want to come and pay him a visit. The younger generation is represented only by an engaged couple, Charles Stratton and Jean Tanner, he a medical student, she an art student.

The staff, or such of them as we see, are Mrs Cooper the manageress and two waitresses, Mabel the old one and Doreen the young one.

The first play is called 'Table by the Window'. This is the table that is to be occupied by John Malcolm, a one-time junior Minister in a Labour Government who went to prison after assaulting his wife, has had to resign and is now living by contributing pseudonymous articles to a left-wing magazine. Here he is flushed by his wife, now Anne Shankland, who, after divorcing him, married again and divorced again. She has come, she says, for a rest cure, and she kids her ex-husband that she did not know he was there. 'John Malcolm', under which he was registered, were only his Christian names, so how could she have known?

But as we soon find out, she is still in love with him and has come to get him back. This will not be simple, as he is carrying on a modest affair with Miss Cooper, the manageress; but her secret in their marriage was that she was capable of 'enslaving' him. In an important speech, John describes what it was like to be on the receiving end.

> None of your tame baronets and Australian millionaires, too well-mannered to protest when you denied them their conjugal rights, and too well-brought-up not to take your headaches at bedtime as just headaches at bedtime. 'Poor old girl! Bad show! So sorry. Better in the morning, I hope. Feeling a bit tired myself, anyway.' No, Anne, dear. What enjoyment would there have been for you in using your weapons on that sort of a husband? But to turn them on a genuine, live, roaring savage from the slums of Hull, to make him grovel at the vague and distant promise of delights that were his anyway by right, or goad him to such a frenzy of drink and rage by a locked door that he'd kick it in and hit you with his fist so hard that you'd knock yourself unconscious against a wall – that must really have been fun.

Her first attempt to win him over is lost when he, foreseeing the possibility of giving in to that kind of life again, restrains himself from repeating the former asault and walks out into the night. But he is back in the morning, and this time, though there is enough reconciliation in their talk to suggest that they really have got a chance of settling down peaceably with one another, John gives in.

To Aunt Edna, this must seem a happy ending, but a moment's thought reveals that it is as indeterminate as the end of *The Deep Blue Sea*. If Anne Shankland was capable of provoking a junior minister to try and kill her when he was still young and capable of wielding power if he wanted to, there was no ghost of a chance that she would settle down to be a dutiful wife with no headaches at bedtime.

Rattigan was on close terms at the time he was writing *Separate Tables* with a successful model, Jean Dawnay, who would sometimes act as his hostess when he was entertaining. Jean Dawnay told him once about an affray she had had with a boyfriend that caused enough disturbance to bring the police in. The nuts and bolts of *Table by the Window* may have been based on this story; indeed Jean Dawnay besought Rattigan to change some of the details in the play when he gave it her to read, lest anyone should imagine themselves depicted in it. But Anne Shankland, though she may be a model and the victim of an assault by her lover, is not Jean Dawnay, but someone nearer home.

After the 1977 revival of the plays, Rattigan, who was in Bermuda, wrote me a letter which, with respect, I cannot quote from extensively. I think I can allow myself a brief extract, though: quoting Michael Franklin, he wrote '*Our* audience (lumped together in his mind as Binkie, Noël, you – indeed all my friends) *longed* for your ending up with "Miss Cooper" and they all *hated* your ending up with me again.' The fact is that *Table by the Window* is as much based on personal experience as *The Browning Version,* though I must say at once that it is situations that are involved, not personalities. ('Not a *portrait* of course,' the letter says specifically, 'nothing is ever a portrait.') Whether or not the play has a happy or an unhappy ending is irrelevant. 'Binkie, Noël and I' thought it unhappy because we were equating the fictional characters with real people; the abundant representatives of Aunt Edna, including a fair slice of the press, saw it as happy because it was dramatically satisfying. Certainly the breakfast table reconciliation and the request to Doreen the waitress to lay for them both at the same table in future bring a turbulent love story to a graceful end.

Miss Cooper is still in charge in 'Table Number Seven', which takes place eighteen months later than the other piece. The regulars are still in residence, though Charles Stratton and Jean Tanner have got married and have an infant son. John Malcolm and Anne Shankland have moved on, but Major Pollock, mentioned before but not seen (he telephoned to leave a forwarding address and said he would be back on Tuesday), is now present in the flesh, boring everyone with his accounts of service in the Black Watch. We sense something fishy about him almost at once, not so much because he quotes Horace, but because he speaks Latin in the old pronunciation and believes it to be Greek. Worse follows. The local paper reports that he has been bound over by the magistrates for insulting behaviour in the cinema. Moreover, he is not a retired major in the Black Watch, but a retired lieutenant in the RASC, and never got nearer to the 'sharp end' of the war than an Army Supply Depot in the Orkneys. When charged, however, the paper reports, he replied, 'You have the wrong man. I am a colonel in the Scots Guards.'

In spite of the efforts made by the major (as it is convenient to call him for the moment) to conceal the *West Hampshire Weekly News* from the other guests in the hotel, Mrs Railton-Bell reads all about it and makes her mind up at once that 'If there's a liar and fraudulent crook and a – I can't bring myself to say it – wandering around among us unsuspected, there could be – well – there could be the most terrible repercussions'. Lady Matheson replies, with Civil Service detachment, that 'he's been wandering around among us for four years now and there haven't been any repercussions yet', adding wistfully, 'Perhaps we're too old.' (And perhaps he hadn't quoted Horace to Mr Fowler.) But Mrs Railton-Bell has a more driving stimulus. Her daughter Sibyl, the spelling of whose name is unusual but correct, has formed a certain friendship with the major. They go for walks together.

So Mrs Railton-Bell determines that the hotel must get rid of the major before any repercussions are felt. With commendable promptitude, she collects the other guests, excluding her victim, tells them the news, and proposes that as their representative she should go to Miss Cooper and demand that the major be asked to leave.

The kangaroo court is worth analysis. Charles Stratton is opposed to any action, though his wife disagrees with him. Mr Fowler reluctantly agrees. Miss Meacham says she doesn't care a damn. Lady Matheson is talked into agreement by Mrs Railton-Bell. Sibyl, who has been sitting in a condition of suppressed hysteria and saying nothing, is pressed by Stratton to give her own judgment rather than let her mother give it for her. She reacts unexpectedly with an increasingly frenzied outburst, 'It made me sick, it made me sick, it made me sick.' Mrs Railton-Bell goes off on her mission and the party breaks up to watch television.

The major comes in by the French windows and begins to look for the *West Hampshire Weekly News*; and at the other side of the room, Sibyl enters by the door. They look at each other for a moment as if transfixed. Then Sibyl tells him what has been going on.

Sibyl has been sketched for us by Lady Matheson when the question arose of whether she should be asked to join the jury sitting on the major's case. 'She's such a strange girl – so excitable and shy – and so ungrownup in so many ways.' The stage direction calls her 'a timid-looking, wizened creature in the thirties, bespectacled, dowdy and without makeup'. Her mother is berating her about something when she first comes on; and a moment later, when she asks the major, still in the clear as far as he knows, if she may go for a walk with him and he declines, Mrs Railton-Bell chides her for letting people think she is running after him. This is something she is very unlikely to do. 'I hate that side of life,' she says, 'I hate it' – and her mother has to beg her not to get into 'one of her states'.

Now she has been actively brought into contact with 'that side of life', and she is confronted with the man who has been labelled as the miscreant in the case. Instead of getting into one of her states, she listens as the major admits all the offences and all the deceits he knows himself guilty of. Stop, she says, I don't want to hear it, it makes me ill; but in a moment, weakened by the major's first, involuntary use of her

Christian name, she is overcome with sympathy. As the major tells her, 'We're both of us frightened of people, and yet we've somehow managed to forget our fright when we've been in each other's company.'

Miss Cooper retains the managerial expertise she displayed eighteen months before. She assures the major that there is no need for him to go if he doesn't want to, but gives him the address of another hotel if he does. And she turns her attention to Sibyl, once the major has gone to pack, and encourages her to show a little more independence, try and find a job like the one she once had until her nerves got the better of her.

SIBYL: Mummy says no.

MISS COOPER: Mummy says no. Well, then, you must just try and get Mummy to say yes, don't you think?

SIBYL: I don't know how.

MISS COOPER: I'll tell you how. By running off and getting a job on your own. She'll say yes quick enough then.

The next scene is dinner time. Table number seven, where the major sits, is empty, and the other guests are talking among themselves. 'What a really nerve-racking day it's been, hasn't it?' says Mrs Railton-Bell to Lady Matheson. 'I don't suppose any of us will ever forget it. Ever. I feel utterly shattered myself', and as she says it, the major walks in and sits down at his table. Then this happens:

CHARLES: (*to the MAJOR*) Hullo.

MAJOR: Hullo.

CHARLES: Clouding over a bit, isn't it? I'm afraid we may get rain later.

MAJOR: Yes. I'm afraid we may.

MISS MEACHAM: We need it. This hard going's murder on form. (*To MAJOR POLLOCK*) You know Newmarket, don't you.

And then this:

Mr Fowler gets up quietly from his table and walks to the door. To do this he has to pass the major. A step or so past him he hesitates and then looks back, nods and smiles.

135

MR FOWLER: Good evening.

MAJOR: Good evening.

MR FOWLER: Hampshire did pretty well today, did you see?
Three hundred and eighty-odd for five.

Then this:

*Suddenly and by an accident the major's and Lady Matheson's eyes
meet. Automatically she inclines her head and gives him a slight smile. He
returns the salute.*

LADY MATHESON: Good evening. (*And after a whispered rebuke
from MRS RAILTON-BELL*) I advise the apple charlotte. It's very good.

Before Sibyl can join in this chorus of forgiveness, Mrs Railton-Bell,
perceiving the danger, rises from the table and commands her
daughter to leave with her. 'No, mummy,' Sibyl says, 'I'm going to stay
in the dining room and finish my dinner.' And that is not all she says.
Turning towards the major, 'There's a new moon tonight, you know,'
she reminds him. 'We must all go and look at it afterwards.'
    'Breakfast usual time,' Mr Pollock tells the solicitous waitress
Doreen.
    It was commonly assumed that the major's offence was not against
women but against boys, but from the dramatic point of view the
offence against a woman served equally well, 'If I had written the man
as a homosexual,' Terry said in an interview in the *New York Times*, 'the
play may have been construed as a thesis drama begging for tolerance
specifically of the homosexual. Instead it is a play for the understanding
of everyone.' As Eric Portman, who played the part, said in *The Stage*, 'I
believe that Rattigan is helping to open up fresh paths for the treatment
on the stage of all sorts of topics and emotions, that, so far, have not
been allowed in our theatre. But, like any expert and intelligent man of
the theatre who wishes to command an audience, he never chooses the
wrong psychological moment, or goes beyond the capacity of his
audience's understanding.'
    The argument at the 'trial scene' works either way. Lady Matheson
begins with a valid point: this respectable lady who complained that the
major was nudging her arm seemed to have behaved oddly. 'Why didn't
she just say straight out to the major: "I do wish you'd stop doing
whatever it is that you're doing?" That's what I'd have done.' Charles
Stratton took a logical viewpoint in his speech for the defence:

The major presumably understands my form of lovemaking. I *should* therefore understand his. But I don't. So I am plainly in a state of prejudice against him, and must be very wary of any moral judgments I may pass in this matter. It's only fair to approach it from the purely logical standpoint of practical Christian ethics, and ask myself the question: 'What harm has the man done?' Well, apart from possibly slightly bruising the arm of a certain lady, whose motives in complaining – I agree with Lady Matheson – are extremely questionable – apart from that, and apart from telling us a few rather pathetic lies about his past life, which most of us do anyway from time to time, I really can't see he's done anything to justify us chucking him out into the street.

Whichever way one chooses to interpret the play, it was an immense success with Aunt Edna, if indeed it was the multifarious incarnation of that lady that packed the theatres not only in London but in New York. Runs of 726 performances in London and 322 in New York (Rattigan's longest after *O Mistress Mine*) suggest that audiences were becoming more broadminded, for in both plays both the hero and the heroine, to use those words loosely, were unsympathetic characters who would not attract automatic sympathy. Eric Portman as John Malcolm kept his representation common, almost coarse, and ended his first romantic scene with physical violence. Almost all the more influential London critics found the 'happy' ending of *Table by the Window* unconvincing (as Rattigan said his friends had), and this is not only because of the unlovable personality that Eric Portman gave John Malcolm, but the selfish and inconstant personality that Rattigan gave Anne Shankland, who was played by Margaret Leighton with an incomparable blend of magnetism and egotism. Miss Cooper, whose diction is occasionally described by the author as 'managerial', was given a wholly managerial performance by Beryl Measor, who had the uphill task of demonstrating her fondness for her difficult guest without ever losing her official manner. In the first play, only Mrs Railton-Bell has any notable individuality among the smaller parts. She is clearly the boss over all those people that Rattigan painted with one quality apiece, lest one should become so much interested in them that one's attention is disengaged from the bigger parts. The two waitresses are given stock waitress conversation on stock waitress subjects, with the kind of stock joke ('I shouldn't have that, if I were you. I saw what went into it') that is given to servants by people who have never known one well.

Eric Portman and Margaret Leighton were utterly transformed in the second play. The major is a beautifully observed part, adorned with all the mannerisms of his type executed convincingly enough to deceive anyone who did not happen, like Mr Fowler, to have some special knowledge. Sometimes the mask slips: 'Cheeribye till dinner,' he says to Sibyl, and this gives Mrs Railton-Bell her opportunity to remark on his commonness. (Was this his first slip in four years?) There is a moving line where the major is discussing his future with Miss Cooper. 'Quite the philosopher, what,' he says, and then corrects himself: 'I must give up saying what.'

Sibyl Railton-Bell gave Margaret Leighton a rare opportunity to show how a potentially dull character could be presented so that, while she might still be dull to the other people in the play, she was never dull to the audience. Her face was sallow and shiny, her eyes deadened behind unfashionable glasses, her voice low and uninteresting until hysteria gave it a shrill edge. But she was the centre of attention whenever she was on the stage. It was an historic performance, and Rattigan became so attached to her that his next play was written for her and dedicated to her.

The theme of the first play, as I have suggested, springs not only from Terry's friendship with Jean Dawnay but also from his own personal issues. The second play springs from the personal issues of one of his close friends. As usual, little private details crop up here and there: the hotel is situated in Morgan Crescent, John asks Anne Shankland why she didn't go to the Branksome Towers, where Michael Franklin's father lived. But the one overall burden is pity for the lonely. 'Loneliness is a terrible thing,' Miss Cooper says to Anne Shankland; and Anne Shankland, John Malcolm, Major Pollock and Sibyl Railton-Bell are all people who are cut off by some quirk from free association with wider society. Despite the ostensibly happy endings of both plays, there is no suggestion that those quirks are conquered.

Modified belief in those happy endings did not keep most of the critics from expressing approval of the plays, and in due course they crossed the Atlantic, retaining the two leading players and the director, Peter Glenville. The New York critics were kind enough to ensure a tolerable run at the Music Box Theatre, where it opened in October 1956, some of them expressing a pronounced preference for *Table Number Seven* ('a little masterpiece of low-keyed eloquence' wrote Wolcott Gibbs in *The New Yorker*). This naturally confirmed Rattigan in his belief that American theatregoers preferred a *drame à thèse* to a plain story. Brooks Atkinson in the *New York Times* also called this play a masterpiece.

It might be said that the plays reached New York just in time, for

138

1956 was the year when the new wave broke over the English theatre. There was not a new Rattigan play in London until 1958, and this was a critical disaster. There was not a new Rattigan play in New York until 1963. This was a critical disaster too.

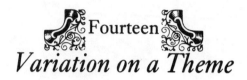

Fourteen
Variation on a Theme

The three-and-a-half-year gap between *Separate Tables* and *Variation on a Theme*, its eventual successor, does not indicate that Terry had abandoned the creative ways of his former days. But he had, though he did not notice it, reached an artistic change of life.

Once *Separate Tables* was established on its run, he went to Paris to work on the script of the film of *The Deep Blue Sea* with Anatole Litvak, the director. It was not a good script, nor did it turn out to be a good film. Kenneth More played Freddie, but Hester was given to Vivien Leigh, a quite unsuitable choice. Kenneth More, whose success in the play had engendered in him a new confidence, nearly decided not to go on with the film. 'The script is no good,' he insisted. 'There's too much Litvak in it and not enough Rattigan. I'd almost go so far as to say that all Rattigan has come out and all Litvak has gone in.' Terry and the producer Alexander Korda persuaded him to carry on, and the film was made by and large according to the Litvak script. Once shooting had begun, Terry had a relaxing tour in Australia, where he was acclaimed as a great man. He returned by way of the Middle East.

This part of his trip was not so indulgent. T. E. Lawrence's estate had just published an accessible edition of *The Mint*, his account of his time in the Royal Air Force, where he served under the name of Ross. (The book had originally been published in a limited edition at a vast price.) Ronald Storrs, Lawrence's sponsor in the Arab Bureau in Cairo, had been a friend of Frank Rattigan, and Lawrence, the great self-made hero of the revolt in the desert who chose to abandon the prospects of fame and fortune and hide himself as a pseudonymous airman, had about him such an aura of mystery that Terry felt an urge to write a piece that would explain him as a human being. He and Puffin Asquith worked intermittently together on a film script that would elucidate the puzzle. Terry claimed to be doing some background research on the picture, but he does not seem to have penetrated far into the Arabian desert. When he came home, work continued in the same desultory way as before.

It was in September 1955, when he had nothing urgent on the schedule, that William Wyler called him to report Marilyn Monroe's interest in *The Sleeping Prince*. The offer was a dexterous one, for the play had not even been seen in New York. It took Terry a very short time to make his agreement with Marilyn Monroe, and he came back to London with a promise, not of thousands of dollars, but of hundreds of thousands of dollars, and the privilege of telling people that he was working for this almost unique sex symbol.

Clearly, so that American filmgoers should know something of what they were in for, a New York production of *The Sleeping Prince* would have to be laid on, and a company was assembled. The play was to open in November of the following year, at about the same time as the New York production of *Separate Tables*.

Meanwhile, in London the new wave in the English theatre was beginning to make its presence felt, though characteristically with a French play. *Waiting for Godot* played at the Arts Theatre that autumn, and was such a success that it moved across Piccadilly Circus to the Criterion, where it continued to be a success. Its hold on the public interested Terry, and he wrote a piece about it in the *New Statesman*. As if to demonstrate that the play was not to be taken seriously, he chose to present Aunt Edna's point of view. It need hardly be said that Aunt Edna was against it.

> Even a middlebrow like myself could have told [Samuel Beckett] that a really good play had to be on two levels, an upper one, which I suppose you'd call symbolical, and a lower one, which is based on story and character. By writing on the upper level alone, all Mr Beckett has done is to produce one of those things that thirty years ago we used to call Experimental Theatre – you wouldn't remember that, of course, and that's a movement which led absolutely nowhere.

It was clear that Terry and the theatrical Establishment were going to be taken by surprise when the new wave broke over them. John Gielgud admitted that *Waiting for Godot* was something he couldn't understand. Somerset Maugham dismissed it as 'two dirty old men picking their toenails' (which at least shows an element of imagination).

What happened the following spring was more significant. The Royal Court, whose first season of new plays for the English Stage Company was not going very well, put on a piece by a young actor, John Osborne, called *Look Back in Anger*, and surprised everyone when it became a success.

In retrospect, we can see that at least a part of *Look Back in Anger*'s appeal was its innate romantic content. Jimmy Porter, its hero, who has a degree at what used to be called a 'red-brick' university, has settled down to running a sweet-stall in a provincial town. His behaviour compels his wife, who comes from a higher stratum of society, to leave him in the first act, whereupon he embarks on a substitute relationship with her best friend. All is forgiven in the end, Jimmy's wife is reconciled, the conclusion may be regarded as a happy one, and if Aunt Edna had found her way to Sloane Square she would have had nothing to complain of but the crudity of the language.

What made the play noteworthy was the social level at which it moved. There were no French windows or tennis rackets in the wretched little house where the Porters lived. Jimmy, in a vivid performance by Kenneth Haigh, talked – and how he talked! – about the kinds of thing that interested a young generation beginning to take advantage of the Welfare State. Routine living had to do, not with hunt balls and skiing in the winter, but with ironing shirts and practising the trumpet and reading the Sunday papers. Love revealed itself not in sighs and embraces but in blunt demands.

Terry could see nothing in this. Later he was to concede a modicum of talent in the play, but it is likely that his opinion was swayed by the fact that Olivier had spoken well of it (though it took him two visits to make up his mind), and had even chosen to act in the author's next piece. But in private he insisted that this was not what the theatre needed.

It was certainly not what he needed, for in February there had been an official announcement of the filming of *The Sleeping Prince*, and he was kept busy working on the script. In July, Marilyn Monroe and her retinue arrived and the shooting began, in the unhappy circumstances I have described.

On the last day of August, Terry gave a party in his Eaton Square flat. This was to mark his impending departure for the United States, where it seemed likely that he might stay for a good time. *Separate Tables* and *The Sleeping Prince* were both on tour preparatory to opening on Broadway, the first at the Music Box on 28 October, the other four days later at the Coronet.

Naturally there was a trickle of hope among the guests that Marilyn Monroe might be coming, for filming was still not finished. She didn't come, but her entourage was represented by Milton Greene's wife and Irving Stein, who was working on his English studies. 'I read *Punch* every week,' he confided, 'and I understand nearly all of it.' More significant, as it turned out, was the presence of Margaret Leighton in the company of Laurence Harvey.

Laurence Harvey, né Skikne, was born in Lithuania and brought up in South Africa. He came to England after the war, paid a three-month visit to RADA, and embarked on a mercurial career in the English theatre. He was twenty-six. Margaret Leighton was thirty-four.

Terry, with his mother and his secretary, Mary Herring, made a leisurely journey via Cannes and Naples. When he had seen his two plays on to Broadway, he came home for Christmas, but at once went back, this time to Hollywood, where he moved in with Rex Harrison in Beverly Hills. He was to do a filmscript of *Separate Tables*, and discuss a possible film of *O Mistress Mine*. Enough other offers came his way to have kept him there for years, but he found Hollywood more than he could take. There were story conferences all day, and what he found even worse, as soon as he was free from front office conferences, he was expected to attend innumerable star-oriented parties. To hear him talk about it, you would think he had been as unhappy as he had been in the old days at Warner Brothers studios in Teddington, with their long and rigid hours. There was no point in his staying. He was unable to do much work. As soon as he could get free, he sailed home to England where he could live according to his own pattern.

There was still enough to be done on the *Separate Tables* script to keep him busy for a few months, and he also began some desultory work on a play derived from the Christie mass-murder case. He had attended the trial at the Old Bailey the previous year and found it deeply interesting.

The play did not progress very far. Christie was not in himself a dramatic individual, except to a psychiatrist, a journalist or a policeman, and his murders were no more than acts of gratification, with no hint of romance to be squeezed from them. It seems possible that Terry may have visualized some kind of relationship between Christie and his younger fellow lodger Ellis, who was also tried and hanged – many say wrongly – for murder. He had the title *Man and Boy* loosely attached to the work; but in the end he dropped the whole thing, for which we may be thankful. There was pathos in the case of Ellis, and drama too in the subsequent finding, after he had been hanged, that he may very well not have been guilty; but nothing else in Christie's case has the makings of a Rattigan play. The first author to have made use of the Christie case was the very different writer Howard Brenton, and his play *Christie in Love* is a far more suitable rider to the case than anything Terry could have devised.

What he did next was much more characteristic, and much more close to his own life.

His decision to write what was to become *Variation on a Theme* shows how confident he was that Aunt Edna ruled the stalls. Terry had long since put behind him his angry youth. When he was at Harrow he had written a letter to *The Times* questioning the right of the authorities to hold compulsory parades in the OTC. He had voted in the Union for the motion that 'This House will in no circumstances fight for its King and Country'. Since then he had seen at first hand the occasional need to fight for his King and Country, and learnt to understand the value of parades if discipline is to be maintained. What is more, he had been, by the standards set by Wesker and Arden and Pinter, a tolerably wealthy young man ever since the success of *French without Tears*, and the problems of the young post-war generation had never seriously brushed his existence. If he still had any left-wing tendency, it only showed itself in his preference for the *New Statesman* over other weekly reviews.

There was something almost defiant in the decision to jettison Christie and turn his attention to Dumas's sentimental tale. *La Dame aux Camélias* is a totally romantic play, and its setting in the Paris demi-monde of the 1840s had no conceivable parallel in England of the 1950s. Clearly Terry had been moved by something.

The variation stays pretty close to the theme. Marguerite Gautier has become a successful, tuberculous divorcée named Rose Fish. Why 'fish', no one has ever satisfactorily explained. Rattigan had a way of attaching the names of his friends to characters in his plays, when they were not called after towns in the Home Counties, like Taplow or St Neots. His current secretary was Mary Herring, but apart from a reference to Rose's having begun as a secretary, a claim that she has to make good by typing a dictated note, no easy task for the average actress, there's nothing to connect Rose Fish with Mary Herring. Rose is living in Cannes on the profits of four well-concluded marriages, and preparing to embark on a fifth, to a wealthy German black marketeer, Kurt Mast, the equivalent, if you like, of Varville in Dumas's play. She has a companion, Hettie, or in full, a symptom of Rattigan's weakness for the aristocracy, Lady Henrietta Crichton-Parry. She corresponds with Dumas's Prudence dramatically, but not socially.

Rose falls in love with a young ballet dancer who has rescued her when she found she had not enough money to pay her losses at the Casino. He dances under the name of Anton Valov, but is actually called Ron Vale. (Some of us tried to get Rattigan to change Ron's Christian name. It is not a sound that can be made romantically. But he was adamant. Perhaps he recalled the success he had had with Ronnie Winslow.) Ron Vale solicits Rose as earnestly as Armand Duval solicited Marguerite. There are two differences, though, between Ron and Armand. The first, unimportant, is that Ron is rather common when he leaves off his phony Russian accent, and has to be kept out of the way when Rose has her smart friends, a social reversal from Dumas. The second, which is vital, is this. It is Rose, rather than Ron, who is helplessly in love, and for an interesting reason.

She has a teenage daughter, Fiona, whose affection she hopes for, but who thinks her a crashing bore. Fiona is always making excuses to get away from her mother and her friends at the Villa Auguste. She would much sooner be with the younger set at the Café Ciel et Enfer. Now what Rose particularly longs for is someone to whom she is necessary, someone who can't get on without her. Ron really seems to care for her in this way.

One evening, the day before he is due to dance the Blue Bird at Monte Carlo, Ron is light-heartedly demonstrating some ballet movements with Fiona, and he falls and breaks his ankle. Rose is just about to leave for dinner with Kurt Mast. Then this happens:

ROSE: In a few moments, would you ring Maxim's and tell Kurt that I'm not coming down tonight?

HETTIE: Shall I tell him what's happened?

ROSE: No.

HETTIE: Then what *shall* I tell him?

ROSE: Whatever you think best, in the circumstances.

HETTIE: What are the circumstances?

ROSE: I'm needed by Ron.

'Needed by Ron.' Rattigan thought this line immensely important. It expressed exactly the nature of the feeling that Rose had for Ron. It was also the nature of the feeling that was the nearest Terry came to love.

The play continues fairly firmly on Dumas's lines, with the difference that it is Rose's love which is most closely followed rather than Ron's. Ron, at any rate, settles down in Rose's villa, until there is a visit from Sam Duveen. Sam is a choreographer who has been keeping Ron in private as well as promoting him in public. 'Father figure,' he says when Rose asks him about his relationship with Ron, and he is in fact the

145

equivalent of Armand's father in *La Dame aux Camélias*. Instead of persuading Rose to write a dismissive letter, as Monsieur Duval did, he suggests that she leave a message for him on a handy tape recorder. The message achieves its intent, and Ron, his ankle mended as also his friendship with Sam, returns to the ballet, where he has a fair success.

But like Armand Duval, he resents his dismissal, and one evening he makes a dramatic entry to a party where they are playing chemmy. He wins a lot from Kurt, and offers it to Rose. 'God knows it's not all I owe you, but you'll get the rest back one day – every bloody penny – with interest too.' He does not go as far as Armand, and throw her to the ground before chucking the money at her; indeed, before a moment has passed Kurt is on to him – not challenging him to a duel, but provoking a vulgar fight in which he is armed with a garden chair and Ron with a broken tumbler.

By this time, we know that Rose is so ill that her doctor has ordered her to take three months in a sanatorium in Switzerland, and to avoid the excessive sunlight of the south of France. She is not the kind of woman to allow doctor's orders to interfere with her pleasures, though. When Ron comes back to apologize, she soon agrees to give up her standing engagements, and to go out and dine with him. The ending has the outward appearance of happiness. But the final stage direction is more characteristic of the Rattigan liking for open ends. *They have disappeared. Hettie makes a hopeless gesture after Rose, but she has not looked back.*

Dumas finished his play more definitely:

ARMAND: Marguerite! Marguerite! Marguerite! (*Un grand cri. Il est forcé de faire un effort pour arracher sa main de celle de Marguerite.*) Ah! (*Il recule épouvanté.*) Morte! Mon Dieu! Mon Dieu! que vais-je devenir?

From Aunt Edna's point of view, I think Dumas wins that hand.

After the opening on 8 May 1958, at the St James's, there was a party at Eaton Square. Rex Harrison and Kay Kendall were there, Vivien Leigh, Margaret Leighton and Laurence Harvey. It was a happy party. As I left, Terry said to me, 'I know they all hated it.'

And he was right. The reviews were terrible. *The Times*, the *Telegraph*, the *Herald*, the *Star*, condemned it; in the weeklies, they were followed by *Punch*, *Time and Tide*, *The Stage*, the *Observer* (Kenneth Tynan, who imagined Rattigan interviewed by his Muse). Only T. C. Worsley in the *New Statesman* and Derek Granger in *The Financial Times* came to his rescue. There were a few passing words of praise in some reviews – one critic liked the scene where Rose had her typing test; in the *Evening Standard*, fellow-dramatist John Mortimer reckoned the last scene with Rose and Ron the equal of *Separate Tables*.

No one at any rate failed to praise Margaret Leighton, who played Rose opposite the Ron of Jeremy Brett. (The part was originally given to Tim Seely, but a change was made before the West End opening – to Miss Leighton's private displeasure.) There was an opulent set by Paul Anstee, and direction by John Gielgud, of which Rattigan said rather unfairly, 'As all he does is turn his back on the players and correct their intonations, it doesn't have very much effect' – though he only said that in private.

It cannot be contradicted that there was something in the common feeling that the play was about a bunch of squalid people in a squalid situation. Rattigan's variation on his theme was a canon by inversion. Marguerite Gautier is a traditional 'tart with a heart', but it is the heart that Dumas emphasized, not the professional infidelities. Armand, though he had the bad luck to love a *fille de joie*, stands out as rather nicer than the young Paris *rentiers* among whom he moved. Neither Ron nor Rose is nice enough to attract sympathy.

Both of them are unashamedly on the make. The final scene that so satisfied John Mortimer is an Aunt Edna conclusion like that of *Table by the Window*. It is too much to believe that Rose would settle down with a fifth husband equipped, as Sam Duveen has warned, only with the prospects of a second-class dancer ('a couple of minor roles at Covent Garden'.) He would have had to retire at about forty. How would he enjoy life with a woman whose tastes have been built on the more or less endless spending of money? It simply was not enough to reproduce the plot and not to people it with suitable characters.

In the *Manchester Guardian*, Gerard Fay suggested that the affair was a concealed homosexual liaison. The same line was put forward in the *Sunday Times* by Harold Hobson, who wrote discreetly that the play 'was about something not its ostensible subject'. In the *Spectator*, Alan Brien laid his cards on the table:

> Why do sizable stretches of the play still grip and shock as a real play should? Because the subject should be a homosexual relationship between a bored and ageing *rentier* and a sharp, oily male tart.

T. C. Worsley came to the rescue somewhat hamhandedly in an article in *The London Magazine*. The suggestion that the play concerned a homosexual duo was, he said, 'a personal smear', as if the suggestion had been that it concerned Terry's own life. In fact, he protested, the story in the play, far from dealing with a homosexual connection, was modelled on an actual affair, in which he personally knew the people concerned. Now the truth is that in theatrical circles and well-informed critical circles, a considerable number of people would know the people concerned, even if they didn't know them personally. They were Margaret Leighton and Laurence Harvey.

The mutual attraction between these two, that ended in a short and unhappy marriage, raised problems which Miss Leighton all too often took to Terry. They had worked together since 1954, in *Separate Tables* both in England and America, and a mutual confidence had been established. Rattigan was not happy to see her enmeshed with a younger, and a very frivolous, man. One Sunday evening the two of them arrived unheralded at Sunningdale for advice: Harvey had set his mind on buying a castle in Surrey where they could live as beautifully as the Oliviers, but he couldn't buy it without using Margaret Leighton's money, and she didn't want it. The two of them were ushered into an empty drawing room and furnished with champagne cocktails, and a financial expert who had been playing golf with Terry that afternoon was sent in to see them. He came out in ten minutes to report that the castle was not to be bought. 'There were floods of tears, of course,' he reported – 'his, not hers.'

It was as well that no such joint extravagence was embarked on. Two years later, when Margaret Leighton was playing in John Mortimer's *The Wrong Side of the Park*, the marriage came to an end. Its conclusion has been described by John Mortimer in his autobiography, *Clinging to the Wreckage* (Weidenfeld and Nicolson, 1984).

> In return for her superb acting in my play, I conducted Miss Leighton's divorce. She arrived at the High Court of Justice in full mourning, very pale, supported on the arm of Terence Rattigan who also seemed to be dressed for a State funeral. It was one of the most theatrically effective 'undefendeds' I have ever done.

Terry's use of the relationship for a play was characteristic; his plots were always taken from life, and often from the lives of people close to him. *Variation on a Theme* was dedicated 'With deep gratitude and affection, to Margaret Leighton, for whom this play was most eagerly written and by whom it was most brilliantly played.' Rose Fish was as closely tailored to Margaret Leighton as Olivia Brown in *Love in Idleness* had been to Gertrude Lawrence and was then to Lynn Fontanne. She was even given an origin in Edgbaston, like Margaret Leighton's. 'I spent the first twenty years of my life,' Rose tells Ron, 'in Frogmore Road, off Five Towns Avenue, and I can spot a Brum accent a mile away . . . I'd guess you come from somewhere much more posh than Frogmore Road. Say the North Side? Am I right?'

She was nearly right. 'You got the district wrong. Acacia Avenue.'

'Off Leamington Road? Oh, that's real posh. Did you ever go to the Warwick Arms? . . . That's when they had "Harry's Hotspurs" playing in the lounge.'

Actually, Margaret Leighton was born in Barnt Green, in Worcestershire, but she went to school in Edgbaston, and her first work in the theatre was at the Birmingham Rep. All that geographical detail is Leightonismus.

On the other hand, Ron is not a portrait of Laurence Harvey except in so far as he fulfils the functions Harvey carried out. You might argue that the change of name from Ron Vale to Anton Valov represented the change from Skikne to Harvey, that the adopted pseudo-Russian voice was South African Harvey's acquired RADA accent, but these are unimportant things. Ron's conduct is borrowed from elsewhere.

The knowing observers who detected a concealed homosexual liaison in *Variation* were not altogether mistaken. Whoever the characters in the play might be said to represent, their behaviour was the behaviour of an older man with his younger man friend. Terry never came nearer to a real love affair in his life than his affection, his adulation if you like, for Kenneth Morgan. He had to present the relationship between Rose and Ron in the terms he knew, and these were homosexual ones. Besides the current long-standing attachment already mentioned, there was another short-term affair going on, and with a dancer. This one doesn't seem to have added anything to the play besides some technical advice about dancing and the Christian name of a minor character; but it was Terry's friendship with those two young people that patterned the affair between Ron and Rose. Sometimes the young ones had to be persuaded not to be present at a party where there was important company. Here is Ron:

> Have you ever thought what it's been like for me, asked over here a couple of odd evenings a week whenever there're no important people around – because common Ron mustn't meet important people – oh dear no – that'd never do – and then when I'm here I'm shoved around, needled, sent up, everyone talking about people I don't know, and things I don't understand.

And here is Ron explaining why he is there:

> I don't understand it. I hardly ever see you, when you call me in the mornings, we don't say much to each other, just gossip, your

friends treat me like dirt and so do you, only more polite, and yet I can't damn well do without you. I need you in my life. For some bloody silly reason which I can't explain, I need you in my life.

It is hardly surprising that the relationship did not convince the critics on its own terms, let alone the audiences. To anyone who had any suspicion of the actual situation, it was as clear as could be. Probably the trouble is that Terry had written with his heart rather than his head. On previous occasions, his heart had been concerned, as in *The Browning Version*, for example, with different emotions, like nostalgia. He could not write convincingly about love between a man and a woman, because this was something he had never known at first hand. What he offered in its place was his own form of affection, which reached its peak in the curtain line of the first act, the line that he found so important: 'I'm needed by Ron.'

Variation on a Theme ran only for 132 performances, the shortest London run of any Rattigan play so far. Michael Franklin sent him a first-night telegram 'from Michael, without whom this play would never have been written'.

Terry was awarded the CBE in the Birthday Honours.

Fifteen
Ross

The preponderantly bad notices for *Variation on a Theme* distressed Terry. He always read his reviews with care; even before he had had the luxury of a secretary to do it for him, he cut them out and stuck them in a book for reference. 'I take my notices seriously,' he wrote in the first of his prefaces; but he added, 'I don't for a moment admit that I have ever been guided by them in my subsequent work, or influenced by them in my own judgment of it.'

Whatever the cause, there is no doubt that the unkind reception of *Variation* marks the beginning of Terry's post-climacteric career. The next four plays he wrote were *Ross*, *Man and Boy*, *A Bequest to the Nation* and *All on Her Own*, the last two for television. Only the last, a comparatively slight piece scrutinizing the reactions of a woman whose husband has been found dead, is built on an original plot. *Ross* was a personal interpretation of the life of Lawrence of Arabia. *Man and Boy* was an extravagantly fanciful piece about the fall of a crooked financier, stimulated by, if not based on, the death of the Swedish tycoon Ivar Kreuger. *A Bequest to the Nation* took a romantic look at the relationship of Nelson and Lady Hamilton.

After *Variation* had opened, Terry went to the South of France for a holiday – the very place to keep it in his mind; by the time he came back, its bastard child was on view, Shelagh Delaney's *A Taste of Honey*, which she claimed to have written because, when she saw *Variation* in Manchester on its preliminary tour, she reckoned that she could write something better. Ironically, when it came to the West End after a successful opening in Joan Littlewood's Theatre Royal in Stratford – Stratford-atte-Bow, not Stratford-upon-Avon – it went to the Criterion, the house where Terry's own reputation began.

Terry was truly surprised at the way people had written about *Variation on a Theme*. He said when he was at work on it that it was 'going to blow up the Establishment'; and he complained afterwards that no one had understood how he had tried to 'kick Aunt Edna downstairs'.

Both these misjudgments stemmed from his lack of involvement in life outside that of his own circle. When he showed up the gambling set in the south of France as the vapid wretches they were, he certainly blew *them* up; but people like these had nothing to do with the Establishment, and their happiness or misery was not a matter of concern to the middle-class audiences of the West End. As for Aunt Edna, far from having been kicked downstairs, she had again been provided with the kind of unhappy affair she had shown herself so addicted to before, when it concerned people she recognized, as in *Table by the Window*, for example, or *The Deep Blue Sea*. To make the principals so uncharming was not to break new ground, only to paint the picture in less attractive colours.

Now *Ross* was virtually written in advance. Work had been going on for two or three years on the film that it was meant to become. Rank had set aside three quarters of a million for it. Then, with no warning, the money was withdrawn and Terry, Puffin Asquith, the director designate, and Dirk Bogarde were left without a film.

All the same, there was a story, and there were scenes already written for it that were too good to throw away. Terry decided that they would make an epic piece for the theatre. He had, after all, written a play on the same lines, *Adventure Story*. There would be the same opening scene focussing on the leading character; then the battles, seen not on the battlefield but in the commander's camp; then a conclusion with the hero's personal problems examined anew. This time, instead of the conquest of the world, the Arab revolt to clear the Ottoman Empire away from its domination of the Middle East. On his deathbed, Alexander had asked, 'Where did it all go wrong?' Lawrence's enigma was not concerned with his campaigns; they had not gone wrong. But something, Terry believed, had happened to him while he was a prisoner of the Turks at Deraa that had robbed him of his calm self-satisfaction and put in its place an inexplicable aversion to fame and success and the company of others. He brushed aside offers of eminence or authority, and 'backed into the limelight', as the current phrase had it, by enlisting in the RAF under a false name.

Terry had more reliable material to work on than he had in Plutarch. There was Lawrence's own account, as he wrote it in *The Seven Pillars of Wisdom*. Easier to read, and more reliable in narrative, there was B. H. Liddell Hart's *T. E. Lawrence: in Arabia and After*. Neither book hints at the theory that Terry presents in his play.

He worked on the play until the spring of 1959. Then he went on a long tour round the world, coming home, inevitably, by way of Hollywood, where he was offered profitable film work, and conscientiously turned it down. On his arrival back in England, he found the Lawrence play, which he had christened *Ross*, after Lawrence's first RAF pseudonym, facing more trouble.

When the news had broken that Rank was not backing a Lawrence film, the producer Sam Spiegel decided to make one of his own; and he was anxious that no other Lawrence story should be in the field. The Lord Chamberlain's powers of censorship would allow him to forbid on the stage any representation of a real character without the permission of his family; so Spiegel went to Lawrence's brother and suggested that he should ask the Lord Chamberlain to forbid any portrayal of Lawrence. Well advised by his lawyers, Terry replied that if the Lord Chamberlain would not allow Lawrence to be played on the stage, he would have his work done on television, over which there was no censorship. By way of further insurance, they went to Liddell Hart and asked him if they could use his name an an 'official source', so that any shortcomings Lawrence's brother found in the script could be attributed to the book. The play as published is prefixed with a credit running, 'The Author gratefully acknowledges his debt to Captain B. H. Liddell Hart, both for the illumination afforded by his book *T. E. Lawrence – in Arabia and After* and for his help in checking the script.' (Liddell Hart evidently did not check the punctuation of his book's title.)

So the Lord Chamberlain, Lawrence's family and Sam Spiegel were seen off and production could go on. Glen Byam Shaw was to direct, and Lawrence would not be played by Dirk Bogarde, as (rather to Terry's disapproval) he was in the film, but by Alec Guinness. At the same time, Terry had other things on his mind, the chief of them being a musical cobbled from *French without Tears*. There was also the possibility of a play about Kay Kendall's death from leukaemia; but nothing came of that until many years later.

Ross opened at the Haymarket on 12 May 1960. It was received generously, but with some reserve, by the critics; generously, with no reserve, by the public, though it is likely that a fair proportion were not altogether sure what was the point in the crucial Act 2, Scene 4.

We begin with Lawrence as 352087 AC2 Ross, on a charge for being late on pass. His excuse was that he had fallen off his motor bike coming home from an evening with friends. Terry weaves a pretty little joke into this scene:

FLIGHT LIEUTENANT: Why did you go to this place in Buckinghamshire?

ROSS: To have a meal with some friends.

F/LT: Close friends?

ROSS: Some of them.

F/LT: Give me their names.

ROSS: But have you the right —?

F/LT: Yes, I have the right. I want these people's names *now*. That's an order, Ross.

ROSS: (*with a faint sigh*) Very well, sir. Lord and Lady Astor, Mr and Mrs George Bernard Shaw, the Archbishop of Canterbury —

The flight-lieutenant rates this as a piece of gross insubordination; but Ross's escort, an intelligent man, adds it to the bag of suspicion he already has and accuses him straight out of being Lawrence. His aim is blackmail; if he can get nothing from Ross/Lawrence, he will sell his story to the press. But before he does so, Terry gives us a transitional scene. In his sleep, Lawrence sees a screen in the barrack room, with a dinner-jacketed lecturer beside it and his own photo on it. On to the screen there come Field Marshal Allenby, Ronald Storrs, General Barrington, the Arab chief Auda Abu Tayi and a nameless Turkish General. The lecture begins, but Lawrence laughs at it. 'You make it sound so dull.' 'Dull?' 'Yes, it wasn't like that at all. Not in the beginning. It was fun.'

For the rest of the first act, we are with Lawrence on his desert campaign. He sets off, with no authority, to ride across the desert to Wadi Safru where he means to prompt Prince Feisal to lead his Arabs against the occupying Turks. From here on, the dialogue has to be taken as being spoken in Arabic, and Terry has given it a faintly false note, rather as Kipling gave the conversation of his jungle animals. Here is Auda Abu Tayi, whom we saw on the lecturer's screen, when Lawrence (el Aurans to the Arabs) proposes his scheme for the assault on Akaba:

'A march in the worst month of the year against the worst desert in Arabia – el Houl – the desolate – that even the jackals and vultures fear – where the sun can beat a man to madness and where day or night a wind of such scorching dryness can blow that a man's skin is stripped from his body. It is a terrible desert – el Houl – and terrible is not a word that comes lightly to the lips of Auda Abu Tayi.'

This was new territory for Terry. There was nothing quite like it among the Greeks; and of course it leads to difficulties when there must be talk between monoglot Arabs and monoglot British, but Terry ignores the difficulties as blithely as Lawrence ignores the difficulties of marching through the desert and keeps the conversation in English without seriously provoking disbelief.

The assault on Akaba is of course successful, and Lawrence reports it on the telephone at the nearest British camp he can find. There have been enormous Turkish casualties and two Arab casualties, plus five men who died on the march. One of those five was Lawrence's orderly Rashid. He had two Arab orderlies, Rashid and Hamed, who were friends, and we may well believe that he was fond of them, but no more.

After he has reported the capture of Akaba to Admiral Makepeace at Suez, Lawrence 'raises his head in fierce and glowing pride', as the stage direction says. He begins to talk to his invisible other self:

'Ross, can you hear me? I've done it. I've captured Akaba. I've done what none of the professional soldiers could have done. I've captured the key to Southern Arabia with five hundred inefficient, untrustworthy Arab bandits. What makes you so unhappy? Is it that Moroccan I shot in the desert and couldn't kill cleanly because my hand was shaking so much? The mangled Turkish bodies in the dynamited trains? Those men that died in the desert? . . . Rashid? . . . Is it Rashid?' [This is the proud, confident Lawrence of the days before Deraa.] 'What is wrong in trying to write my name in history? Lawrence of Akaba – perhaps – who knows? (*Pause*) Oh Ross – how did I become you?'

This is something we may think about in the interval, for there is no hint of a loss of confidence in that act; and when the second act begins, in General Allenby's office in Cairo, Lawrence, in an ill-fitting army uniform, is still what Storrs has called him – over-meek, over-arrogant or over-flippant. He sounds Allenby out with a trick remark about a twentieth-dynasty perfume jar, and they soon settle down as fellow intellectuals. When he is offered the command of a great Arab operation, with four Arab forces supporting the British offensive through the Gaza Gap, he is reluctant to take it on. It needs a man with more faith in the purpose. It's not enough to like the Arabs, he maintains. Your man must believe in them and their destiny. Allenby, who has plumbed the measure of Lawrence's mind as exactly as Lawrence has his, tricks him into accepting the appointment. Lawrence says to him:

> 'You're a trained commander, you see. When you send men out to die, you don't question whether it's *right* – only whether it's *wise*. If it's unwise, it's wrong, and only then your conscience pricks. My conscience isn't Sandhurst trained. It's as undrilled as my salute, and so soft it must have the armourplating of a cause to believe in. How on earth can one *think* oneself into a belief?'

And Allenby says: 'I suppose one can't. But mightn't it be possible to *will* oneself into it?'

With such a challenge, Lawrence cannot refuse.

Terry does not venture to represent the campaign of railway bombing that Lawrence then embarks on; instead he shows him captured by a Turkish sergeant as he is making a sketch of the airfield at Deraa.

We are now at the dramatic centre of the play, which Terry treats characteristically by concentrating on the figures on the touchline rather than the players on the field. He has already given us a glimpse into the office of the Turkish Military Governor of Deraa, a wise old sybarite who remarks to his staff captain that if he should capture Lawrence he would try persuasion – not torture – to change his views on Arab independence. When we next look into the office, the persuasion is going on, out of sight, almost out of earshot, in the guardroom. Here is Liddell Hart's account of what happened:

> Lawrence was marched off to an office where in reply to questions he 'admitted' he was a Circassian. That might explain his white skin, but it drew him deeper into the mire. For the second time in his life he found himself forcibly incorporated in the Turkish Army, and this time for a purpose for which Turkish officers have notoriously been apt to use their recruits. That night the ordeal came and when Lawrence resisted he was handed over to the tender mercies of the guard to be brought to a suitable frame of mind. After various unpleasant forms of

coercion had failed, he was thrashed into senselessness. But his gory state at least saved him from further attentions, and during the night he managed to escape from the hospital to which he had been carried.

Terry's Turkish general admits to his captain that he knows all that is happening outside, that he ordered it. When in due course the guard sergeant brings Lawrence into the room, only half-conscious, the general explains why he has done what he has done:

> 'You must understand that I know. I do pity you, you know. You won't ever believe it, but it's true. I know what was revealed to you tonight, and I know what that revelation will have done to you. You can think I mean just a broken will, if you like. That might have destroyed you by itself. But I mean more than that. Far more.'

Leaving Lawrence on the floor, he tells him how to get out into the street and leaves him. Lawrence drags his way back into freedom.

Freedom from the Turks, that is; but as soon as he finds his way back to Allenby he finds his freedom constricted by military necessity. His request to be sent back to England is accepted, but almost at once cancelled by Allenby's cunning. And by the time the next scene opens, Lawrence has taken part in a triumphant entry into Jerusalem and rejoined the conflict, captured Deraa and utterly defeated the Turkish Fourth Army, which feats he describes in a situation report that is read back to him by the pilot who is to deliver it. The report makes a brief reference to his having killed one of his own men, too badly wounded to be evacuated. When he describes the same event to Auda Abu Tayi, who makes a dramatically convenient arrival, the man proves to be his orderly Hamed, and Lawrence gives a moving account of his death. Hamed has progressed from a punctilious refusal to speak to him to a complete devotion. When he saw Lawrence's pistol ready to end his pain, he said 'God will give you peace', and it is his voice that Lawrence hears when he is consumed in a half-hysterical disquiet over his indifference to the appalling savagery of his recent activities.

In the next scene we are back at the RAF station and AC Dickinson has done what he said he would do. The press have all got the story, and the Air Ministry have sent orders that Ross is to be discharged and got off the station as soon and as secretly as possible. We catch our last sight of him at mid-morning, wearing civilian clothes and packing his kitbag. There is a demonstration of loyalty from his fellow airmen. 'What are you going to do?' the Flight Sergeant asks him. 'I'm going to get back into the RAF as soon as I can,' says Lawrence. 'I'll have to change my name, I suppose. Ross won't do any more. Shaw. I thought of that this morning.' The men go back to their duties, the Flight Sergeant goes to collect the key to the Group Captain's private gate so that Lawrence/Ross may leave unobserved by the press. (Terry clearly didn't realize what the press can do when its mind is made up.) 'God will give you peace,' Ross says to himself as he ties his kitbag.

Terry's theory, never expressed in words but clearly intimated, is that the beating and buggery to which Lawrence was subjected at Deraa revealed in him a secret pleasure in these things that he had always tried to keep away. It may have been at least half right, for we know now that in his later life Lawrence used to hire a young man to beat him. But the truth or unreality of the theory is irrelevant; there is no more reason why Terry should not advance his own ideas about Lawrence than Shakespeare his ideas about Richard III. The narrative as he recounts it is convincing enough, the self-satisfied confidence of Lawrence before Deraa ably contrasted with the reluctant confidence of the later man.

No doubt there are people prepared to come to the defence of Lawrence over the question of his private weaknesses, as there are those who like to condemn Shakespeare's portrait of the 'faultless' Richard III. This is a concern for psychologists; *Ross* may be based on a psychological plot, but fundamentally it is a romantic adventure tale of the kind one used to read in boys' papers such as *Chums*, the *BOP*, *The Captain*. The characters are more interestingly conceived than in any of Rattigan's earlier plays except *The Deep Blue Sea*. They are all people such as he seldom met in his own life, except perhaps Ronald Storrs, a diplomat and a friend of his father's; and what is more, they have already been sketched out in *The Seven Pillars* and in Liddell Hart's biography. So they had to be invented, with little help from his own circle. Rashid and Hamed and Auda Abu Tayi had to be almost invented from scratch, and they are characters from *The Jungle Book*. The airmen's talk and behaviour is much better contrived than Terry's working-class activity usually seems; the men are given individualities, not in any depth, but enough to keep us interested in them.

Lawrence and Allenby are both presented as great men, intellectual and practical, but they are great men as seen in popular eyes. It is hard to see how they could have been shown with more of their genius on the surface; they have their parts to play in the story, and if they are given admirable things to do and say, in the language of the current theatre, that is all that could be hoped for. Some critics complained that Terry's Lawrence was not a clear, determinate figure; but Lawrence's Lawrence wasn't that either, except to himself. Terry had worked immensely hard on the story, which was intended to be a movie of outstanding quality. When it failed to be a movie of any quality, it had to be truncated, but it still contains an immense amount of information about Lawrence and his campaigns, and there is no point in the play at which information outweighs entertainment. Alec Guinness played the part to everyone's satisfaction, and when he had to leave the company, was capably replaced by Michael Bryant. Glen Byam Shaw was the director, and the London run, which began at the Haymarket on 12 May 1960, lasted for 762 performances. It opened in New York eighteen months later, with John Mills as Lawrence, and had a run of 159 performances.

To the American critics, *Ross* did not have the same pride in British achievement as to the British critics, and Lawrence remained to them a somewhat inexplicable figure. What was generally admired was the construction of the play, the manner in which the facts were presented through the medium of emotions familiar to theatre audiences in other contexts. There are good jokes (Hamed's resurrection of the dead camels when he learnt that Lawrence was not leaving but going with him to Jerusalem); there is sentimental pathos (the friendship of Rashid and Hamed, Hamed's death at Deraa); there is fine melodramatic tension (Auda Abu Tayi's temptation to betray Lawrence to the Turks when he learns of the £10,000 reward). Above all, there is a strong continuing narrative. If the film had been made, it seems likely that it would have been a pretty good one.

The change in Lawrence's personality after his experience at Deraa is not a matter of serious dramatic concern. It is all very well to affirm that one couldn't allow the sudden discovery of a personal imperfection to change one's life in that way, but it is another thing to say that such an effect had not worked on Lawrence, or at any rate to the fictional Lawrence that Terry had created.

What does seem slightly wrong, though, is Lawrence's sigh at the end of the first act, 'Oh Ross – how did I become you?' This is no more than a trumped-up curtain line. Becoming Ross was exactly what Lawrence wanted. He wanted it so much that when circumstances prevented him from being Ross any longer, he decided, before he had even reached the barrack gate, that he would become Shaw, who was Ross with a different name and number. If the Lawrence who asked himself what was wrong in trying to write his name in history had to be contrasted through dramatic artifice with the Lawrence who was unhappy about his spiritual condition, a more appropriate comparison would have been with the Colonel Lawrence, in Arab dress at the Peace Conference in Paris in 1919, with a hysterical crowd waiting to see him leaving his hotel.

Sixteen
A Death Sentence and a Reprieve

The first rumours that Rattigan was suffering from leukaemia were floated, quite wrongly, in the spring of 1960. He had a bad go of flu, which he neglected to attend rehearsals of *Ross* and of its successor, *Joie de Vivre*. The result was a fortnight in The Clinic with pneumonia. Leukaemia was a current anxiety in theatre circles since Kay Kendall's death. It is not impossible that Terry may have mentioned it himself at the time. However, pneumonia was what he had, and when he came away from The Clinic he was ordered to rest. He chose Brighton for his recuperation. It was a favourite place for theatrical people; he would be near Laurence Olivier and John Clements and others of his friends, and he liked it well enough to rent a flat there.

However, he had to be in London again by July for the opening of *Joie de Vivre*. This was the musical that had been made out of *French without Tears*, with music by Robert Stolz and lyrics by Paul Dehn, and an updated script that was only partly his own work.

Musicals were increasingly highly estimated at the time. Even John Osborne, when he wanted to write about the gossip writers of the press, wrote a musical about them, *The World of Paul Slickey*, a somewhat underrated show. *Fings Ain't What They Used t'Be* was doing well, and on the day after *Joie de Vivre*'s scheduled opening, *Oliver* was due to begin its long and successful career. It was natural that Binkie Beaumont should encourage his most successful writer to enter the game.

161

Joie de Vivre was not a well thought out creation, however. Robert Stolz was an able musician in the Viennese tradition (and indeed has a memorial statue in Vienna next to Schubert's), but he lacked the popular touch for that period. His last great success had been *White Horse Inn*, a romantic piece with nothing in common with the farcical *Joie de Vivre*, which had become more farcical after the libretto had been brought up to date with contemporary catchwords and references and a new character, the call-girl Chi Chi, who in the original play is heard of but not seen. The lyrics by Paul Dehn were witty enough, but the songs were generally considered only to interfere with the comedy. The dress rehearsal, by Paul Dehn's account, was as disastrous as the dress rehearsal of *French without Tears* had been. The conductor had fallen off the rostrum; two of the principals had developed laryngitis; and the pianist went out of his mind, announcing that he had been in touch with Napoleon and Jesus Christ and had had a great revelation which he would announce on the opening night. This was on 14 July 1960, at the Queen's.

Whether it was the result of the pianist's revelation or not, the first performance got the bird from the audience. The perilous line that had been seized on by the New York critics of *French without Tears* – 'It isn't funny, it's a bloody tragedy' – met with wholehearted agreement from the house. There were four performances altogether, then it came off.

Only the faithful T. C. Worsley was able to write kindly of *Joie de Vivre*. The rest of the critics were, at the best, regretful. The generous Harold Hobson, having allowed himself to use phrases like 'peculiarly revolting', made up for it by praising Terry's other work. The author went back to Brighton and contemplated the play he had promised to write for Rex Harrison. Then he went to New York to discuss a Broadway production of *Ross*, and – with notable courage – the possibility of a musical to be made out of *The Sleeping Prince*, with music and lyrics by Noël Coward. From New York he flew on to Hollywood, where he sold an idea that was to become the film *The VIPs*.

When he came home, he began to change his life as fundamentally as he had changed it after his father's death in 1952. He sold Little Court, and began looking for a house in Brighton. Meanwhile he went to stay in a villa in Ischia, rented from Sir William Walton. Lady Walton was a great businesswoman, and there were several villas there for rent.

In Ischia he went to work more seriously on the play he had promised Rex Harrison. It had now become two plays, another double bill, to be called *Like Father, Like Son*. *Like Father* never came to anything, though its theme of a successful avant-garde artist and his conservative son was, somewhat changed, incorporated in *After Lydia*, half of yet another double bill, *In Praise of Love*. Rex Harrison did get to play this in the

162

end. *Like Son* turned into a television play called *Heart to Heart*. Ironically, since the whole project had begun with the idea of a play for Rex Harrison about the death of his wife Kay Kendall, *Like Son* was to include a part written for Rachel Roberts, her successor in his affections.

Heart to Heart, which was broadcast by the BBC on 6 December 1962, is a very good play indeed, but, as we know it now, it could never have played on the stage. It is set in a television studio, and the script is written with much knowledge of how things go on in television studios, unlike *The Final Test*, which clearly depended very much on the producer.

Terry had two current interests that prompted him to write the script he did. The first was a television series called *Face to Face*, in which eminent people were interviewed by John Freeman (who subsequently became our ambassador in Washington) with all the urgent intensity of a prosecuting counsel. The other was the performance of Richard Nixon on television in 1960, when he countered an accusation of taking bribes with a sentimental appearance, accompanied by his wife and his dog, justifying an occasional slip on the ground that he had devoted so much of his time to political good works.

Terry's Nixon was a newly-appointed Labour minister, and his John Freeman was the handsome and popular David Mann. There is a sub-plot about David Mann's married life, of secondary importance; it has one interesting feature, all the same, and that is that David's wife Peggy was born in Riga, and so was Lydia in *In Praise of Love*. Sir Stanley Johnson, the minister, was formerly a junior minister in a department where there had been a bribery scandal, and the question arises whether David should bring this up in his interview. The decision is virtually taken from him when a woman accosts him in a teashop and hands him a document that appears to prove that a rogue financier has paid an hotel bill for 257,852 francs at a Cannes hotel for Sir Stanley and a woman. David is reluctant to use such testimony against a cabinet minister without being certain that it is correct, and he telephones the hotel, where the payment is confirmed by the cashier. The confirmation is of course taped.

It happens that the controller at the television station is a friend of Sir Stanley's, and is so convinced of his innocence, and so intent on seeing him succeed in his new appointment, that he instructs David that there is to be no mention made of the bribery affair, and he will have the programme blacked out if David disobeys him. David is too clever to include questions about it in his interview, but while he and Sir Stanley are waiting in the studio for the programme to begin, he gives instructions to the production secretary to be ready to track in on the photostat of the hotel bill, which he has ready, and prepare to insert the tape of the talk with the cashier. Sir Stanley, convinced that he is about to be revealed as having accepted a bribe, quits his part in the interview and turns straight to the camera to confess his error.

It seems, when the broadcast is over and the telephone calls start coming in, that David has lost his attempt to prove to the nation, or to the fifteen million of them that listen to *Heart to Heart*, that Sir Stanley is too dishonest a man to sit in the cabinet. The calls go the other way. Out of 288 calls, only three take the line that he must resign. But Jessie, the production secretary, knows the value of immediate opinions like these. 'I only know,' she says, 'that those three tonight are going to mean 3000 tomorrow, and 300,000 the day after, then – hell, why not? – three million on the day it really matters.'

The characters are all Terry's own inventions, apart, perhaps, from the supporting parts that come from the stock he always has ready on the shelf. They are real and convincing, and had the advantage of performances by Kenneth More as David and Ralph Richardson as Sir Stanley. It had been hoped that Richard Burton would play David; Terry took Alvin Rakoff, the director of the play, to meet him and Elizabeth Taylor in Rome, where they were working on the film of *Cleopatra*. But *Cleopatra* went on too long.

Terry spent so much time abroad in this period that he might as well not have gone to the trouble of buying himself a house in Brighton. In fact, he hardly ever used it. He had had it decorated by a friend, who had been allowed to exercise his own preferences. I met Terry one day in July 1962, walking along the Brighton front on his way to a party given by T. C. Worsley, to which we were both bidden. 'I've just moved into my new house after waiting for eighteen months,' he said mournfully, 'and it's uninhabitable. There isn't a single room I can bear to sit in.'

He was not really a happy man that summer, though among other things he sold the idea that was to become the film *The Yellow Rolls-Royce*. (His own Rolls Royce now bore the registration number TR 100 – a vulgarity that attracted endless mockery from us all.) In the autumn, while *Heart to Heart* was being made at the BBC Television Centre, he fell ill again, this time with hepatitis. No doubt this was a by-product of his drinking, which had become pretty indulgent. It sent him back to The Clinic, and when the play was transmitted, on 5 December, he had to watch it from his bed.

He emerged determined to take a break, and got Michael Weight, the designer, who also looked after his villas in Ischia, to book a passage for the two of them to Hong Kong. This trip, he decided, had pulled him together wonderfully, and in the spring he paid another visit to New York.

The last time he had been there, a little over a year before, he had taken with him the draft of a new piece on which he had been working at Noël Coward's house in Jamaica, a play intended, of course, for Rex Harrison. In the event, Rex Harrison never had it, for one evening the draft was read by the French actor Charles Boyer, and Boyer believed that the leading part, a middle-aged Romanian tycoon, would suit him. Might he play it, he asked, and permission was given at once. The play was called *Man and Boy*, and this is what it continued to be called.

The arrangements were now completed. Charles Boyer would play *Man and Boy* in London for a limited season that autumn, and then take it to New York. With the arrangements settled, Terry came home, not to Brighton, but to Ischia.

He was not as fully recovered as he thought he was, however. In Ischia he continued to feel ill, and to run up vast temperatures night and morning. It was not, his doctor told him, a recurrence of his jaundice. It was not the old virus pneumonia. A specialist was called in. Somehow his diagnosis seemed like the fulfilment of a prophecy. Terry had leukaemia.

Confronted with a pronouncement that he knew, from what he had seen of Kay Kendall, might mean death in quite a short time, Rattigan accepted his fate with an almost dramatic imperturbability. He told a few friends of his illness, but insisted that they should not tell anyone else. (It need hardly be said that a lot of them did.) His mother spent a summer holiday in Ischia, but nothing was said to her.

Out of sight, though, he was making his preparations. His specialist told him that he would probably have about six months more to live. He continued to work on *Man and Boy* and on the film script of *The Yellow Rolls-Royce*, for which he had had only vague ideas when he sold the original notion. He decided to sell his house in Brighton, where he had never lived, and stay on in Ischia as long as he could.

This was not as long as he had counted on, for he was urgently asked by Binkie Beaumont to come home. Some business discussion had been made the pretence for this, but the true cause was concern for his health. Expert medical advisers had told Binkie that if Terry had leukaemia, the one thing he should avoid was a hot, sunny climate. People knew, moreover, that he was dying. He should be back among his old circle.

His London medical advisers checked his symptoms. Tell me, he asked, just how much longer have I got? The reply was definite. He would die some time in September. It was then July.

There was less imperturbability this time. He worked as if he had to finish a lifetime of work in a hurry, which indeed was the case. But he was pressed to get a second opinion; and the second opinion contradicted the first. The illness was not leukaemia at all, much though the aggregation of symptoms suggested it.

He cancelled his proposals to sell his Brighton house, and began to live a life of renewed activity. *Man and Boy*, after a fortnight at Brighton, opened at the Queen's Theatre on 4 September.

This ultimate possessor of the title Rattigan had so long wanted to attach to something was a curiously ill-made play by his usual standards. It opens in a basement apartment in Greenwich Village, the kind of place a New York Freddie Page might have lived in. Its current tenant is a young man, Basil Anthony, who plays the piano in a bar. We do not see him at once, because the lights do not come up until the radio has announced the six o'clock news bulletin. Then we see him, half-way into his tuxedo, listening to the latest developments in the case of Gregor Antonescu, an international tycoon whose great empire is on the verge of collapse. It is not long before we learn that Antonescu is Basil Anthony's father.

Basil is living in his little apartment and has a girlfriend, Carol, of little interest, though she fulfils the necessary function of indicating Basil's heterosexuality. Their initial duologue is interrupted by the unexpected arrival of the fugitive Antonescu, who wants to borrow the apartment while he tries to sort out his problem. His personal filing system is so comprehensive that he knew where he would find Basil, and knew that Basil had a girl, and that her name was Carol Penn. Soon we can add the information that Basil is illegitimate, that he is against capitalism, that five years earlier he made an unsuccessful attempt to shoot his father, that he is now an American citizen, though he went to school in England and his father remains Romanian. With the arrival of Antonescu's associate Sven Johnson, the story is about to take off.

While Carol is making coffee for Basil, and Basil is telling a sentimental tale about his father's poverty-ridden childhood, Antonescu, in the next room, is explaining to his London office the details of the crisis, and the way in which he will solve it. It is rumoured that a merger between Manson Radios (one of Antonescu's companies) and American Electric would fail. If it did not fail, Antonescu would be better off by seventy-five million dollars cash, and as the period we are in is 1934, seventy-five million dollars was a sum of real significance. What Antonescu proposes to do, before the markets open in the morning, is to make sure that the merger goes through.

His infallible files have given him useful information about Mark Herries, the President of American Electric. He is invited to call on Antonescu at Basil's apartment, where he is to be given the impression that Basil is Antonescu's boyfriend; and that moreover he could become his own boyfriend if the cards were played right. Basil is induced, though of course not told why, to take his tuxedo off and put on his campiest slacks and shirt. Carol has already left for her job in the theatre. 'Oh,' says Antonescu, 'better not call me father. Our friend is a little – straitlaced about such things.'

Antonescu's files do not show Herries as straitlaced at all. He had a friend called Mike Larter, in his early twenties, who a year before had killed himself in his Park Lane basement with an overdose of sleeping pills. In an ingeniously written act, Terry enables Antonescu to postpone to the collapse of the merger, if no more than that, and at the same time to suggest that he had himself been a friend of Mike Larter's. He even persuades Herries to give Basil his telephone number and his card, while also arranging a statement about the merger, which he has cunningly altered to suggest success rather than postponement.

Basil kept out of the way in his bedroom during the business talk, and only realized what his father was up to when it became so clear what was going on. With faithfully preserved family loyalty, he restrains himself from blowing up the whole plot, as he might have done; but once Herries has gone, he turns on his father in contempt and slams out of the room. The act ends with family gossip between Antonescu and his friend and assistant Sven; but this is of little consequence, serving only to add depth to Antonescu's portrait, and to pass some time before the arrival of Antonescu's wife.

She is a former mistress, who has been made into a countess by the purchase of a Holy Roman title, and into the President of the Antonescu Foundation so that she can sign cheques for large sums when required. On this occasion, it is a blank cheque. 'I've signed about twenty of those in the last three weeks,' she protests. 'Just how much *are* you snitching from the Foundation?'

There is no good answer to that, for while Antonescu and his wife are discussing his sex life rather than his finances, Basil comes back with two newspapers. Their headlines pronounce that there is a warrant out for Antonescu's arrest. A British bank has discovered that the securities he deposited against a loan for six million dollars are worthless. The effect of the news on Antonescu is unfortunate: he has a slight stroke and has to be helped onto Basil's bed, where he is temporarily helpless.

There follows a very unlikely scene. Basil tells Sven that he has always known that the securities were valueless. What is more, he has known for a long time about his father's dishonest practices, more than Sven has ever been told, 'Like all the four hundred other Antonescu banks. A set of portable books, a board of directors who don't know what they're directing but accept because it's Antonescu who asked them, and a local crooked accountant, paid a hundred dollars a week.'

The radio tells that a warrant has been issued by the FBI; all ports, airfields and frontier posts are being watched. Basil says he will go and get a friend's car and drive him to the Mexican frontier; but while he is out, Gregor makes another plan. He sends Sven to borrow a gun from one of the Antonescu staff, he tries vainly to get his wife to stay with him, and when Basil returns he tells him that he will be able to escape in a private plane. There is a scene of family affection with Basil, his earnest offers of help persistently refused, and a scene of business efficiency with Sven, who insists on there being a farewell note clearing him of blame. Basil leaves. Sven leaves. Antonescu struggles into his coat as the radio reveals that Mark Herries will come to the microphone and tell listeners how he discovered Antonescu's frauds, and walks out into Greenwich Village, the cocked pistol in his pocket.

I said this was an ill-made play, but that does not mean that it is not dramatically exciting. What is wrong with it is the number of loose ends. The girl Carol, built up as the potential good influence in Basil's life, is never seen again. Basil's suggestion that his father might take refuge in her apartment on West 23rd Street is clearly no more than an excuse to bring her name in again; it never leads to anything. At the other end of the play, the Countess is given no function other than an emphasis on her husband's multiple sex life, all heterosexual. Her presidency of the Foundation is not a serious issue, in spite of the twenty-odd blank cheques she claims to have signed.

The plot involving a homosexual influence over the President of American Electric fades out. It is hard to see where it was meant to lead. Was Herries, whom we know to have had a keen staff of accountants, expected to allow the merger to take place in the hope of being accorded sexual gratification? If not, what was he to do? He had only delayed affairs by twenty-four hours. And in the end, American Electric plays no part in Antonescu's downfall, which is the result of an action brought by the Bank of the City of London.

Basil's wandering loyalty is hard to explain. At the end of Act Two, fresh from being offered as a human sacrifice to his father's dangerous competitor, he simply tells him, somewhat melodramatically, 'You are *nothing*. You live and breathe and have being and you are my father – but you are *nothing*.' It is easy to believe that such an insult, to a man who is prone to describe himself as the man who gave roads to Yugoslavia and electricity to Hungary, who will always be put through on the telephone to Mussolini in the middle of the night, might be irritated by such a remark. But if Basil had wanted to anger his father, he had all that other ammunition in the store – not the man who gave roads to Yugoslavia, but the man who set the livelihoods of thousands at risk, who retained the loyalties of his four hundred crooked accountants with their portable books by blackmail. It is hard to believe that he would not have released a round or two from that armament in the almost physical anger that posessed him at the moment.

There is nothing of Terry's own circle to be traced in the characters of the play. He had at this time an able accountant of his own, Bill Forsyth, who must certainly have provided him with the necessary financial talk, but one does not see him either as Antonescu or Herries. There is a sad echo of the death of Kenneth Morgan in the death of Mark Herries' friend Mike Larter. Usually when Terry was writing about characters constructed entirely from his imagination, such as Hester in *The Deep Blue Sea*, they are given a touch more reality than those built up from familiar components, but it is not so here. Antonescu was devised when Terry had been reading about Ivar Kreuger, but there is no sign that he was intended to resemble him. He is a truly original character, who no doubt took on his Romanian characteristics when he was adopted by Charles Boyer instead of the notional Rex Harrison. Basil is a fairly average young English boy, transferred to America for dramatic purposes; and the rest of them, Carol, Sven, Herries, Beeston the accountant, the Countess, are as ordinary as Rattigan's supporting characters deliberately are when he does not want them to distract attention from their betters.

Nonetheless, Terry has a great talent for handling his chessmen without giving them a chance to show off, and there are moments in the play where the oft-praised sense of theatre shows. Basil's entry with his fatal newspapers when Antonescu and the Countess are arguing about how many mistresses he has is a genuine *coup de théâtre*, even if the argument, never forecast in any way up till then, has only been marking time. There is real pathos in the wavering relationships of father and son. The revelation of what is to Basil his father's final dishonesty, a lifetime's sympathy extracted from a tale of begging as a child exploded as no more than a pretty biographical decoration, is momentarily distressing. A line of good moments, however, does not make a genuinely coherent story, especially when none of the characters is interesting enough to rouse in an audience a genuine desire to know what is coming next. Antonescu is fine at the centre of a scene like the seduction of Mark Herries, but in spite of the immense abilities that we are constantly told of, in spite of Carol's description of him as a charmer, he is not a man you would want to spend your leisure with.

The notices in the London press were cool on the whole. Bernard Levin described it as 'a play that outdistances all but a handful of authors writing in England today.' Yet even T. C. Worsley complained that the relationship between Antonescu and Basil was not deeply enough explored. But he came to the rescue when the old line of criticism came up again, that the play was not about what it purported to be about, but about an affair between a boy and a man. Cuthbert Worsley, whose own preferences as outlined in his autobiography *Flannelled Fool* (Alan Ross, 1966) were not very different from Terry's, always interpreted this line as a personal insult: 'This seamy line of personal smear is not criticism; it is gossip journalism,' he insisted.

Terry was as much disappointed by the reviews as he had been about *Variation on a Theme*. Had he not been taking a swipe at the Establishment? Had he not written a story basically unacceptable to the middle-aged, middle-class ladies whom he had served so faithfully in his earlier days? He had indeed done both of these things, but he had done nothing more to put in their place. When Bernard Hollowood, the current editor of *Punch*, wrote and asked him for a contribution, he replied, not only to say that the subject (I forget now what it was) was not one that interested him, but to add no less than four pages attacking the criticism of the play by Basil Boothroyd.

The play was only scheduled for a short run, and it played for 69 performances at the Queen's, after its initial fortnight at Brighton. Then on 12 November it opened at the Brooks Atkinson Theatre in New York, with only one change of cast (in the unimportant part of Carol) and with the same director, Michael Benthall. The New York critics were not excited. Some of them found it, as Basil Boothroyd had done, too light for its subject. Howard Taubman of the *New York Times* was concerned about a lack of commitment. 'One does not ask for a tract in the theatre, especially from Mr Rattigan. But his play has the appearance of being serious about an arresting theme. It is almost impossible to believe that it could be restricted so completely to the personality of Antonescu and that it could avoid so thoroughly the meaning of such a life in its relation to society.'

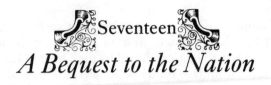

Seventeen
A Bequest to the Nation

With the New York critics mostly against it, *Man and Boy* had only a short run of 54 performances. But while Terry was there, *The Girl who Came to Supper* – the musical made out of *The Sleeping Prince* opened. The songs added by Noël Coward have not survived on their own merits, but at least the general feeling was that this was a happy show. It ran for 113 performances at the Broadway Theatre. To have been slammed by the press for his last two plays, and praised for one in which the script has been rewritten by someone else, is not the perfect way to induce happiness in a writer, and Terry was not in his best mood when he came back, especially as *The VIPs*, his latest film, had just been released and received only modest notices. He was looking restlessly for some way to occupy himself, for there was no new play on the horizon, nor was he in the mood to start one. He telephoned me once or twice about ideas for *Punch* articles. 'I really do want to write a piece for *Punch*,' he told me one day. 'In fact, I want to go on writing for you.' He put forward a promising idea, on the British mistrust of euphoria, a feeling he was hardly subject to at the time. But he never wrote it. He still had some work to do for *The Yellow Rolls-Royce*; we were drinking one evening at the Eaton Square flat, waiting for another guest for dinner, when his secretary came in with a bundle of typescript. 'Another 20,000 dollars,' he remarked: payment went by the page of script. He didn't check it until we were back from Prunier's after midnight.

In the late spring of 1964 he went to see a new play at the Arts Theatre, Joe Orton's *Entertaining Mr Sloane*. At last he had found a modern play that he could approve of, a well-made drama in three long, developing acts, with a story based wholly on the nature of the characters. He put some money into it and it transferred to Wyndham's.

His own dramatic energy was fired by a contract with the television company ATV. They wanted him to contribute a new play for television, which was to be introduced by the Duke of Edinburgh, and at the same time stimulate funds both for the Duke of Edinburgh's Award and for the rehabilitation of the *Cutty Sark*. Naturally a nautical theme would be appropriate, and what more appropriate than Nelson, in whom Rattigan suddenly discovered a lurking interest. He went to the Palace to talk it over with the Duke.

Terry's last theatrical discussion with the Royal Family had been less urgent. Some years before, there was an RAF celebration at the Albert Hall, for which Rattigan had written some words. His main concern at the time was with *The Prince and the Showgirl*, then being made, but loyalty brought him to the evening. Bidden to go and meet the Queen, he found her and the Duke surrounded by air marshals, none of whom seemed to have anything to say. His arrival broke the deadlock. Formal introductions over, Her Majesty opened the conversation. 'Tell me, Mr Rattigan,' she said, 'what is Marilyn Monroe really like?'

It was the Duke who gave Terry his theme for the play. Terry maintained that when Nelson had enjoyed a career of such uninterrupted success, nothing was left to write about. His heroes (like Shakespeare's) needed a touch of weakness so that he might write about their personality rather than their achievements, a 'play about people' rather than a 'play about things'. Nelson's life seemed to be just a string of victories; he had never had a defeat, either naval or private. But yes he had, the Duke said. He had wanted England to accept Emma Hamilton as his consort; and it never did.

Terry began to study accounts of the Nelson–Emma Hamilton affair; but characteristically he introduced a sub-plot almost on the scale of the plot. Young George Matcham, son of Nelson's sister and another George Matcham, was sixteen, and Nelson was as great a hero to him as Kitchener would have been if he had been around in 1914, or Montgomery in 1943. An accidental meeting with Lady Nelson, the discarded wife, led him to wonder why such a great man should treat her so badly and another woman so well. Terry's decision was that Emma was an intolerable woman; so when the boy saw her at close quarters, his hero worship suffered.

172

This is not, of course, the whole story of *Nelson: A Portrait in Miniature*. With Michael Bryant as Nelson and Rachel Roberts as Emma Hamilton, it was broadcast by ATV, to general approval, in March 1966. Then it was later made into a play for the stage.

Rattigan was still in a discontented mood. An old friend told me in the winter of 1964 that he was 'completely round the bend', but this was no more than an ordinary man's reaction to a rich man's eccentricities. He bought a house in Scotland, which he asked Michael Franklin to decorate for him, but in which he never lived. Now that it was established that he was not suffering from leukaemia, he decided to live in a warmer climate. And his accountant advised him that, with the money that was due to come to him from outstanding film commissions, it would be advisable to live out of England for the statutory tax year.

He moved between Ischia and Hollywood, and, when his mother was ill in the London Clinic, he took an apartment in Paris in order to be near home if there were any bad developments. Finally he rented a house in Bermuda, and ultimately decided to become a genuine tax exile and stay there permanently. He put the Brighton house on the market. The Eaton Square flat he had already relinquished when the landlords warned him that they were going to increase his rent.

There was still work to do. He was converting *Nelson* into *A Bequest to the Nation*; he was working on the script of a musical film version of *Goodbye, Mr Chips*; and he wrote a short monologue for Margaret Leighton, *All on Her Own*. This was the soliloquy of a woman trying to persuade herself that the death of her hearty, hard-drinking husband had been an accident and not suicide. It had one transmission on BBC2, and ten years later it was played by Barbara Jefford at the King's Head Theatre in Islington.

The unhappy run of illnesses followed him to Pompeii in the summer of 1968. *Goodbye, Mr Chips* was being filmed on location there, and Terry went down with acute appendicitis. He was taken to a hospital in Naples for an operation, where the attention was so poor and the surroundings so dirty that gangrene set in. At his own request, the whole affair was kept quiet, but by great good fortune his doctor was on holiday in Italy. He came to add what assistance he might; and Terry's secretary, Sheila Dyatt, flew out from England in case there were serious problems to be dealt with. There might well have been, for Terry was reckoned close to death. But he had a capacity for recovering that was almost the equal of his capacity for catching things, and after two or three weeks he was removed from his unattractive Neapolitan hospital and taken to a healthier place in Switzerland. After that he went to recuperate in Baden Baden.

There was a seven-year gap between *Man and Boy* and his next play in London. This was partly due to his own sense of disillusion. 'I did not write *Man and Boy* to be successful,' he told an interviewer. 'I do not want to go down simply as a matinée playwright.' If the public did not want *Variation on a Theme* (in which he reckoned he had got rid of the Aunt Edna syndrome), or *Man and Boy*, which dealt, however romantically, with current affairs, it was not easy for him to make up his mind what they did want. When his voice was heard, it was muted. The third volume of collected plays was published in 1964, and in that there was the new preface, justifying a continued adherence to the standards of Aunt Edna, because Aunt Edna had altered her tastes to keep up with the current theatre. There was the little television monologue for Margaret Leighton, *All on Her Own*. There was an ill-advised revival of *The Sleeping Prince*. And of course there was the television portrait of *Nelson*. It was an adaptation of this, and not a new play, with which he made his next appearance.

It does not seem as if he took an immense amount of trouble over this, and yet it contains more of him than many of his earlier and better plays. Basically, it is the television piece in three dimensions, with a permanent set on which the scene changes are indicated by the lighting. It is worth reproducing the note on the set at the start of the published text:

> The play is set in a permanent and open architectural structure which will include a staircase and different levels for the various acting areas. Neither doors nor windows will be shown although both are sometimes referred to in the text . . . the sets are not naturalistic, and the scene changes are indicated more by the use of lighting than by physical transformations.
>
> There are four backcloths to represent, in order, Bath, London, Merton and Trafalgar.

In the first scene of the first act we meet young George, who is to be so much at the centre of affairs. His father and mother are off to Merton to stay with Nelson and Emma, but he must stay behind for a while to finish his term at school. This leaves him open for an ambush by Lady Nelson, whom the family call 'Tom Tit' because her rheumatism has given her a comic, birdlike walk. Lady Nelson persuades the boy to take a letter from her addressed to Nelson, which she once sent through the public post, to have it returned with a cruel message on the cover. When George joins his family at Merton, she can be sure that he will deliver the message personally.

The scene gives a lot of useful information about the set-up. Emma considers Merton to be her house, Nelson his, and Matcham (George's father) points out that it is mortgaged to him. Nelson, we learn, has been recalled by the Admiralty, presumably from leave, for no definite period. George, at this moment, believes his uncle to be 'the greatest man on earth', and, less positively, that Lady Hamilton is 'one of the most beautiful and gracious ladies who ever lived'. He is a young man with pronounced respect for the concept of honour. All of this information is to be helpful later, but why Terry should have used seven characters to impart it, three of whom are never seen again, and two only in the background, suggests either a lack of consideration or an over-indulgent producer.

We meet Nelson in the next scene, telling the First Lord of the Admiralty, first how to conquer Napoleon on land, second, and more practically, how to destroy the French at Cadiz, an operation in which he makes it clear he will not take part, being, as he claims, on indefinite sick leave. And in the next, we meet Lady Hamilton, receiving young George, and later Lord Minto, in her bedroom in Clarges Street, and talking with exaggerated vulgarity in language thick with four-letter obscenities. Into this scene comes Nelson, fresh home from the Admiralty in his much-bemedalled uniform, with the cheering crowd outside that it always fetches; and then his flag captain, Hardy, who has only shop talk to offer – shop talk, however, that just once overflows into a kind of rude poetry, when he tells George in a long speech what it is like to be a British seaman:

> Pressed into service, as like as not – four-fifths of them are – and pressed means kidnapped in Chatham or Portsmouth, knocked on the head and thrown into a life as brutal and slavish as any in the world. In Newgate gaol they get better to eat than maggoty biscuit, and they don't get two hundred lashes for a back answer to their gaoler. Two hundred multiplied by nine? That's a lot of bloody flesh off a man's back, Master Matcham, and the threat of it keeps 'em servile enough – as it'd keep you – and Lord Minto I don't doubt. And a bumper tot of rum would make you both drunk enough to fight a battle. But would you care overmuch who won it?

The stage has been set, extravagantly enough, but little has developed so far. George, advised by Minto, has agreed to postpone delivering his letter; and, more significantly, Nelson has virtually confirmed to Hardy that he will not sail with the Fleet to engage the French outside Cadiz:

HARDY: So when does the *Victory* sail?

NELSON: It must be soon – for it's sure that they'll need every ship they can spare.

HARDY: Every *ship?*

NELSON: And every Captain, too. I don't doubt you'll have your orders to sail the *Victory* south in a few days.

HARDY: Yes, my lord.

NELSON: She's still a good enough ship for the kind of pell-mell battle this is likely to be. Perhaps Collingwood will choose to fly his flag in her rather than the *Royal Sovereign.*

'Collingwood's flag in the *Victory?*' Hardy fumes when Nelson is out of earshot. 'I'll shoot it down myself.' But the rivalry between Nelson and Collingwood is not to be a contention. The true rivalry has already made its appearance. It is the rivalry between the Fleet and Emma Hamilton for the allegiance of Admiral Nelson.

The first act ends with a short meeting between Minto and Lady Nelson. This adds nothing much to the situation, save that Lady Nelson gives Minto a note to give to George. He may read the letter she asked him to give to her husband, and if there is anything in it that will cause him 'any distress whatever', he may, if he wishes, not deliver it. Otherwise, the scene is simply an amen to what has gone before.

With the first scene of the second act we see precisely what course the play is to take. It is a love story on a classic triangle situation, and a love story of the pattern Terry liked to describe, in which a sexual obsession may drive a lover into excesses unthinkable in other circumstances. We are seeing repeated the infatuation of Rose Fish for Ron, the determined passion of John Malcolm for Mrs Shankland, the inexplicable craving of Hester Collyer for Freddie Page. But Rose Fish, John Malcolm and Hester Collyer had no serious rivals, and Nelson's situation is unlike theirs. He has to make a choice, between Emma Hamilton and the command of the Fleet.

The scene begins with Emma performing one of her attitudes, for which, historically, she was well known. With his new-found extravagance, born no doubt of writing for films and television, Terry has given her a numerous audience. All three Matchams are there, Mrs Matcham giving melodramatic assistance at the harpsichord. Besides the Admiral, who sits a little apart from his guests, we have his brother the Dean, with his wife and teenage son; Minto, Hardy and another captain. Some of the servants are there too, including Emma's maid Francesca, who acts as stage manager. Emma is being Andromache, and the performance has allowed Terry to incorporate some vulgarisms that he had written in to add substance to the television script, not, in this case, vulgarisms of language, but vulgarisms of characterization. Into her words, written for her by Nelson's brother the Dean, she adds some lines from Shakespeare's *Antony and Cleopatra*, 'The crown o' the earth doth melt, and there is nothing left remarkable beneath the visiting moon', and so on. The interpolation is designed to diminish the general admiration, for just before Emma slips it in we have heard Minto ask who wrote the words, and Nelson tell him, 'My brother William.'

But the choice of quotation is deliberate. 'Dearest Emma,' says the Dean, 'is sometimes inclined to insert certain passages of her own finding, and Shakespeare's Cleopatra, it seems, is one of her favourite heroines.' Then:

MINTO: Of course.

EMMA: What do you mean by that, Minto?

MINTO: Of course Emma Hamilton would have as her favourite that other 'lass unparallel'd'.

EMMA: 'Lass unparallel'd'? Well, I'll accept 'unparallel'd' at any hour and at ten in the evening I'll even believe in 'lass'. You think quick, Minto. If you'd said something about 'this dotage of our Admiral', you'd have had this in your face.

The evening degenerates into a morass of misbehaviour that leads to a great quarrel between Emma and Hardy in which Nelson takes Hardy's side and asks Emma to apologize to him. To show that she meant no disrespect, she says, she will sing the National Anthem; but what she sings is a current patriotic version beginning 'Join we great Nelson's name, First on the rolls of fame,' and concludes with a 'God save my King' that is clearly addressed by her to Nelson rather than to 'that old madman of Windsor', as he calls her monarch.

Courteous but clearly unsatisfied, Nelson excuses himself to go and discuss tactics in the next room with Hardy, while Emma talks with the patient Minto about her shortcomings and her hold on Nelson:

When I get up in the mornings and look at myself in my glass, don't you think I don't say to myself – but he can't love *that*! Not *that*! So Francesca fills me up with a few tankards of porter and brandy at breakfast, and by the evening I'm the Divine Lady again and I'm saying – but, of course Nelson loves me, and he's damn lucky to have me. But tonight's different, I don't know why.

177

She sits at the harpsichord and plays the notes that have always stood for a signal between them, the opening bars of 'Rule, Britannia'. After a meagre pause, Nelson leaves his tactics and joins her. Forgiveness and passion are the order of the moment. In five more minutes he will join her upstairs. But before he can do so, young George comes to say goodbye, and to fulfil his promises to Tom Tit.

The effect is disastrous. 'I thought, whatever's happened, a husband can still read a letter from his wife,' says innocent, honest George, 'especially when the husband is you, of all people in the world.' Nelson is unmoved by this. 'Thank you for the compliment, but this is a husband of all husbands in the world who happens to prefer to think his wife is no longer alive.' George plays the wrong card. He accuses Nelson of bad manners in not answering his letters, and this time Nelson is moved indeed. He takes a quick look at the letter. 'You double-dealing, traitorous dog!' he thunders. 'It's a plot! I'll have you kicked out of this house tonight, and never come back.'

Commanding the Matchams to take their son away, fending off Emma, alarmed by the sounds of anger, Nelson insists on going out into his rainy garden. But his last words are for George's forgiveness. 'He will not be harmed in any way at all. Anyone who dares to do so – or orders it done – anyone at all (and that was directed at Emma) – will leave my house tonight.'

We are in the presence of Rattigan's old conviction, the dominance of the weak over the strong, 'the worst form of tyranny the world has ever known', as Oscar Wilde called it.

When Nelson returns, cold and wet but a little more collected, he goes back to his talk with Hardy, but the subject has changed. It is not possible any longer for Nelson to ignore the fact that many people, even the officers of the Royal Navy, believe that he has shamefully deserted his wife and set up with a common, drunken middle-aged woman. Terry told the New York critic Holly Hill that he had found no historical evidence that Nelson knew how vulgar Emma was, but he thought it impossible that a really sensitive man, and especially a man as vain as Nelson, would not have known. In the play, he knows only too well:

NELSON: God in heaven, Hardy, when Emma throws a glass of champagne, after an insult to my King, don't you think I see exactly what you see, a drunken, middle-aged woman making a fool of herself and me? Do you think I relish the gutter talk, don't wince at the vulgarity, and have lost the capacity to smell liquor on the breath? Do you think I don't feel blasted with shame nearly every day that I spend at Emma's side?

HARDY: Then why have you so long endured such days?

NELSON: Because after the days there are the nights. And now of course you are asking the question: how can any love be respected that begins and ends in the bed?

HARDY: Yes. How can it?

NELSON: To me, very easily. To the forty-year-old Admiral who had never known or enjoyed what most other men have enjoyed and long since forgotten – that in the release of the bed there lies an ecstasy so strong and a satisfaction so profound that it seems that it is everything that life can offer a man, the very purpose of his existence on earth – well, to that poor crass innocent of an Admiral in Naples Bay the question was not so easy . . . I was still the rector's son who, from the cradle, had been preached the abomination of carnal love, and the ineffable joys of holy wedlock. But when at last I surrendered to Emma, I found – why should I be ashamed to say it? – that carnal love concerns the soul quite as much as it concerns the body. . . . You must understand that there is nothing in Emma I would change, Hardy. I love her and I want her exactly as she is – because I am obsessed and I want her absolutely.

There, give or take a stripe or two round the sleeve, is the complete analysis of Terry's compulsive lovers, Rose, Hester, John Malcolm, and in due course Alma Rattenbury. It is not enough for Hardy, who is concerned, as young George was, why Nelson could not offer a touch more gentility towards his wife. Life with her, Nelson argues, was a hell of humiliation 'from which I am now so very happily escaped'. 'Did you say happily, my lord?' Hardy asks him. 'Is it so satisfying to be laughed at in Clarges Street?' A few brutish boors, Nelson concedes, probably hired by my enemies. 'I doubt,' Hardy says, 'if Napoleon would hire spies to risk jeering you into going out again to sea.' And at that moment we know that Nelson will go. The conversation turns to battle tactics; but the unexpected arrival of George, proposing an early exit ahead of his family, brings the talk back to the matter of Lady Nelson.

George never hears the explanation he needed, why Nelson should treat his wife so badly; and when Nelson recites to him, from memory, the text of the fatal letter, he is more bewildered than ever. It is a kind and generous letter, the last sort that Nelson wanted, but he tries to expound the difficulty of living on terms with someone who relentlessly forgives you, whatever insults you pour upon her. George is still unsatisfied, but at least he is able to pretend to himself that, in spite of such an error, Nelson is still the great man he believed.

As for Nelson, we have here another example of Terry's talent for unspoken intimation. Often, when he insinuates more than he states, he is praised for the 'economy' of his writing, but there is no economy in *Bequest to the Nation*. The dialogue throughout is a colourful suggestion of Regency conversation. But now, when Nelson is once more joined by Emma, more is suggested in their exchanges than either of them says.

She knows by then that there is no hope of her stopping Nelson from joining the Fleet in the *Victory*. But she is desperately afraid that if he is killed, she will be left 'alone and deserted', and she proposes an oath to him: 'Swear that this time you'll do all that lies in your power not to get yourself killed,' she demands. Nelson cunningly avoids making an oath in exactly those terms. 'I will do all that lies in my power,' he concedes, 'not to leave my Emma alone and deserted, and that I do most solemnly swear to, before God.'

In a short scene on board the *Victory*, we see that Nelson has halfway agreed to her terms. He has put on a plain jacket, so that the array of stars on his breast do not offer a useful target for the sharpshooters in the rigging of the French ships. He has no intention, however, of allowing HMS *Temeraire* to overtake the *Victory* and so meet the worst of the enemy's barrage. Before he leaves his cabin to go to the quarterdeck, he asks Hardy and Blackwood to witness his signature on his will, drawing attention to the last paragraph, reading it aloud.

The paragraph runs: 'I leave Emma, Lady Hamilton, therefore a Legacy to my King and Country, that they will give her an ample provision to maintain her rank in life.'

And before he goes on deck, Nelson shifts into his dress uniform, with all the stars on the breast.

Indications of suicide have already been made. Nelson declined to swear to Emma that he would try not to get himself killed. Later, when Blackwood asks that, after the battle, it might be his ship, the *Euryalus*, that brings the news to London, Nelson ('absently', says the stage direction) says 'Hardy, please remember to tell Collingwood that is my wish.'

'It will be you who will give the order, my lord,' Hardy reminds him.

'Of course,' says Nelson. 'I meant – in case I forget.'

We may deduce from the last scene, a visit by the ever sympathetic Lady Nelson to the already near bankrupt Emma, that King and Country made no such provision as Nelson had requested. The Nelsons, however, were well provided for. The title was raised from Viscount to Earl, and bestowed on Nelson's elder brother William.

Whether Nelson really sought his own death at Trafalgar is not a problem that need be discussed in this connection. What is more interesting is why he should have done so. He was contented with his

liaison with Emma. He had no qualms of conscience about his wife –
until her letter was brought to him by young George. The instrument
that brought him to a proper realization of his duty – that special
responsibility that he confided to his men before the battle – was the
teenage boy who had braved the anger of the man he regarded as 'the
greatest man on earth' to fulfil what he regarded as his unbreakable
promise. He had done what he could (or believed he could) to ensure
that Emma Hamilton was not left in poverty. But the matter of his
wife had become an unbearable load of guilt. There was no middle
course open to him, and death in action was as honourable an end as
anyone of his calibre could think of.

The play opened at the Haymarket Theatre on 23 September 1970
and was received with modest approval. More than one critic accused
it of being old-fashioned, and by the standards of the day, that it
certainly was. There was little in the dialogue of that thraldom of
middle-class English. The language is meant to suggest the courtesies of the Regency period, but there is a feeling about it that the
author had written it down as it came into his head, without concerning himself how it was to sound on the stage. Terry's habitual
middle-class language always has that quality about it to some extent,
but as it is usually the kind of talk that is intended to make its meaning
known as economically as possible, one does not look for elegance of
diction. In this mock-Regency talk, at least an element of gentility is
called for, especially as Terry is writing longer lines of dialogue than
usual. Sometimes they seem positively careless, one thought after
another without a real attempt to make them into practical speech.
Here is Emma consoling Nelson when he comes back from his retreat
into the garden after his reconciliation with George: 'If you'd gone on
trying to catch your death of cold hiding from me outside at night, I
could have nursed you later – as I did at Naples – and meanwhile
learnt solitaire.' Do away with the unhandy relative clauses, and this
resolves into about four speeches in a more natural language.

Some critics found the figure of Nelson, played by Ian Holm, not
credible. There seemed too little about him to have made him 'the
greatest man on earth', not only to a romantic boy, but to the crowds
who came to see him wherever he went. This is hardly a fair criticism.
The play is about a special aspect of Nelson, the established hero
playing a less than heroic role in his domestic life. It is not a
documentary; we hear a little about the battle of the Nile, such as
might come into ordinary conversation, but we are not offered a
review of his achievements. Why should we be? The naval tactics at
Copenhagen or the Nile have nothing to do with the Admiral's love
affairs.

What we have is simply a romantic gloss on history, such as we had seen before in *Adventure Story* and *Ross*. A framework of fact is enrobed with drama of a kind that makes the participants into acceptable, though not necessarily unarguable, historical human figures. Stock characters are inflated to historic proportions, which is not quite the same as reducing historic celebrities to everyday proportions. Emma, like Alexander in *Adventure Story*, shows how the habits and emotions common in ordinary life work when they inhabit exceptional people. For all the faults I have found in it, *Bequest to the Nation* is pretty good theatre. It would have been better if Terry had not been so discouraged by criticism, not always of the best, that he failed to put the same enthusiasm into his plays as he had done twenty years before.

It ran at the Haymarket for 124 performances. Six weeks after it opened, there was a revival of *The Winslow Boy*, with Kenneth More in the part of Sir Robert Morton. Drawing on all the lessons they had learnt from their experience of later Rattigan, critics were not slow in pointing out its faults, and it is true that, just off stage, Aunt Edna was clearly perceptible, calling for romance, and suspense, and middle-class principles. Romance and suspense, however, had by no means lost their hold on West End audiences; and the middle-class standards upheld by Arthur Winslow and Sir Robert were matched by the liberal aspect of Grace Winslow's pursuit of justice and Suffragette laurels in preference to a respectable marriage with John Watherstone and life in the garrison. At any rate, *The Winslow Boy* ran for more than six months.

In the Queen's Birthday Honours in June 1971, Terry was knighted.

Eighteen
In Praise of Love

There were two Rattigan plays in the West End at the start of 1971, Terry's sixtieth year, *A Bequest to the Nation* at the Haymarket and *The Winslow Boy*, though *Bequest* was soon out of the running. A rejuvenated Rattigan announced that he would come back to live in England. He had rented one house after another in Bermuda before he found one that suited him. Much labour was expended in each of them, humping furniture up the stairs to get his study right once more.

Some visitors to the Rattigan households in Bermuda reported that life there was uninteresting, a kind of garrison existence with no ready means of escape. Certainly Terry took life fairly easily. He passed a good deal of time on the golf course, often on his own. This was where he did his thinking. Then the day's work would begin in the evening, and if it were not finished by dinner time it would go on after dinner, sometimes into the small hours of the morning.

Terry was thrilled about his knighthood, an honour that he never shrugged off as lightly as some other theatrical knights have been known to. Stewart Trotter, who directed a fine production of *The Browning Version* some years later, says that he punctiliously addressed him as 'Sir Terence', expecting a characteristic theatrical response that they should work on Christian name terms; but Sir Terence remained Sir Terence throughout, no matter how friendly they became. On the lawn at Spanish Grange, Terry's current home in Bermuda, Brownie, the friendly Bermudian who ran the domestic staff, celebrated the announcement with a home-made banner bearing congratulations to 'SIR TERRENCE'.

On his return to England Terry took a suite at Claridge's and declared that he would look for a house in the country. (Perhaps it had escaped his attention that he already had a house in Scotland.) The first literary work he undertook was trivial in the extreme. Thames Television ran a series of short plays called Armchair Theatre, and Rattigan's agent offered them *High Summer*.

This was one of the unrealized pair of plays that should, in theory, have run in repertory with *The Browning Version* and *Harlequinade* twenty-five years earlier. Rattigan's agent had had it on his shelves ever since, for no one had shown any enthusiasm for it, indeed any interest in it. It was, as I have said, a foolish, melodramatic piece about a bad hat of a Marquess, who breaks his society-imposed exile to return to his stately home in the middle of a cricket week. There are odd hints in the play of what was to come later. The Marquess's return, that should have caused nothing but embarrassment to the company, met instead with almost universal friendliness. A similar conclusion comes at the end of *Table Number Seven*, when the exploded major faces the diners at the Beauregard Hotel. The Marquess resolves in the end to live in Paris with his woman Amy Sprott and settle down as a painter, just as Rose Fish and Ron Vale in *Variation on a Theme* walk out into the sunset expecting to live on Ron's dancing. The relationship between the Marquess and his Amy has even about it a touch of Viscount Nelson and his Emma.

When Peter Duguid, the director appointed by Thames, went to see Terry at Claridge's to solicit some revisions, Terry is reported to have said frankly, 'It's awful, isn't it.' But he allowed it to be played after he had worked a little on the script, and he recommended his favourite Margaret Leighton for Lady Margaret, the leading woman's part. Margaret Leighton was no more enthusiastic than the author had been. But she played the part, and honest Roland Culver played Lord George and Christopher Gable played the wicked Marquess. The broadcast went out in September 1972 – hardly a good beginning to a Rattigan revival.

Nevertheless something better was in the air. In December, there was a pleasant revival of *While the Sun Shines* at the little Hampstead Theatre, with Alec McCowen as the Earl of Harpenden. Terry and McCowen led the audience in a discussion on the stage after the performance on the first night; there was indeed little to discuss about the play, but there was talk about wartime life in London and Terry's own charm won everyone over to the belief that they had been seeing some kind of masterpiece. Before returning to Bermuda, he visited

Cuthbert Worsley in a nursing home; Worsley was ill after an ambitious but unsuccessful attempt to sail across France on the inland canals.

Terry was back in the spring, and spending time with the actress Marti Stevens. She was at the birthday party he gave in June at his new chambers at Albany, and there was optimistic gossip, that he was not averse to encouraging, that they might be married, though how far the proposition was explored from the distaff side is another matter.

The following month there was a revival of *French without Tears* at the Young Vic. Terry went to the first night with Harold French, Stephen Mitchell and Trevor Howard, all veterans of 1966. The next play, it was announced, would be another double bill, to be directed by John Dexter.

A couple of days after the *French without Tears* opening, Terry was at the Garrick Club's annual dinner, a sign of the change in his social attitudes. He was accustomed to choose his own companions rather than to attend a collection picked by others. His apparent sociability was handicapped by a shyness that used to afflict him with people he did not know well. At the dinner, he approached Ronald Harwood, whom he had not met before, to tell him how much he had enjoyed his television play, *The Guests*, in which Margaret Leighton had played. This gave Harwood, still on the fringe of his career, a chance to talk about the theatre with a pastmaster; but Terry's shyness was too much. He spent the rest of the evening talking about cricket – talking specifically about the rival merits of Amiss and Hammond, although Harwood had never seen Hammond play.

The new double bill was *In Praise of Love*, composed, as *Playbill* was, of a farce and a romance. At the opening night at the Duchess Theatre on 27 September, the farce was put first. This was called 'Before Dawn', and the second play, 'After Lydia'; but later, when the romance was somewhat extended to make it fill an evening on its own, the title 'After Lydia' was dropped and the title *In Praise of Love* was transferred to the single play.

'Before Dawn' was another variation on a theme, this time on Sardou's *Tosca*. The play is mocked with such crass and tasteless disrespect that it is hard to think what was in Rattigan's mind when he wrote it. When he had last transformed a French *pièce bien faite*, in *Variation on a Theme*, he may have produced a work of a quality inferior to its original, but at least it showed the 'sense of theatre' on which he prided himself. The mockery of *Tosca* is crude in its treatment of the plot, and crude in the workmanship employed to carry the plot.

Tosca is given the notorious choice by Scarpia; if she wants to save Mario Cavaradossi she must sleep with Scarpia. She makes, in due course, the notorious response: she stabs him in the back. But Terry's Scarpia wears a knife-proof leather jacket. So the threatened seduction must take place. It is not so dreadful as it might have been, for Scarpia proves impotent. This means that, to conceal such a terrible state secret, Tosca will have to be shot beside Cavaradossi. They would be shot with blanks, and carriages would be provided afterwards to take him to Milan, Tosca to her home. The love between the two of them is in any case of a spiritual rather than a physical nature, for Cavaradossi much prefers his boyfriend Angelotti.

This farrago is decorated with music-hall jokes of the most basic kind. There has been endless confusion between Scarpia and the young captain, Schiarrone, about which orders are to be obeyed, and which only to appear to be obeyed. So there are exchanges like this:

SCHIARRONE: Isn't he to be shot with blanks?

SCARPIA: Balls, Schiarrone, balls.

During rehearsal, John Dexter had made some twelve minutes' worth of cuts and put in a bridging passage. Donald Sinden, who played Scarpia, said to me after my visit, not to the first night but to the final preview, 'Did you wonder why my warrant was propped up on the pork pie? It had my lines on it.' Once the run had begun, it was decided to run 'After Lydia' first and the farce afterwards; no one attuned to the standards of 'Before Dawn' would be able easily to reattune himself to the subtleties of the other play. When it was played first, audiences listened to 'Before Dawn' in almost total silence; when it was played second, it went on five minutes longer to accommodate the laughs.

'After Lydia' was descended from the play about the left-wing painter and his conventional son that had been meant to form part of the duo, *Like Father, Like Son.* It was based on what Terry knew of the life of Rex Harrison and Kay Kendall, and he knew a good deal, having watched developments as they evolved. Briefly, the plot concerns a husband trying to hide from his wife the fact that she is going to die from leukaemia – the situation through which the Harrisons lived. It was a subject that Rattigan had meant to write about for a long time. Now he was able to amplify the detail from his own experience.

The play is a masterpiece of deceit, though for once no one abused it on the ground that it purported to be about one thing and was really about something else. The deceit is part of the ingenious dramatic structure. The eponymous Lydia is the wife of Sebastian Cruttwell, a successful literary critic whose domestic life is represented as boorish. He has been married to Lydia for twenty-eight years, but it was no love match. As an Intelligence Officer in the army, he met her at the end of the war, working in a brothel and avid for a British passport. She had no passport at all at the time; she was an Estonian from Tallinn and had had to endure successive invasions from Russians and Germans, neither of which regarded the Estonians as anything more than convenient labour. The arrival of their son Joey, now twenty, ensured that the marriage continued on reasonably conventional lines.

Sebastian and Joey are the legacies from the earlier play. Sebastian is a successful critic who once wrote a successful novel but ceased writing novels when his second was critically dismissed. He is a devoted Marxist, but lives in a style a little above that of the workers. Considering how easily Terry threw off a few thousand pounds' worth of drama when he had to, he has made Sebastian's labours appear very difficult; they don't seem to amount to more than one critical article a week for a Sunday paper, yet he spends a great deal of time in his study. Joey seems to be able to pass his days as he wishes; he is currently canvassing for the Liberals (as his creator did) in a bye election, but has also written a half-hour television play, for which he will be paid £300 (as his creator was for *The Final Test*). Sebastian regards the Liberal Party as crypto-fascists and the play as pseudo-Kafka crap; the relation between him and his son is as cool as relations between fathers and post-adolescent sons habitually are.

The all-purpose family confidant is Mark Walters, an American writer of thrillers who has become a millionaire by his practical use of formulae and now lives in England, in a luxurious apartment in Eaton Square (like his creator). Mark is a man of boundless charm and generosity. Once he was tempted to lure Lydia away from Sebastian; but that was long ago, and now the three of them live in an atmosphere of friendly compatibility.

The main story is this: Lydia, as the result of malnutrition during the war years, is suffering from terminal poly-arteritis. (It had begun as leukaemia, and is treated as if it were, but Rattigan made the change for some reason that he never disclosed.) Because she knows where to find the documents in her doctor's surgery, she knows that she may, with luck, last as long as two years more. But she conspires with the doctor, a fellow-Estonian refugee, to have false reports sent so that Sebastian will believe that she is recovering.

The doctor, however, is a double agent. Besides the encouraging reports that he sends to Lydia, he sends honest reports to Sebastian. Sebastian has been trying desperately to find a cure, but he knows that Lydia will probably not last beyond another three or four months. With the help of his generous newspaper, he has had high-grade specialists attending Lydia's consultations without divulging their true functions there. He is hiding his knowledge of Lydia's illness as doggedly as she is hiding hers. His dismay on receiving a biopsy

187

report makes him forget a vital assignation, and links the main plot with the sub-plot.

Joey's pseudo-Kafka crap is to be broadcast on the evening after Mark's first visit. Mark will come and watch it with the three members of the family. But this is the day on which Sebastian hears the news of Lydia's inevitable death, and he forgets to turn up and hear the broadcast. It leads to a great row with Lydia and sulks with Joey. Mark restores some kind of peace while Sebastian is in his study trying to compose an apology to his son. Only Mark knows everything, that Sebastian is aware of Lydia's terminal condition, that Lydia knows of it. He solves the problem by telling her where her husband hides the genuine reports. Then he leaves them.

The play ends with a scene of resigned quiet. Lydia has agreed to go with Mark for ten days' holiday in Cannes, during which time Joey will look after his father. As Sebastian and Joey play chess on the expensive new chess set that Mark has brought from Hong Kong, Lydia prepares to retire. Here are the last few lines:

SEBASTIAN (*to Joey*):   Well, well, well. Do you know those ten days without her might be quite fun. (*He sees LYDIA on the stairs*) Oh sorry, darling. Didn't see you were still there.

LYDIA: I know you didn't.

SEBASTIAN: Go on. Move, Joey. (*LYDIA goes on slowly up the stairs*) We haven't got all night ahead of us. (*LYDIA disappears from sight*) Except, I suppose, we have.

Terry, who claimed that he never wrote curtain lines, never wrote a better one than that.

'After Lydia', to my way of thinking, is the best-written play in the whole of Terry's work. Casual as the language is in which the dialogue is couched, it gives an impression of care that is missing from the earlier plays. The characteristic I mentioned earlier, of seeming only to write down thoughts as they occur, without apparent effort to turn them into fluent conversation, is gone. Here is Caroline in *Who Is Sylvia?* explaining her feelings about her husband's double life:

You see, from the beginning I thought to myself – well, this Mark Wright business must go rather deep. I'm his wife, and if he really wants to change his identity from time to time, then it must, in some way, be my fault. Something that I can't give him, that he wants and can find elsewhere.

This is perfectly clear and explicit and made out of middle-class English. But it is written English, not spoken English, and this is one of the weaknesses in Terry's work when it becomes too fluent.

On the other hand, here is Sebastian telling Mark about Lydia's experiences in wartime Estonia:

> Lydia *was* reported dead, you know. That's how she managed to stay alive. When the Russians came back she was officially a non-person. Labour Camp material, perhaps, but not worth killing.

There you have true conversational speech, with a fresh phrase for each fresh idea. It even continues in the description of the mass execution, its dramatic intent restrained behind the ordinary talk of one man to another:

> Well, the drill was, they take them out at dusk into the open country, about a thousand at a time. And then they'd be made to dig this big ditch. It had to be pretty big to take in a thousand bodies. Of course, they knew what it was for. No 'You're all going to the baths to be deloused,' as in the gas-chambers. No. The 'untermensch' knew what they were digging.

That is the language of the old Flying Officer talking to his friends.

But the ability to reproduce everyday conversational English is the least of the merits the play exhibits. It is a technical masterpiece. A good deal of the dialogue is comic; Terry considered calling the play a comedy. 'After Lydia' is not a comedy, however, so much as a thriller. There are as many hidden clues in the story as in an Agatha Christie detective play, but the clues are psychological rather than practical. What on earth was there about Sebastian to induce Lydia to stay with him? He is thoughtless; his very first lines are to complain that his room is cold, when the explanation is that he has not turned the heating on; he continues to address the cleaner as Mrs Mackintyre, although Mrs Mackintyre was replaced by Mrs Reedy three months back; he asks Mark to dinner and forgets the invitation. He is something of a domestic bully, constantly asking why this thing or that has not been done properly; and he is an intellectual bully as well, putting others right over little things such as an American pronunciation of 'Gladstone' or holding political views different from his own. And yet Lydia has lived with him for twenty-eight years, and clearly worships him.

And we see that his overbearing manner is no more than a disguise for his possessive affection. We are not told in the first act that Sebastian knows how ill Lydia is; yet suddenly, in the middle of a game of chess, he breaks into a quotation from Shakespeare (whom he has just condemned as 'that complacent old burgher of Stratford-on-Avon'):

> Ay, but to die and go we know not where;
> To lie in cold obstruction and to rot;
> This sensible warm motion to become
> A kneaded clod.

That is a useful clue. A moment later, Lydia carelessly observes, 'So all I'm entitled to say about Britain today is that it has been rather a pleasant place for an Estonian to have lived in.' 'To *have* lived in, mum?' Joey challenges her, knowing nothing. 'I meant up to now, Joey, of course,' she corrects herself. There is another clue.

What is so interesting is that the problem is a different one for each character. Sebastian knows Lydia will die and must not say anything about it. Lydia knows she will die and may tell Mark but not Sebastian or Joey. Mark knows that Lydia will die but does not know at first that Sebastian knows it. Joey never knows it. So often praised for his stagecraft, Rattigan never wrote so clever a play as this.

The double bill opened at the Duchess Theatre on 27 September 1973. On the press nights, 'Before Dawn' opened the evening, and no doubt biased the critical palate, for there was a good deal of antipathetic judgment. 'Before Dawn' was not a satisfactory hors d'oeuvre for a play like 'After Lydia'. What is more, in spite of the many lines that John Dexter had taken out of the farce, a good deal also had to be taken from the other play. There were enough enthusiastic notices to keep the bill on, but the run was confined to 131 performances, and this at a small theatre.

For the New York production, Rex Harrison played the part of Sebastian. (In London it was done by Donald Sinden, with Joan Greenwood as Lydia.) Rattigan was ill with pneumonia while the Broadway production was on the road, and did not see it until just before it went in. It had been considerably amplified from the London version, and now played as a full-length two-act play. Mostly the extra material was fairly trivial stuff, but one passage showed some importance, the account by Sebastian of Lydia's escape from execution by machine gun. These additions were genuine Rattigan, but one thing was not, and it made him very angry. Instead of concealing his love under the veil of indifference, Rex Harrison went out for sympathy from the start. Soon after the first act begins, this new, affectionate Sebastian is sneaking a look at Lydia's latest medical report, so telling the audience of his hidden concern for her condition. He emphasizes what he now knows by paying her courtesies that, in the authorized version, he treats brusquely. Lydia's slight stroke at the end of the first act, which Sebastian pretends to believe is the effect of too much vodka, is made to seem a matter of importance to him; inebriated she may be, but at least he can help her walk to the staircase.

Rex Harrison's defence of his sympathetic playing was that, without it, 'people will think I'm an absolute shit' – an explanation that Rattigan seemed to find rather funny. But its insensitivity is clear from the script, for there are the identical words, used by Sebastian about himself, 'an absolute shit'. This was precisely what people were supposed to think.

The play opened at the Morosco Theatre on 10 December 1974, and ran for 199 performances, sixty-eight more than in London. The notices were chiefly friendly, though 'sentimental' and 'old-fashioned' were two epithets thrown at it by several critics. Clive Barnes in the *New York Times* thought it 'facile', and difficult to believe in. On the other hand, Rex Reed in the *Daily News* reckoned it 'the kind of play Broadway has been waiting for – an extraordinary evening of rare perfection'; and in the *Post*, Richard Watts rated it moving and beautiful.

None of the New York reviews, and none of the London reviews either, were as adverse as that in the *Financial Times*, which Rattigan was expecting to have been written by myself. In fact, I went to a preview, spoke afterwards, with enthusiasm, to John Dexter and Donald Sinden, wrote, with enthusiasm, to Rattigan, and went on a long-delayed holiday. My substitute, Michael Coveney, decades younger than I, disliked both the plays very much. I received a six-page letter from Rattigan; so did Michael Coveney. I, at any rate, was forgiven. Rattigan sent me a copy of the play, inscribed with an injunction not to go on holiday when he had a first night in prospect.

Alas, I had few opportunities to do such a thing. His next London first night was not until 8 January 1976, a revival of *The Browning Version* at the King's Head in Upper Street, Islington. The next after that was in July 1977, *Cause Célèbre* at the Haymarket. Terry survived this by less than six months.

Nineteen
Cause Célèbre, His Last Play

The evident pleasure with which young audiences had received the revivals of early comedies, *While the Sun Shines* at Hampstead and *French without Tears* at the Young Vic, maintained Terry's enthusiasm for work. After *In Praise of Love*, he went back to his Bermuda home, Casa del Cevro in Tuckerstown, with a BBC commission which was close to his heart.

This was for a television play about the life of the dancer Vaslav Nijinsky. This was ideal material for him. He could at last write about a homosexual love without disguising it as anything else. He had already considered dramatizing Romola Nijinsky's biography, but she wrote and asked him not to; this time he turned to a more recent biography by Richard Buckle. The script that he produced, covering the whole of Nijinsky's ill-fated life, culminating in the rivalry between Diaghilev and Romola de Pulszky for Nijinsky's love (and it is presented truthfully as love, not a mere bodily possession), is sensitive and beautiful. But Romola was still alive, and she had no intention of allowing anyone but herself to write about Nijinsky. A long, ill-tempered correspondence between her, Terry and the BBC ensued, in which the BBC insisted that Terry should fulfil his contract. He knew only too well what it was like to have a beloved person snatched from you, by suicide in his case, by madness in hers, and he compromised in the end and persuaded the BBC to promise not to produce the play until after Romola was dead. Romola is dead now, but up to the time of

192

writing there is no indication that the Corporation is to broadcast the play.

However, at the start of 1974, another commission came, from a different arm of the BBC. This was for a play for radio, to be included in a series that would be given international transmission, thus enabling the BBC to offer a rather higher fee than usual. The subject Terry chose for this was one that he said had been in his mind since he had read about it in the newspapers almost forty years before. It had so fascinated him, he said, that he had always intended to write about it.

His treatment of the story was highly unconventional. As the public knew the case, Alma Rattenbury, the wife of an elderly, comfortably-off retired businessman, fell in love with the seventeen-year-old houseboy George Wood (as he is called in the play). As Terry elaborated it, George Wood murdered the old man because he believed that he was still having sexual relations with his wife, to whom he now felt he himself had exclusive rights. Wood and Mrs Rattenbury were tried jointly for the murder. Wood, the actual manipulator of the fatal mallet, was found guilty, but Mrs Rattenbury was acquitted. Not long after, she killed herself, a particularly distressing decision, for Wood was reprieved.

Such a tale was too straightforward for Terry to use unadorned, and moreover he was stimulated by the abilities given by radio to flick suddenly from one event to another, parallel, one. So he ran the murder story simultaneously with a sub-plot based on imaginary characters whom he could employ to highlight the emotional angles he found in the Rattenbury–Wood case.

He imagines Mrs Davenport, a member of the jury of about Mrs Rattenbury's age, who, like Mrs Rattenbury, finds her husband sexually incompatible. Unlike Mrs Rattenbury, however, she is something of a sexual puritan, as we learn from her relationship with her seventeen-year-old son Tony, a boarder at a public school. The play then follows the story of the murder and the subsequent trial, while in the background fall Mrs Davenport's commentary and, more important and very characteristic of Terry, an account of Tony's first, unsuccessful, essay at sexual experience. Terry has said that Tony's adventure closely follows an early, equally unfortunate, adventure of his own. It would be good to say that the two plots mesh together in a complementary pattern of contrasted erotic experience, but the truth is that they run side by side without any very important contact. We can study them better when we come to the stage play that Terry made, not without difficulty, from his radio script.

This, however, did not materialize for some time – time that was filled with adversities that he always seemed to meet with good humour. Before *Cause Célèbre* was broadcast, in October 1975, he had had three more operations, and, though everyone was careful not to mention the word, it was generally believed that he was suffering from cancer. In September I met him lunching, very uncharacteristically, possibly for the first time, at the long table in the Coffee Room at the Garrick. He turned round to greet me.

'I expect you've been asked to "do" me,' he said.

'I've already done you.'

'Flatteringly, I hope.'

In fact, I had written a new, updated obituary ten days before, after hearing a report from Pegs French, Harold French's wife, who had been his faithful hostess and companion for the past ten years. It was indeed flattering, but I had no intention of telling him so.

He went back to Bermuda for Christmas. He was receiving hormone treatment that had made him unusually fat, and he was walking with a stick. One day he dined at the Garrick with Laurence Olivier. Olivier was also walking with a stick, and moreover had had a good deal of his hair shaved off for his part in the film *Marathon Man*. Rattigan reckoned that if they went into dinner together with their sticks, they would attract a slightly comic attention, so he left his at the porter's lodge. In the event, they attracted no attention at all. After ten minutes during which no one came to talk to them, Olivier reacted. 'I don't believe anyone knows who the hell we are,' he said.

After Christmas in the sun, Terry came back to England again for more treatment. In January he was greatly delighted with a production of *The Browning Version* at the King's Head pub in Upper Street, Islington. The director, Stewart Trotter, had been to see him at Claridge's, where he had taken a suite, and persuaded him to come to a performance in the crowded little room at the back of the pub. He recalls the occasion:

> Sir Terence was very moved by the evening, but still kept a critical distance. He shied away from any confrontation during rehearsals. If he disagreed with anything, it was his agent who got in touch with us. He actually wanted to rewrite *The Browning Version* when he saw it. He felt that some of the language, particularly in the love-interest scenes, was old-fashioned. He also suggested putting an interval into the play. His notion for an effective first-half curtain was something of a lift from *Hedda Gabler*. Crocker-Harris asks about his translation of the *Agamemnon* and Millie reveals that she has burnt it.
>
> At the Kings's Head he was like a little boy at a pantomime. We, of course, were all scared stiff and had put on ties to greet the Master. Rattigan, in concession to the Fringe, had come without.

The play really took off that night, and at the end it was difficult to say who was crying most – a group of trainee teachers at a table to our left or Rattigan himself. Naturally he wanted to meet the cast afterwards – but the treatment he was having made him pee a lot. So first I took him upstairs to the grotty King's Head loo. Standing outside, I heard a gurgling sound that made me happier than I can say. It was Rattigan singing.

The production, in which Crocker-Harris was played by Nigel Stock, won the year's H. M. Tennant Award as the best Fringe production.

I had supper with Terry at Claridge's a few days after his visit. In my notice for the *Financial Times*, I had criticized the flatness of some of the dialogue. Terry, who still read every notice, agreed with me about that (as he had with Stewart Trotter) but made an effort to justify it. The affair between Millie Crocker-Harris and Frank Hunter, he maintained, must not be allowed to attract too much attention, and Hunter was deliberately made rather colourless – a justification that would have been more convincing if Hunter were indeed colourless.

We watched television for a while, first a political programme ('they really should have had a script and actors'), then some of the Olympic skating. Then he pulled himself out of his chair and crossed the room to take a slip of paper from a drawer. 'Not a very good notice,' he said, passing the paper to me to read. It was virtually his death sentence. He seemed quite reconciled to dying.

John Gale had commissioned him to make a stage version of *Cause Célèbre* (which at that time Terry was calling *Crime Passionelle*), and this was his main concern when he returned to Bermuda. He was also nursing a project to write a play about the Asquith family, something he had had in his mind for quite a long time. Puffin Asquith was the son of Herbert Asquith, later the Earl of Oxford and Asquith, who was prime minister during the first world war until he was shouldered out by Lloyd George. No finished scenario had been devised, but the play was to hinge on a meeting at General Haig's headquarters between Asquith and his son Raymond, a young officer then engaged in the battle of the Somme. Raymond was killed on the Somme (as Terry's uncle had been), and Terry had a notion that if the prime minister had not been so much upset by the death he might have been able to contrive a negotiated peace with Germany, and so change the course of European history. In the event, Asquith had other worries – the Irish rebellion, the shortage of munitions – that ensured his departure, and Lloyd George continued the war as energetically as he knew how.

195

However, the main effort had to be put into *Cause Célèbre* (or *Come to Judgment*, the next temporary title), for this had to be finished in the available time, and this was short. The doctors did not give Terry more than another year to live, and already he was finding writing a difficult pursuit.

He was to have worked on the script with the director Robert Chetwyn, but they did not get on. He then worked for a while with Peter Coe, but Peter Coe was unenthusiastic about the secondary plot and would have preferred the play to become more of a documentary account of the actual murder case. Terry insisted on retaining this feature, which he believed to be his most individual contribution to the play, and in due time a third director was found.

The Peter Coe script was shown to Robin Midgley, who liked it no more than its author had and declined to work on it. Then he was shown Terry's own earlier script, on which he had proposed to work with Robert Chetwyn, as well as the original radio script, and this changed his mind. By now, Terry was virtually immovable in Bermuda, and a long-distance agreement was made, that Robin Midgley should make a version from the three scripts he had seen, and when he had this ready he should fly out and discuss it with Terry there. It took longer to get ready than either of them had expected, but Midgley arrived in Bermuda in January 1977. He and Terry got on well together, and after two weeks' work a final script was prepared (by now entitled *A Woman of Principle*, though this name lasted no longer than *Crime Passionelle* or *Come to Judgment*).

Armed with this, Midgley flew home to England, and it was arranged that the play should open at the Leicester Haymarket (where Midgley was Artistic Director) for a three-week run, and then go in to London. Glynis Johns was cast as Alma Rattenbury, and her defending counsel, O'Connor, was to be played by Charles Gray.

Terry was determined to see the play at the earliest possible moment. He flew home at the end of April and moved into a room at the King Edward VII Hospital, where he was soon living a much more active social life than he should have been. But he hardly felt active enough to spend an evening in Leicester, and he asked if he could go to the first available matinée. This was on Saturday, 31 May.

But before then Glynis Johns had to drop out; and because his contract stipulated that he was to play opposite Glynis Johns, Charles Gray dropped out too. Fortunately, his contract also obliged him to play for the whole Leicester run, so the play as Terry saw it included him as O'Connor, but as Mrs Rattenbury it had Heather Sears as a courageous but not entirely suitable substitute. When the play moved into Her Majesty's Theatre in London, Glynis Johns was able to return; but Charles Gray departed and was replaced by Kenneth Griffith, a very different kind of player but one equally able to give the necessary weight to the part.

Terry was driven up to Leicester for his Saturday matinée, had some talk with Robin Midgley about the London production, and was driven back to hospital. The London opening was to take place on 5 July. Terry decided that if his next operation were scheduled for 1 June, he would be ready to attend by then, and on 4 July he duly went to the first night at Her Majesty's, sitting in the Royal Box with Michael Franklin. It was the last first night he ever attended.

What sort of play was this much worked over drama?

In many ways, it was not very different from the radio play. Setting the scene, Rattigan writes at the beginning of the script:

> The stage represents at various times Court Number One at the Old Bailey and other parts of the Central Criminal Court in London, a villa at Bournemouth, the drawing room of a flat in Kensington, and other places. Changes of scene are effected mainly by lighting, the curtain falling only at the end of each of the two acts.

The principle was similar to that used for *Bequest to the Nation*.

Adrian Vaux did what he could to design a set on which this might happen, but one can only say that he made the best of a bad job. Terry's paragraph only touches the edges of what is required. 'A villa at Bournemouth' had to be reinterpreted as meaning the outside of the front door, the hall, the sitting room, the bedroom; and the Kensington flat has a bedroom too. But with the judicious help of the lighting, all the necessary scenes were presented, if not with as much luxury of detail as Terry and Robin Midgley would have desired in other circumstances.

Time in the play is as flexible as scenery. Spotlights pick out Mrs Rattenbury and Mrs Davenport on either side of the stage, to emphasize the relationship that Rattigan put into their different lives. We move to Mrs Davenport in her drawing room, explaining to her sister Stella the complexities of her married life – separated from her husband and resolved on a divorce because of his adulteries, her son Tony living with her but currently on holiday with his father. She has just received a jury summons.

Flash to Tony and his father in Cannes, where we hear the other side of the marital situation. Then flash to the front of the Rattenburys' villa in Bournemouth, where Wood has just come to the front door in answer to an advertisement for a house boy. In a long scene that shows most of the house, room by room, he is engaged, with every possible indication of subsequent seduction.

Then back to the Davenports in Kensington, where Tony is talking to his mother about the Rattenbury case. In a moment he is in his bedroom, with his school friend Randolph Brown, son of a bishop. They are talking about sex, about the relative merits of a tart and Jones Minor. More daring than his friend, Tony resolves to go to the West End and try an experiment with a prostitute, a resolve which will cost him £1 7s 3d, the total resources of himself and his friend.

This sequence of short, instant scenes follows four stories that are wrapped around one another like the strands of a rope. There is the trial, much of it shown with the lawyers in the foreground. Alma Rattenbury's defence counsel wants to get her into the witness box, where he can persuade her to give evidence incriminating Wood, but she will not go until she has a visit from her son Christopher, who has been coached by counsel. 'He said that as I was nearly grown-up I should understand that when a woman has a choice between her lover and her children she's almost bound to put her lover first.'

ALMA: Christopher's not going to be in court?

O'CONNOR: Of course.

ALMA: Will he be there every day?

O'CONNOR: That depends. Say au revoir to your mother, old chap.

Christopher is taken out to his seat in court. Then, in a telling curtain line:

ALMA: Don't think you've won, Mr O'Connor.

Meanwhile, Casswell, the junior for Wood's defence, is trying to keep his client from saying that he was under the influence of cocaine. Wood is determined not to say that Alma made him do the murder, and will go into the box with his shaky defence, resolute not to shop the only woman he has ever loved.

The trial is followed with some skill. Alma is persuaded to go into the box, and her evidence includes her affirmation that she no longer has sex with her husband. O'Connor then, very exceptionally, reads from Wood's sworn statement (to his counsel's indignation). Wood has said that he heard the sounds of lovemaking between Alma and her husband, and goes on to confess to the murder, done in revenge for what he regards as infidelity to himself. 'Is there any part of that statement that is in any way inaccurate?' O'Connor asks her, and she has to admit that there is not. The 'mad, ludicrous story' that she told to the police when they came to the house, that she had done it to please her husband, was the result of shock. Wood's counsel, Croom-Johnson, endeavours only to show her as a woman of bad character. His case for Wood depends only on the suggestion that he was under Alma Rattenbury's influence.

We are shown Mrs Davenport, foreman of the jury, give a verdict of guilty for Wood, with a recommendation to mercy, and of not guilty to Alma; and we see the judge pronounce the death sentence.

Now whenever there is any evidence given of what happened on the fatal night, we switch from this story and follow the second, the actual-moment, story that began with Wood's arrival at the door of the Rattenbury house, and has continued, as it were offstage, until the sergeant's description of what he found, with a flashback to the point where Wood made his fatal misunderstanding, and where, in court, his statement is read. This obviates the need for stretches of question and answer such as often slow down trial scenes, and reveals in real life the characters of the people whose characters counsel are trying to establish.

The third story is barely a story on its own, but is involved in the parallel Terry is establishing between the Wood–Rattenbury trial and the private life of the Davenports. Mrs Davenport has sought to be excused from jury service on the ground of her deep prejudice against Alma Rattenbury. Not only is she not excused, she is elected foreman, no doubt because, as she has told the judge, her father was a judge in India (like Terry's grandfather).

The fourth story concerns the Davenport married life. Tony's trial of West End commercial sex has resulted in gonorrhoea. He tells his mother of this on the night before the opening of her jury service, and insists on going to see his father, something forbidden by the decree nisi. When he comes back, he brings his father with him; and, decree or no decree, he goes off to live with him. The factor that was intended to connect the Davenport story with the Rattenbury story was domination. Much is made of domination in the trial, the domination of the old by the young; and the collapse of the Davenport marriage is due to the domination of Mrs Davenport over her son. The comparison of the two cases is not very illuminating, and it seems likely that Terry was anxious to write two separate plays, one about the Rattenbury trial and one about the discovery of sex, and could not find a truly convincing link. What we have occurs on the night before the verdict:

MRS DAVENPORT: All the time, all the time that man was on at her: 'You were twenty years older, madam. Twenty years older. I put it to you, you dominated that boy.' Do you know what she answered? 'When an older person loves a younger, it's the younger who dominates because the younger has so much more to give.'

STELLA: And you thought of Tony?

MRS DAVENPORT: Of course.

STELLA: My God, to think that a murderess could go free because a jurywoman overloves a son who doesn't give a damn for her.

Of the generally friendly notices, the weakness of this sub-plot was the point taken by the less friendly. It is easy to say that, considering the circumstances in which the play was composed, the fault is easy to excuse – though that is not the kind of thought that Terry would have cared for in his good days. It is as easy to say, and kinder, that the presentation of the trial, and the painting of the characters involved, is brilliantly done, in Terry's best manner.

Terry's last departure from England was properly theatrical. He had a uniform edition of all his plays prepared and sent to the Queen. He had a car to drive him all round London's theatreland, where, as in earlier days, there were two Rattigan plays running, *Cause Célèbre* at Her Majesty's and a revival of *Separate Tables* at the Apollo. Then he flew back to Bermuda – to die, as we all thought, recalling his constant pain on his hospital bed.

But he was not ready for that. He spent a week in his house, and was then taken to hospital once more, this time with meningitis. He coped with this for three months, even recovering sufficiently to be discharged from hospital. He died on 30 November 1977. He would have been pleased by his press.

Terry had always wanted to be cremated, but in Bermuda there were no facilities. Pegs French, to whom no domestic problem came amiss, made arrangements for a cremation in Canada, but then found, with no Rattigan relations available for consultation, that she was left with the ashes. In due course they were laid in the family vault at Kensal Green, but Pegs French set herself to organize a suitable public memorial.

In St Paul's Church, Covent Garden, the 'actors' church', there was a handsome white marble tablet on the west wall commemorating Charlie Chaplin, and above it a similar tablet commemorating Noël Coward. They have now been joined by a third, lettered simply SIR TERENCE RATTIGAN, CBE, with the dates of his birth and his death.

Epilogue

How are we to assess this popular playwright, so constantly disparaged by the critical intelligentsia, so determined to go on writing the kind of play he liked, fashionable or not?

'If,' wrote C. P. Snow in the *Guardian* in October 1957, 'Terence Rattigan had received the kind of serious criticism that has since been showered on one or two other playwrights – the sort of criticism that many novelists expect to get – he would certainly have become a much more important dramatist than has been his lot so far.'

Terry's score at that date was one that should have satisfied him fairly well. Fourteen plays had been produced in the West End, counting pairs of double bills as single plays, and nine of them had achieved above average success. Of those that had not, *First Episode* certainly had above average success for an undergraduate play. *After the Dance*, a play that deserves a revival, was a victim of the war. *Follow My Leader* was a victim of the Lord Chamberlain, who banned it when it should have been played and released it when it was too late. *Adventure Story*, admired still by devoted Rattiganists, was the author's cherished experiment. *The Sleeping Prince* was the victim of its stars. There are many people in the theatre who would account a dramatist with a record like this as reasonably important.

It is as well, incidentally, that Terry never was subjected to the sort of criticism that novelists expect to get, for dramatic standards are only distantly related to literary standards. I have mentioned the casual way, as I see it, in which Rattigan threw his dialogue down on the page, caring only for its gist rather than its style. (Some of his stage directions are even more inelegant, but the phrasing of a stage direction can hardly be included in an estimate of a drama.) If Terry had written the novels and short stories he had threatened in his youth, it is unlikely that they would have been very good. The 'sense of theatre' is a priceless attribute in a dramatist, but it has little to do with English literature; and even when Terry did turn to prose, in his prefaces, for instance, and essays on dramatic content – none of it imaginative, only critical – he was not very good at it, however interesting his ideas.

Luckily, however, he never did try his hand at novel or story. I doubt if his writing habits, longhand against a writing board, would sustain a serious, extensive creation. And in any case, if he had been offered serious literary criticism of any of his work, he would have been convinced that it was mistaken, and might very well have written to the critic to explain why what he had done was what ought to have been done, if for no other reason than that it was to his own taste. There is nothing wrong with this attitude, which he shared with James Joyce and others, except that if, by any chance, the writer has strayed into an unproductive path, he is likely to stay there. The question is, then, was Terry an important *dramatist?*

A successful dramatist, certainly, and his record of misses is very small in comparison with the hits. Yet he had it in his mind to write at least one play that would still be current after fifty years. This is a more modest target than, I suspect, he was really aiming at. *The Second Mrs Tanqueray* and *The Magistrate*, for example, have lasted longer than that, the first of them a play inferior to *The Deep Blue Sea*, the other a comedy no better than *While the Sun Shines*. I believe he was thinking of a play that would last, as it were, for ever, a play like *The Rivals*, *The Importance of Being Earnest* or *Arms and the Man*. Yet all those were written to please the contemporary equivalents of Aunt Edna.

We cannot get away from that grim figure. Aunt Edna was one of Terry's supreme mistakes; or rather, dragging her out into the public view was his mistake. When critics needed a stick to beat Rattigan with, there was Aunt Edna waiting in the wings. She only had to be brought on the stage and more serious critical ideas could be put back in the cupboard. Yet the truth is that her influence on Terry was almost entirely beneficial.

She is presented as a woman of intelligence and, if not of discriminating taste, at any rate interested in the arts that separate the active patrons from the supper-on-a-tray television addicts. She does not always like what she sees and hears, a sign of her capability of judgment. Moreover, before she can come out with a damnatory judgment, she will have had to buy a seat, and possibly a seat for a friend, a companion, a clutch of nephews and nieces. Terry ascribes to her a dislike of Kafka, Picasso and William Walton, and the superficial reasons that arouse her dislike would have been shared by her creator if he had shown more interest in any of those three. However, on the strength of those opinions, he labels her 'a hopeless lowbrow'.

And he adds, 'The great novelist, the master painter, and the composer of genius are, and can afford to be, as disregarding of her tastes as she is unappreciative of their works.' (I am quoting from the preface to Volume 2 of the Collected Works, where Aunt Edna made her debut.) Not so, he insists, the dramatist, and there is a good reason why, in 1953, he should possess this belief. He knew exactly what Aunt Edna wanted, because he was himself Aunt Edna.

He is frank about it. 'Aunt Edna,' he writes, 'or at least her juvenile counterpart, was inside my creative brain, and in pleasing her, I was only pleasing myself.' His rightly admired 'sense of theatre' was gained, at an early age, among galleries, or stalls if money sufficed, full of Aunt Ednas. 'If my neighbours gasped with fear for the heroine when she was confronted with a fate worse than death, I gasped with them ... when my neighbours laughed at the witty and immoral paradoxes of the hero's bachelor friend, I laughed at them too ... and when my neighbours cheered the return of some favourite actor I cheered with them.' That passage is about the sub-teenage years. But there's more.

'As I composed my feeble lines' (he had matured into a young Harrovian here), 'I had quite genuinely visualized them as being spoken by the actors and actresses of my choice.' And though in later times he may not always have been so specific about which players were in his head, he always heard the lines spoken as in a theatre when he wrote them. What he wrote was what he meant to hear, and what he meant to hear was what he might hear as he sat in the stalls.

It was entirely to his credit that he should continue to write what he thought the public wanted to hear, when the critics were attacking him for it. Up to the fatal date of 1956, popularly associated with *Look Back in Anger*, though plenty of other new theatre was around at the time, he had followed his own line successfully. Now it seemed that he should be following other people's lines. If he had tried to do so, he might have ventured into territory strange to him, territory, moreover, in which he had no belief. I have recorded what he said about *Look Back in Anger* to George Devine. Was he to compete in that league? It was inhabited by people whose way of life he did not understand, whose interests he did not share, whose motives were not his motives, whose very way of speaking was fundamentally different from the middle-class argot he had put to every use he needed.

He did not shrink from inventing characters in unfamiliar worlds, but when he did so, those characters were transformed into people from his own world. There are those Macedonians, like officers from the Staff College. Lady Hamilton belongs firmly in the twentieth century. Even the Arabs Hamed and Rashid are young National Servicemen under the skin. His characters, and his situations, remained in his own world, and attempts at forking them out were never very successful.

Variation on a Theme was claimed by himself as an attempt to 'kick Aunt Edna down the stairs', and indeed it displeased the audiences that had been so loyal to *Separate Tables*. But it displeased them not so much for its content as for its dramatic inadequacy. That much-vaunted 'sense of theatre' had let him down, and in doing so, had warned him that his aunt was not lightly cold-shouldered. There had been almost a four-year gap between *Separate Tables* and *Variation on a Theme*. There were two more years before *Ross*, and *Ross* had brought him securely back to the position from which he might continue to work at pleasing the audience – not Osborne's, or Arden's, or Pinter's audience, but his own.

Certainly he deserted that audience again in *Man and Boy*, which pleased some of the critics but few of the theatregoers; but he was back with the faithful with *A Bequest to the Nation*, even if he was misled by other, less experienced, writers in his use of foul language, which appeared to be the small talk of the current theatre, but was certainly not the small talk of a Rattigan play. With *In Praise of Love* (by the time people had finished messing about with it) he had returned to his most likeable form.

When Dr Samuel Johnson wrote a Prologue for Garrick to read at the opening of the Drury Lane season in 1747, this is what he wrote:

> The stage but echoes back the public voice;
> The drama's laws, the drama's patrons give,
> For we that live to please, must please to live.

Aunt Edna was born at that moment. As long as Terence Rattigan was faithful to her, he was, by any standards, an estimable playwright. *French without Tears* has already lasted fifty years. *The Browning Version* and *The Deep Blue Sea* have a decade or so to go. I do not doubt that they too will make their half centuries, not out.

APPENDIX

APPENDIX

Appendix

London and New York openings

FIRST EPISODE (in collaboration with Philip Heimann)

Comedy Theatre, 26 January 1934

ALBERT ARNOLD	Max Adrian
PHILIP KAHN	Angus L. MacLeod
JOAN TAYLOR	Meriel Forbes-Robertson
TONY WODEHOUSE	William Fox
DAVID LISTER	Patrick Waddington
MARGOT GRESHAM	Barbara Hoffe
JAMES	Vincent King
A BULLER	Jack Allen
Directed by Muriel Pratt	

Ritz Theatre, New York, 17 September 1934

ALBERT ARNOLD	Max Adrian
PHILIP KAHN	Statts Cosworth
JOAN TAYLOR	Gerrie Worthing
TONY WODEHOUSE	John Halloran
DAVID LISTER	Patrick Waddington
MARGOT GRAHAM	Leona Maricle

JAMES	Stanley Harrison
A BULLER	T. C. Dunham
Directed by Haddon Mason	

FRENCH WITHOUT TEARS

Criterion Theatre, 6 November 1936

KENNETH LAKE	Trevor Howard
BRIAN CURTIS	Guy Middleton
ALAN HOWARD	Rex Harrison
MARIANNE	Yvonne André
M. MAINGOT	Perry Walsh
LT-CDR ROGERS	Roland Culver
DIANA LAKE	Kay Hammond
KIT NEILAN	Robert Flemyng
JACQUELINE MAINGOT	Jessica Tandy
LORD HEYBROOK	William Dear
Directed by Harold French	

Henry Miller Theatre, New York, 28 September 1937

KENNETH LAKE	Philip Friend
BRIAN CURTIS	Guy Middleton
ALAN HOWARD	Frank Lawton
MARIANNE	Simone Petitjean
LT-CDR ROGERS	Cyril Raymond
DIANA LAKE	Penelope Dudley Ward
KIT NEILAN	Hubert Gregg
JACQUELINE MAINGOT	Jacqueline Porel
LORD HEYBROOK	Edward Ryan, Jr
Directed by Harold French	

AFTER THE DANCE

St James's Theatre, 21 June 1939

JOHN REID	Martin Walker
PETER SCOTT-FOWLER	Hubert Gregg
WILLIAMS	Gordon Court
JOAN SCOTT-FOWLER	Catherine Lacey
HELEN BANNER	Anne Firth
DR GEORGE BANNER	Robert Kempson

JULIA BROWNE	Viola Lyel
CYRIL CARTER	Leonard Coppins
DAVID SCOTT-FOWLER	Robert Harris
MOYA LEXINGTON	Millicent Wolf
LAWRENCE WALTERS	Osmund Willson
ARTHUR POWER	Henry Caine
MISS POTTER	Lois Heatherley

Directed by Michael Macowan

FOLLOW MY LEADER (in collaboration with Tony Gold-schmidt)

Apollo Theatre, 16 January 1940

KARL SLIVOVITZ	Walter Hudd
QUETSCH	Frith Banbury
PAUL	Kenneth Morgan
RISZKI	Erik Chitty
MAJ OTTO BARATSCH	Francis L. Sullivan
MARIE PILAWA	Eileen Peel
HANS ZEDESI	Reginald Beckwith
ANNOUNCER	Bush Bailey
FIRST PHOTOGRAPHER	Geoffrey Clarke
SECOND PHOTOGRAPHER	Raymond Leigh
CHILD	Odile de Chalus
POLICEMAN	Ronald Fortt
KING STEPAN OF NEURASTHENIA	Athole Stewart
SIR COSMO TATE-JOHNSON	Marcus Barron

Directed by Athole Stewart

GREY FARM (in collaboration with Hector Bolitho)

Hudson Theatre, New York, 3 May 1940

MRS IRON	Evelyn Vardon
STEPHEN GRANTHAM	John Cromwell
JUDITH WEAVER	Jane Sterling
JAMES GRANTHAM	Oscar Homolka
MAVIS	Maria Temple
LADY WEAVER	Adrienna Morrison
ELLEN	Vera Mellish

Directed by Berthold Viertel

FLARE PATH

Apollo Theatre, 13 August 1942

PETER KYLE	Martin Walker
COUNTESS SKRICZEVINSKY	Adrienne Allen
MRS OAKES	Dora Gregory
SERGEANT MILLER	Leslie Dwyer
PERCY	George Cole
COUNT SKRICZEVINSKY	Gerard Heinz
FLT LT GRAHAM	Jack Watling
PATRICIA GRAHAM	Phyllis Calvert
MRS MILLER	Kathleen Harrison
SQN LDR SWANSON	Ivan Samson
CORPORAL JONES	John Bradley

Directed by Anthony Asquith

Henry Miller Theatre, New York, 23 December 1942

PETER KYLE	Arthur Margetson
COUNTESS SKRICZEVINSKY	Doris Patston
MRS OAKES	Cynthia Latham
SERGEANT MILLER	Gerald Savory
PERCY	Bob White
COUNT SKRICZEVINSKY	Alexander Ivo
FLT LT GRAHAM	Alec Guinness
PATRICIA GRAHAM	Nancy Kelly
MRS MILLER	Helena Pickard
SQN LDR SWANSON	Reynolds Denniston

Directed by Margaret Webster

WHILE THE SUN SHINES

Globe Theatre, 24 December 1943

HORTON	Douglas Jefferies
THE EARL OF HARPENDEN	Michael Wilding
LIEUTENANT MULVANEY	Hugh McDermott
LADY ELISABETH RANDALL	Jane Baxter
THE DUKE OF AYR AND STIRLING	Ronald Squire
LIEUTENANT COLBERT	Eugene Deckers
MABEL CRUM	Brenda Bruce

Directed by Anthony Asquith

Lyceum Theatre, New York, 19 September 1944

HORTON	J. P. Wilson
THE EARL OF HARPENDEN	Stanley Bell
LIEUTENANT MULVANEY	Lewis Howard
LADY ELISABETH RANDALL	Anne Burr
THE DUKE OF AYR AND STIRLING	Melville Cooper
LIEUTENANT COLBERT	Alexander Ivo
MABEL CRUM	Cathleen Cordell

Directed by George S. Kaufman

LOVE IN IDLENESS

Lyric Theatre, 20 December 1944

OLIVIA BROWN	Lynn Fontanne
POLTON	Margaret Murray
MISS DELL	Peggy Dear
SIR JOHN FLETCHER	Alfred Lunt
MICHAEL BROWN	Brian Nissen
DIANA FLETCHER	Kathleen Kent
CELIA WENTWORTH	Mona Harrison
SIR THOMAS MARKHAM	Frank Forder
LADY MARKHAM	Antoinette Keith

Directed by Alfred Lunt

(as O MISTRESS MINE)
Empire Theatre, New York, 23 January 1946

OLIVIA BROWN	Lynn Fontanne
POLTON	Margery Maude
MISS DELL	Esther Mitchell
SIR JOHN FLETCHER	Alfred Lunt
MICHAEL BROWN	Dick van Patten
DIANA FLETCHER	Ann Lee
CELIA WENTWORTH	Marie Paxton

Directed by Alfred Lunt

THE WINSLOW BOY

Lyric Theatre, 23 May 1946

RONNIE WINSLOW	Michael Newell

213

VIOLET	Kathleen Harrison
ARTHUR WINSLOW	Frank Cellier
GRACE WINSLOW	Madge Compton
DICKIE WINSLOW	Jack Watling
CATHERINE WINSLOW	Angela Baddesley
JOHN WATHERSTONE	Alastair Bannerman
DESMOND CURRY	Clive Morton
MISS BARNES	Mona Washbourne
FRED	Brian Harding
SIR ROBERT MORTON	Emlyn Williams

Directed by Glen Byam Shaw

Empire Theatre, New York, 29 October 1947

RONNIE WINSLOW	Michael Newell
VIOLET	Betty Sinclair
ARTHUR WINSLOW	Alan Webb
GRACE WINSLOW	Madge Compton
DICKIE WINSLOW	Owen Holder
CATHERINE WINSLOW	Valerie White
JOHN WATHERSTONE	Michael Kingsley
DESMOND CURRY	George Denson
MISS BARNES	Dorothy Hamilton
FRED	Leonard Mitchell
SIR ROBERT MORTON	Frank Allenby

Directed by Glen Byam Shaw

PLAYBILL

Phoenix Theatre, 8 September 1948

The Browning Version

JOHN TAPLOW	Peter Scott
FRANK HUNTER	Hector Ross
MILLIE CROCKER-HARRIS	Mary Ellis
ANDREW CROCKER-HARRIS	Eric Portman
DR FROBISHER	Campbell Cotts
PETER GILBERT	Anthony Oliver
MRS GILBERT	Henryetta Edwards

Harlequinade

ARTHUR GOSPORT	Eric Portman
EDNA SELBY	Mary Ellis

DAME MAUD GOSPORT	Marie Lohr
JACK WAKEFIELD	Hector Ross
GEORGE CHUDLEIGH	Kenneth Edwards
FIRST HALBERDIER	Peter Scott
SECOND HALBERDIER	Basil Howes
MISS FISHLOCK	Noel Dyson
FRED INGRAM	Anthony Oliver
JOHNNY	Henry Bryce
MURIEL PALMER	Thelma Ruby
TOM PALMER	Patrick Jordan
MR BURTON	Campbell Cotts
JOYCE LANGLAND	Henryetta Edwards
POLICEMAN	Manville Tarrant

Directed by Peter Glenville

Coronet Theatre, New York, 12 October 1949

The Browning Version

JOHN TAPLOW	Peter Scott-Smith
FRANK HUNTER	Ron Randell
MILLIE CROCKER-HARRIS	Edna Best
ANDREW CROCKER-HARRIS	Maurice Evans
DR FROBISHER	Louis Hector
PETER GILBERT	Frederick Bradlee
MRS GILBERT	Patricia Wheel

Harlequinade

ARTHUR GOSPORT	Maurice Evans
EDNA SELBY	Edna Best
DAME MAUD GOSPORT	Bertha Belmore
JACK WAKEFIELD	Ron Randell
GEORGE CHUDLEIGH	Harry Sothern
FIRST HALBERDIER	Peter Scott-Smith
SECOND HALBERDIER	Tom Hughes Sand
MISS FISHLOCK	Olive Blakeney
FRED INGRAM	Frederick Bradlee
JOHNNY	Bertram Tanswell
MURIEL PALMER	Eileen Page
TOM PALMER	Peter Martyn
MR BURTON	Louis Hector
JOYCE LANGLAND	Patricia Wheel

Directed by Peter Glenville

215

ADVENTURE STORY

St James's Theatre, 17 March 1949

PTOLEMY	Raymond Westwell
PERDICCAS	Anthony Baird
MAZARES	Marne Maitland
ALEXANDER	Paul Scofield
PYTHIA OF DELPHI	Veronica Turleigh
HEPHAESTION	Julian Dallas
PHILOTAS	Robert Flemyng
AN ATTENDANT	Natasha Wills
DARIUS, KING OF PERSIA	Noel Willman
BESSUS	William Devlin
QUEEN-MOTHER OF PERSIA	Gwen Ffrangcon-Davies
PRINCESS STATIRA OF PERSIA	Hazel Terry
CLEITUS	Cecil Trouncer
PARMENION	Nicholas Hannen
PALACE OFFICIAL	Walter Gotell
ROXANA	Joy Parker
GREEK SOLDIERS	Stanley Baker, John van Eyssen
PERSIAN SOLDIERS	Terence Longdon, David Oxley, Frederick Treves

Directed by Peter Glenville

WHO IS SYLVIA?

Criterion Theatre, 24 October 1950

MARK	Robert Flemyng
WILLIAMS	Esmond Knight
DAPHNE	Diane Hart
SIDNEY	Alan Woolston
ETHEL	Diana Allen
OSCAR	Roland Culver
BUBBLES	Diana Hope
NORA	Diane Hart
DENIS	David Aylmer
WILBERFORCE	Roger Maxwell
DORIS	Diane Hart
CHLOE	Joan Benham
CAROLINE	Athene Seyler

Directed by Anthony Quayle

THE DEEP BLUE SEA

Duchess Theatre, 6 March 1952

PHILIP WELCH	David Aylmer
MRS ELTON	Barbara Leake
ANN WELCH	Ann Walford
HESTER COLLYER	Peggy Ashcroft
MR MILLER	Peter Illing
WILLIAM COLLYER	Roland Culver
FREDDIE PAGE	Kenneth More
JACKIE JACKSON	Raymond Francis

Directed by Frith Banbury

Morosco Theatre, New York, 5 November 1952

PHILIP WELCH	John Merivale
MRS ELTON	Betty Sinclair
ANN WELCH	Stella Andrew
HESTER COLLYER	Margaret Sullavan
MR MILLER	Herbert Berghof
WILLIAM COLLYER	Alan Webb
FREDDIE PAGE	James Hanley
JACKIE JACKSON	Felix Deebank

Directed by Frith Banbury

THE SLEEPING PRINCE

Phoenix Theatre, 5 November 1953

PETER NORTHBROOK	Richard Wattis
MARY	Vivien Leigh
THE MAJOR DOMO	Paul Hardwick
THE REGENT	Laurence Olivier
THE KING	Jeremy Spenser
THE GRAND DUCHESS	Martita Hunt
THE COUNTESS	Rosamund Greenwood
THE BARONESS	Daphne Newton
THE ARCHDUCHESS	Elaine Inescort
THE PRINCESS	Nicola Delman
FOOTMEN	Peter Barkworth,
	Angus Mackay, Terence Owen

Directed by Laurence Olivier

Coronet Theatre, New York, 1 November 1956

PETER NORTHBROOK	Rex O'Malley
MARY	Barbara Bel Geddes
THE MAJOR DOMO	Ronald Dawson
THE REGENT	Michael Redgrave
THE KING	Johnny Stewart
THE GRAND DUCHESS	Cathleen Nesbitt
THE COUNTESS	Nydia Westman
THE BARONESS	Betty Sinclair
THE ARCHDUCHESS	Neff Jerome
THE PRINCESS	Elwin Stock
BUTLER	Sorrell Booke
FOOTMEN	William Major, Martin Waldron

Directed by Michael Redgrave

SEPARATE TABLES

St James's Theatre, 22 September 1954

Table by the Window

MABEL	Marion Fawcett
LADY MATHESON	Jane Eccles
MRS RAILTON-BELL	Phyllis Neilson-Terry
MISS MEACHAM	May Hallatt
DOREEN	Priscilla Morgan
MR FOWLER	Aubrey Mather
MRS SHANKLAND	Margaret Leighton
MISS COOPER	Beryl Measor
MR MALCOLM	Eric Portman
CHARLES STRATTON	Basil Henson
JEAN TANNER	Patricia Raine

Table Number Seven

JEAN STRATTON	Patricia Raine
CHARLES STRATTON	Basil Henson
MAJOR POLLOCK	Eric Portman
MR FOWLER	Aubrey Mather
MISS COOPER	Beryl Measor
MRS RAILTON-BELL	Phyllis Neilson-Terry
MISS RAILTON-BELL	Margaret Leighton
LADY MATHESON	Jane Eccles
MISS MEACHAM	May Hallatt

MABEL	Marion Fawcett
DOREEN	Priscilla Morgan

Directed by Peter Glenville

Music Box Theatre, New York, 25 October 1956

Table by the Window

MABEL	Georgia Harvey
LADY MATHESON	Jane Eccles
MRS RAILTON-BELL	Phyllis Neilson-Terry
MISS MEACHAM	May Hallatt
DOREEN	Helena Carroll
MR FOWLER	William Podmore
MRS SHANKLAND	Margaret Leighton
MISS COOPER	Beryl Measor
MR MALCOLM	Eric Portman
CHARLES STRATTON	Donald Harron
JEAN TANNER	Ann Hillary

Table Number Seven

JEAN STRATTON	Ann Hillary
CHARLES STRATTON	Donald Harron
MAJOR POLLOCK	Eric Portman
MR FOWLER	William Podmore
MISS COOPER	Beryl Measor
MRS RAILTON-BELL	Phyllis Neilson-Terry
MISS RAILTON-BELL	Margaret Leighton
LADY MATHESON	Jane Eccles
MISS MEACHAM	May Hallatt
MABEL	Georgia Harvey
DOREEN	Helena Carroll

Directed by Peter Glenville

VARIATION ON A THEME

Globe Theatre, 8 May 1958

ROSE	Margaret Leighton
HETTIE	Jean Anderson
RON	Jeremy Brett
KURT	George Pravda
FIONA	Felicity Ross

MONA	Mavis Villiers
ADRIAN	Lawrence Dalzell
SAM	Michael Goodliffe

Directed by John Gielgud

ROSS

Theatre Royal, Haymarket, 12 May 1960

FLT LT STOKER	Geoffrey Colville
FLT SGT THOMPSON	Dervis Ward
A/C PARSONS	Peter Bayliss
A/C EVANS	John Southworth
A/C DICKINSON	Gerald Harper
A/C ROSS	Alec Guinness
FRANKS (THE LECTURER)	James Grout
GEN ALLENBY	Harry Andrews
RONALD STORRS	Anthony Nicholls
COL BARRGINTON	Leon Sinden
AUDA ABU TAYI	Mark Dignam
TURKISH MILITARY GOVERNOR	Geoffrey Keen
HAMED	Robert Arnold
RASHID	Charles Laurence
A TURKISH CAPTAIN	Basil Hoskins
A TURKISH SERGEANT	Raymond Adamson
A BRITISH CORPORAL	John Trenaman
ADC	Ian Clark
A PHOTOGRAPHER	Anthony Kenway
AN AUSTRALIAN SOLDIER	William Feltham
FLT LT HIGGINS	Peter Cellier
GRP CAPT WOOD	John Stuart

Directed by Glen Byam Shaw

Eugene O'Neill Theatre, New York, 26 December 1961

FLT LT STOKER	Robert Milli
FLT SGT THOMPSON	Ted Gunther
A/C PARSONS	Bill Glover
A/C DICKINSON	Francis Bethencourt
A/C ROSS	John Mills
FRANKS (THE LECTURER)	Kenneth Ruta
GEN ALLENBY	John Williams
RONALD STORRS	Anthony Nicholls

COL BARRINGTON	Court Benson
AUDA ABU TAYI	Paul Sparer
TURKISH MILITARY GOVERNOR	Geoffrey Keen
HAMED	Cal Bellini
RASHID	Joseph Della Sorte
A TURKISH CAPTAIN	Eric Van Nuys
A TURKISH SERGEANT	Thomas Newman
A BRITISH CORPORAL	Del Tenney
ADC	Nicholas Coster
A PHOTOGRAPHER	Scott Graham
AN AUSTRALIAN SOLDIER	John Hallow
FLT LT HIGGINS	John Valentine
GRP CAPT WOOD	James Craven

Directed by Glen Byam Shaw

JOIE DE VIVRE

Queen's Theatre, 14 July 1960

KENNETH LAKE	Brook Williams
BRIAN CURTIS	Donald Sinden
HON ALAN HOWARD	Barry Ingham
MARIANNE	Anna Sharkey
MONSIEUR MAINGOT	Harold Kasket
LT CMDR ROGERS	Terence Alexander
DIANA LAKE	Joanne Rigby
KIT NEILAN	Robin Hunter
JACQUELINE MAINGOT	Jill Martin
LORD HEYBROOK	James Land
CHI-CHI	Joan Heal
TERESE	Lilian Mowbray
PIERRE	John Leslie
GASTON	Glenn Wilcox
MAYOR	John Moore

Music by Robert Stolz, Lyrics by Paul Dehn
Directed by William Chappell

MAN AND BOY

Queen's Theatre, 4 September 1963

| CAROL PENN | Alice Kennedy Turney |
| BASIL ANTHONY | Barry Justice |

GREGOR ANTONESCU   Charles Boyer
SVEN JOHNSON   Geoffrey Keen
MARK L. HERRIES   Austin Willis
DAVID BEESTON   William Smithers
COUNTESS ANTONESCU   Jane Downs
Directed by Michael Benthall

Brooks Atkinson Theatre, New York, 12 November 1963

CAROL PENN   Louise Sorel
BASIL ANTHONY   Barry Justice
GREGOR ANTONESCU   Charles Boyer
SVEN JOHNSON   Geoffrey Keen
MARK L. HERRIS   Austin Willis
DAVID BEESTON   William Smithers
COUNTESS ANTONESCU   Jane Downs
Directed by Michael Benthall

A BEQUEST TO THE NATION

Theatre Royal, Harmarket, 23 September 1970

GEORGE MATCHAM SNR   Ewan Roberts
KATHERINE MATCHAM   Jean Harvey
BETSY   Deborah Watling
GEORGE MATCHAM JNR   Michael Wardle
EMILY   Una Brandon Jones
FRANCES, LADY NELSON   Leueen MacGrath
NELSON   Ian Holm
LORD BARHAM   A. J. Broan
EMMA HAMILTON   Zoë Caldwell
FRANCESCA   Marisa Merlini
LORD MINTO   Michael Aldridge
CAPTAIN HARDY   Brian Glover
REV WILLIAM NELSON   Geoffrey Edwards
SARAH NELSON   Eira Griffiths
HORATIO   Stuart Knee
CAPTAIN BLACKWOOD   Geoffrey Deevers
MIDSHIPMAN   Stuart Knee
FOOTMEN, SAILORS, MAIDS   Stanley Lloyd, Conrad Asquith, Graham Edwards, Chris Carbis, Deborah Watling, Alison Coleridge

Directed by Peter Glenville

IN PRAISE OF LOVE

Duchess Theatre, 27 September 1973

Before Dawn

THE BARON	Donald Sinden
THE LACKEY	Don Fellows
THE CAPTAIN	Richard Warwick
THE DIVA	Joan Greenwood

After Lydia

LYDIA CRUTTWELL	Joan Greenwood
SEBASTIAN CRUTTWELL	Donald Sinden
MARK WALTERS	Don Fellows
JOEY CRUTTWELL	Richard Warwick
Directed by John Dexter	

Morosco Theatre, New York, 10 December 1974

LYDIA CRUTTWELL	Julie Harris
SEBASTIAN CRUTTWELL	Rex Harrison
MARK WALTERS	Martin Gabel
JOEY CRUTTWELL	Peter Burnell
Directed by Fred Coe	

CAUSE CÉLÈBRE

Her Majesty's Theatre, 4 July 1977

ALMA RATTENBURY	Glynis Johns
FRANCIS RATTENBURY	Anthony Pedley
CHRISTOPHER	Matthew Ryan
IRENE RIGGS	Sheila Grant
GEORGE WOOD	Neil Dalglish
EDITH DAVENPORT	Helen Lindsay
JOHN DAVENPORT	Jeremy Hawk
TONY DAVENPORT	Adam Richardson
STELLA MORRISON	Angela Browne
RANDOLPH BROWN	Kevin Hart
JUDGE	Patrick Barr
O'CONNOR	Kenneth Griffith
CROOM-JOHNSON	Bernard Archard
CASWELL	Darryl Forbes-Dawson

MONTAGU	Philip Bowen
CLERK OF THE COURT	David Glover
JOAN WEBSTER	Peggy Aitchison
SGT BAGWELL	Anthony Pedley
WARDER	David Masterman
PORTER	Anthony Howard
CORONER	David Glover

Directed by Robin Midgley

Index

Index

227

B.A. Young has served as both drama critic and arts editor for the London *Financial Times* and as the drama critic of *Punch*. He sat on the British Council Drama Advisory Committee from 1973 to 1983 and was president of the Critic's Circle from 1978 to 1980. He is now retired and lives in Cheltenham.

27334

LIBRARY
SAMPSON C
P. O. DRAW
CLINTON, N

PR6035 A75 Z98 1988
Young, B. A. (Bertram A.)   SSBK
The Rattigan version: Sir Terence Rattig
SAMPSON COMMUNITY COLLEGE

3 4015 00027 6772

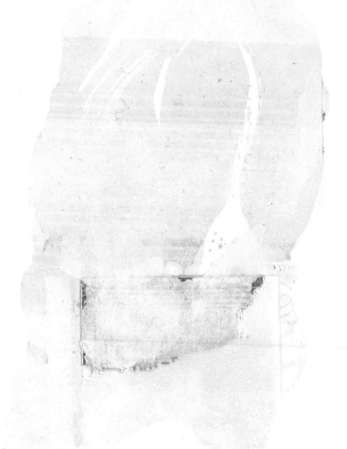